ONE BLINDING VISION

R. James Shupp

He was suddenly dazed by a blinding flash of light.
(Acts 9:3 The Message)

Elk Lake
PUBLISHING™

Elk Lake Publishing
One Blinding Vision
R. James Shupp
Copyright © 2015 by R. James Shupp
Requests for information should be addressed to:
Elk Lake Publishing, Atlanta, GA 30024
ISBN-13 NUMBER: 978-1-942513-75-9

Cover and graphics design: Anna O'Brien
Editing: Jerry Gramckow, Kathi Macias, and Deb Haggerty
Published in association with Jim Hart, Hartline Literary Agency

Unless otherwise noted, all Scripture quotes are taken from the New International Version®, NIV® Copyright ©1973, 1978, 1984, 2011 by Biblica, Inc.® Used by permission. All rights reserved worldwide.
Also quoted are the following:
Scripture taken from the New King James Version®. Copyright © 1982 by Thomas Nelson. Used by permission. All rights reserved.
KJV (King James Version), Public Domain.
The Message (MSG) Copyright © 1993, 1994, 1995, 1996, 2000, 2001, 2002 by Eugene H. Peterson
God's Word Translation Copyright © 1995 by God's Word to the Nations. Used by permission of Baker Publishing Group
Good News Translation (GNT) Copyright © 1992 by American Bible Society

DEDICATION

To church planters everywhere:
You are a special kind of servant in the harvest.
May your dreams be big and your vision loud.

CONTENTS

PART I: THE JOURNEY

*And the world cannot be discovered by a journey of miles,
no matter how long, but only by a spiritual journey, a journey of one
inch, very arduous and humbling and joyful, by which we arrive at the
ground at our feet, and learn to be at home.*

–Wendell Berry[1]

---

[1] *The Unforeseen Wilderness: Kentucky's Red River Gorge.* (Shoemaker Hoard, 1991), 43.

PREFACE

In the mid-1970s, Larry Lawrence played quarterback for the Oakland Raiders and the Tampa Bay Buccaneers. As with most men in the NFL, Larry seemed to be superhuman. He was a prime physical specimen in peak condition. By 2003, however, because of a rare condition called "sticky platelet syndrome," he needed a new heart.

On any given day in the United States approximately 3,000 people are on the official waiting list for a donor heart. But with only 2,000 donor hearts available each year, Larry faced the grim possibility that he might die before one was found for him. He needed two miracles, and he needed them soon: a healthy heart and a successful transplant.

Then it happened. Just three days after Christmas in 2003, the pager Larry carried began to vibrate. This could mean only one thing: Rush to the hospital immediately and prepare for surgery. A twenty-two-year-old organ donor had died suddenly from an untimely stroke. It's a strange irony—and Larry understands this better than most—that his life would be spared by another man's death.

The most unforgettable part of this story happened more than a year after the transplant. It's somewhat rare for the donor's family members to meet with the recipients of their loved one's organs. But Kayree Turner, the grieving mother, wanted to see the man who had her son's heart. Their first meeting and the broadcast interview to follow was scheduled to occur at a radio station in Midland, Texas. My friend, who happens to be a pastor, was there to witness the event.

Kayree did something quite unusual when she saw Larry for the very first time. As her tiny frame moved toward the former quarterback, she lost all sense of his personal space. Standing toe to toe, she cautiously leaned in, ever so close. Any mother can understand what she did next. With tears streaming down her cheeks, she turned her head sideways and placed her right ear on the left side of Larry's chest.

And there she lingered, awkwardly. There she listened, intently. There she treasured each familiar sound of a faint echo—an echo resonating from within a stranger's chest.

Then she looked up into Larry's eyes and said, "I just wanted to hear my son's heartbeat...one last time."

***

At this moment, if someone listened to your beating heart, whose heart would they hear? Have you captured the heart of Jesus Christ? Is it pounding for Him? What about your mind? Does it think like the Carpenter from Galilee? And your eyes? Are they focused on the risen, returning King of Glory?

This book reflects my personal journey to answer these questions in my own life. It is an honor and a privilege to share my discoveries with you.

—James

TAKING AIM

Our plans miscarry because they have no aim.
–Seneca

"Focus," he said in a barely audible voice. The temperature was well below freezing. My heavy goose-down coat, on top of the flannel shirt covering the thermal underwear, was providing little comfort. My skin was shivering and my eyeballs were dancing around inside their sockets.

"Focus on what?" I tried to whisper back.

"Shh! Softer," came the reply.

It was the coldest part of the night, an hour before sunrise. I was twelve. My father was attempting to transform me into a hunter. We were camouflaged inside the front seat of an old abandoned car, rifles pointing directionless into the darkness. A gentle snow drifting downward gave the clue that even the wind was dead.

I remember thinking, *Could I be far behind?*

"Focus on the tree line," were his next words. "Do you see something moving?"

I squinted in the direction of the tree line. The only motion detectable was from the flakes of precipitation accumulating on the barrel of my gun.

In fact, the snow was sooty, just barely visible on account of the faint glow of the moon emanating somewhere up above the clouds in the sky.

"Look through your scope," he said.

I placed my eye in line with the dark tube fastened to the 30.06 rifle barrel. Then I could see what my father saw—the murky shadow of a very large buck nibbling on some tufts of grass. Somehow they'd both survived this bitter winter. He had a rack of antlers that appeared larger than anything I'd seen hanging on the walls of hunting cabins and lodges.

"Line his shoulder blade up with the crosshairs in your scope," my dad said softly. "Take a normal breath, slowly exhale, and gently squeeze the trigger."

Suddenly I was no longer freezing. I couldn't believe he was letting me take the first shot. Little did I know this was my rite of passage, my journey into manhood. A flood of adrenaline rushed through my system. My heart beat faster and I could feel my pulse in my throat. I could already taste the deer sausage as our family sat around the dinner table. They would listen to me regale them with the story of my great hunt, while my little brothers listened in awe as they vowed to follow in my footsteps.

I lined up the crosshairs just like my dad instructed. As I looked at the buck, I realized the proud animal had no idea that I was about to end his life. It hadn't been too long ago that I sat in a movie theater, warm tears streaming down my face, as Bambi cried out for his dead mother. That didn't matter anymore. Something inside of me had already begun to change. This was about survival or so it seemed. Maybe this moment, still frozen in my memory, was about every young man's desire to do "grown up" things, to leave behind the casual days of childhood.

Moment of truth! Time slowed down. I squeezed the trigger.

I hadn't anticipated what would happen next. The butt of the 30.06 hammered my preteen shoulder like a wrecking ball. It was a sharp, startling pain. Simultaneously, a white light blinded my field of vision. Next, I heard the cracking sound of my father's rifle spitting out lead beside me. Then there was silence.

Everything living within fifty yards of our position quickly disappeared. With rifles in hand, my father and I jumped out of the blind and ran to the location where the buck had been standing. He was gone, vanished somewhere in the tangle of the thicket on the other side of the tree line. His escape trail left no telltale signs that he had been shot. He survived. I did too, albeit with no trophy to hang, no bragging rights, and a bruised shoulder—and ego.

Later that day my father and I took the 30.06 to the target range. We were both certain the sights needed adjusting. My dad constructed a handmade target, etched a bull's-eye in the center, and then nailed it to an old tree stump. We stepped back approximately seventy-five yards. We estimated this to be the distance earlier that separated us from the lucky buck. Several rounds were shot at the target. We obliterated the stump.

The conclusion was inescapable. My eye-hand coordination failed during the crucial moment. My aim exceeded the margin of error. My vision was compromised by a tiny miscalculation. As you'll later see, this is not the last time I'd face a similar reality.

As the years have accumulated, my dad and I rib each other when we recall this moment. He laughs as he shares it with the grandkids—my two sons. Although it was nearly thirty-five years ago, it still seems like yesterday. Surely that trophy buck has died and gone to heaven by now. He's not hanging on our wall, but we have something better: we have a shared memory. Most important of all, I have discovered a life-lesson that transcends the past and causes me to think about the future.

For me, our failed hunting expedition has functioned as a personal parable about life and the really big things that matter most. This is a story about peering through the darkness, fixing your eyes on a vision of something you want, taking aim, and pulling the trigger. It's no longer about deer hunting or becoming a man. It's about the high stakes of success and failure on the greatest scale imaginable.

Aim with Precision

It's a fact. Everyone is taking aim and shooting for something in life. What we want to possess or achieve becomes the target locked in our crosshairs. If you pierce the bull's-eye or smack the target with enough force to drop it where it stands, you become the rightful owner of that thing you value most.

But be very careful. I remember hearing once, "Your skin and bone structure determine how you look, but your values determine how you live." The formation of your values is far too important to leave to chance or the urges of appetite. Aim with precision.

Aim High

What we aim for in life reveals our passions. Our aim identifies our ambitions. It determines what dragons we slay or are slain by. As we take aim at what we want, we assign a set of values to what we see in our larger field of vision. Sometimes the achievement of our aim contributes to our sense of self-worth and significance. Other times it doesn't. Sometimes we hit the target; other times we miss.

Over the span of a lifetime, the aggregate of all the things you aimed to acquire and achieve constitutes your legacy. In essence, it's your story—told repeatedly after your own tongue falls silent. In the end we will stand before God to give an account of what we set in our crosshairs.

I've conducted hundreds of funerals. Many of them were for godly people who served the cause of Christ and worked joyfully to advance His kingdom. Others died like they lived, aimlessly and tragically. During funerals, I've watched family members of the deceased struggle to find just one polite thing to say as they were finally laid to rest. Some of the relatives, however, never tried at all.

There is something poignant and tragic about an aimless life, or a life aimed at the wrong target. Hearts will inevitably be broken, but the biggest heartbreak of all must be in the heart of our Creator. God has such high hopes that we will take aim with the unequalled advantage of His guidance. Like the hunting expedition with my earthly father, our heavenly Father whispers in our ear, "Child! Look over at the tree line. There is a blessing I want you to have. Set your eyes on the prize. Take aim. Pull the trigger." It is in transcendent moments like these that we move beyond the monotony of "just living" to the thrill of "*really* living."

So if we are to take aim and set our sights on something to gain in life, let it be for the highest cause. For God's sake, let it be in pursuit of a call worthy of His glory. For your sake, remain in the hunt until you have given your last, best effort to acquire the prize.

It's more than a cliché. It's the truth. Life is too short to waste. It is too precious a gift to squander.

Aim through the Scope

I've searched the entire Bible looking for a passage or a verse to drive this truth home. One day a short sentence of only seventeen words sprang from the pages of the Bible into my imagination. It is a confession that resonates with the force of a trumpet blast from heaven. These are not the words of a man boasting with pride, but revolutionary words from a humble heart in tune with God. They are the words of Paul, the apostle who set men and women free, the former enemy of the Cross who later became its greatest champion. He hit the bull's-eye dead-center in Philippians 3:14 when he said, "I press toward the goal for the prize of the upward call of God in Christ Jesus" (NKJV).

If you know anything of Paul's life, you are not surprised that he had a goal. The Greek word *skopós,* or "goal," literally means "a mark to shoot at." What's really cool about this word is that we get our English word "scope" from it. It's precisely the word Paul would have used to describe the hunting trip with my father. The deer was my skopós, my mark and my goal. Ironically, I used a "scope" attached to a rifle in my failed attempt to attain it.

Also in ancient times, skopós was used of the military as they took aim at their enemies. Sometimes the word described the activity of spies and scouts who had the goal of gathering intelligence. It was even used of runners who set their sights on the finish line in the arena.

This is where you come in. Your personal skopós is the most important thing caught in your crosshairs. It is your all-consuming focus that causes you to be blind to things of lesser importance. Your skopós is what you are shooting at in life. It is what you are running toward. It's the prize at the end of the race. You cannot achieve it by constantly shifting it, or focusing in a variety of directions. You will miss hitting anything if you are aiming at everything.

So aim as though your life depends upon it … because it really does. The stakes are enormously high. You have but one mark to shoot at and limited time to pull the trigger before the goal slips beyond the tree line. When all is said and done, you will have achieved your personal skopós or you will have missed the mark entirely.

It is interesting to note this is the only place in the entire New Testament where skopós is used. As I dug further into my Greek lexicons and dictionaries, I discovered another nuance. Skopós means "to be marked." Whatever you aim for in life and set out to achieve ultimately sears its mark upon your life. Your skopós is the invisible logo that makes up your unique brand. It's your iBrand, your reputation, what you are known for, live for, and perhaps die to achieve.

The Scope of *One Blinding Vision*

Skopós meant one thing for Paul. It was God's unique call upon his life to be the apostle to the Gentiles. Like most of us, however, Paul had to travel through a tunnel of pain before discovering this. Earlier his focus roamed all over the grid map. He was consumed by the desire to acquire personal trophies and feed his insatiable lust for notoriety.

In his misguided effort to earn God's favor, Paul sought to annihilate the fledgling movement of Christianity and eradicate all memory of her Founder. His early success at threatening, arresting, and executing Christians further fueled his intense hatred against Jesus—the executed criminal they stubbornly followed. Paul saw himself sprinting in a race to reach the skopós first, to eliminate this new threat to Judaism. He could see the prize waiting for him as he neared the finish line. There was just one problem: he was on the wrong track.

In what must have been one of the most dramatic turning points in history, God did something electrifying to seize Paul's attention. This came in the form of a blinding light while traveling on the Damascus Road. The force of this phenomenon knocked Paul from his throne to his knees and placed a mist of darkness over his eyes. It was there he finally met Jesus Christ personally. Once Paul was physically blind, he could finally see his aim was skewed. Blindness opened his eyes to Jesus, and then Jesus gave him a new vision. "Now get up and stand on your feet," said Jesus. "I have appeared to you to appoint you as a servant and as a witness of what you have seen of me and what I will show you" (Acts 26:16 NIV).

Immediately Paul stopped persecuting Christianity and started promoting it. He was transformed from an assassin to an apostle, from terminator to teacher, from martyr-maker to missionary. After his new life with Jesus began, he never looked back. This new vision totally eclipsed the old.

17

Paul received a second wind and moved into the fast lane. He "pressed toward" Jesus like a zealot. The words "press toward" in verse 14 literally mean "persecute," "pursue," or "hunt down." Jesus was locked in Paul's crosshairs, but this time it was different. Jesus was now the target of his deepest devotion and love.

As a result, Paul moved the ball down the field for Christianity like no other man in history. It is to his credit that Jesus was preached in places where no one else dreamed of taking the gospel message. He faced opposition, persecution, and finally death. The skopós, the goal, was worth everything. No one could stop him. And no one could take it away. He lived his life for *One Blinding Vision.*

Could you?

2

My Damascus Road

I didn't keep the news of your ways a secret, didn't keep it to myself.
I told it all, how dependable you are, how thorough.
I didn't hold back pieces of love and truth for myself alone.
I told it all, let the congregation know the whole story.
—Psalm 40:10 (The Message)

Is your current skopós worthy of your life?

Suppose someone asked your family, friends, and coworkers what your life is all about. How would they answer? Do you believe others can identify your true passions and commitments? And once they did, would you feel comfortable with those things being published in a biography or even engraved on your tombstone?

The Little Experiment

Not long ago, I was personally interested in the answer to these questions. The church I led at the time was going through some struggles and pains. Conflict was heating up. People were frustrated. As I attempted to analyze the problems from every conceivable angle, I fell short of the one that really mattered most. In other words, was I part of the problem? If the answer was "yes," did I really want to know the truth?

I figured I could do one of two things. First, I could hide under my shell and engage in blame-shifting. Or second, I could suck in my gut, be a man, and tango with the truth. I decided to do the latter before I really knew what the cost would be.

Here's how the process worked. I conducted an informal survey. I asked a select group of friends to engage a cross-section of our church membership in a fact-finding mission. The goal was to solicit information about my personal effectiveness and determine what they understood to be the primary focus for our church. My hope was that the focus would be correctly identified, and I would receive some unfiltered feedback on the effect I was having on the people I led.

Now before you think I'm weird or paranoid for doing this, consider that this is exactly what Jesus did with His disciples. He gathered them in a group one day and posed this question: "Who do men say that I, the Son of Man, am?" The question inspired one of the great confessions of the Christian faith: "You are the Christ, the Son of the living God," said Peter (Matt. 16:13, 16 NKJV).

It didn't go as well for me. As the information began trickling in, I discovered a disconnect between how I viewed myself and how others perceived me. This led to a short-term identity crisis. I pondered, *Am I who I think I am … or who others think me to be?* After peeling back the layers of this onion, I realized my personal influence had not caused even the slightest shockwave to spread throughout the church.

People were still trying to figure me out. They really wanted to discover what was important to me and how they could follow. But nothing inside me was emerging with any force or inspiring them to follow my leadership. I had not become a part of their culture. On several levels I was failing to meet the expectations of nearly everyone around me—my wife, sons, staff, and church members.

I began to pray. In my mind's eye I caught a glimpse of God. He was frowning at me ... or so it seemed.

The Plunge

I've seen video of a place in Mexico called the "Cave of Swallows." It's the biggest visible cave shaft on the entire planet—a type of black hole in the earth, descending 400 meters straight down. The location attracts high-octane, fearless adrenalin junkies who live to BASE-jump into the cave with parachutes. It looks crazy and insane. I have a mental image of myself from this season of life. It's the image of me hiking, having a good time, enjoying nature, loving creation, and then, "Oops!" After one misstep, I stumble. Freefalling through the darkness, I plunge into my own Cave Of Swallows—accidentally of course, but without a parachute.

In the twenty-five plus years I have been leading churches, this led to the deepest, most painful crisis of the soul I had ever faced. I was embarrassed. Frankly, I wanted to walk away. Each day I looked for the exit sign. I felt like I was cracking at the heels. Failure had never been part of my vocabulary or my résumé. The worst part of it was that I didn't know what was wrong with me or how to solve the problem. When you think you're doing well but everything begins to crash in around you, when all fingers are pointing back to you, it's a lonely, miserable, stinking feeling.

People I've shared these feelings with tell me I'm being too hard on myself. "There are other factors," they say. "The economy is weak. The church has been through many transitions of late. We have been let down by former leaders. The seeds of our problems were here before you arrived ..." While I appreciated all the sympathy, it did not diminish the fact that my calling from God was to love and lead His people. No part of the pastor's heart and soul, mind, and strength can be left out of the commitment equation. Like Hudson Taylor and William Carey who'd gone before me, I desperately wanted to pour out my life—yes, a living sacrifice offered upon the altar of service. But for the very first time in my life, I was within a moment of emptying my desk and checking in my credentials at God's throne.

I've seen friends and colleagues go through an experience like this. Many of them have made it all the way out the back door, never to return. Some quietly slipped away; others publicly kicked the dust off their feet before charging for the exit. Many casually drifted through the day with no heart until they were forcefully terminated. Just how often does this happen? The statistics are grim when the numbers are tallied. As many as 1,500 ministers leave the ministry every month in America. There is something about the grind of leading people, fighting against the devil, and living under a bright spotlight that chips away at the soul of a man of God.

You don't even have to look outside the Bible to see this is true. Elijah, Jeremiah, and Jonah all asked God to take their lives. Moses defied a direct order from God and fell short of entering the Promised Land. Even the "man after God's own heart," David, fell prey to lust, adultery, and murder. Whatever you might think of the person leading your church, you should pray for him. He has a bull's-eye painted on his back.

Hitting Bottom

So here I was, experiencing darkness like I'd never encountered before. Was God up to something? Was this one of those bad seasons He promises to "work together for good" (Rom. 8:28)? Should I claim that promise and kick into survival mode until the storm passed? I certainly didn't feel like it. I wanted to hide my embarrassment. The urge to lash out at the people I loved and somehow hold them responsible for my misery was an ever-present struggle.

The worst feeling of all was the realization that I was trapped. Where could I go and what could I do outside of working in a church? If I were to stay in this emotional sinkhole, then I needed to become an expert at hiding my true feelings. Another requirement would be to conjure up a fair amount of fake enthusiasm as I journeyed through life. I had to wear a mask, so I chose mine with the utmost care. The disguise had a gentle smile, just enough warmth of personality, an eager optimism about the future, and a hefty price tag. It fit perfectly. I snapped it on and went about the business of surviving. That was the day the tiny, shriveled-up church in my heart blew away. My own hypocrisy was to blame.

In spite of all the people who extol its virtues, I've never liked failure. I'm a competitor by nature. Losing has never felt good. My head tells me you learn more from your losses than from your wins, but my heart still hates losing. At some point in life, my competitive nature connected with my ministry calling. I viewed ministry like a seasonal win/loss record. I reasoned, as long as each season had a winning ratio, I must be in God's will. Losing always felt like a sign that God was angry and fighting against me on the opposite team.

I needed help. It's a hard thing to admit you're messed up when part of your calling is to fix other people's messes. So I prayed. I cried out to God. I read the Bible. I took long walks trying to sort things out. I listened to the podcast sermons of other preachers. But I didn't want to talk to anybody about this sickening malaise. That would be too risky. I had grown accustomed to my new mask.

At some point, perhaps through divine revelation, I recognized I was suffering from a lack of personal vision. Like the apostle Paul, I needed my own *One Blinding Vision* to consume my focus and rekindle the fire within. I remembered a phrase by G. Campbell Morgan, a great British preacher, who said, "Painted fire doesn't burn." I was growing weary of walking around with a fake fire.

Search and Rescue

Little did I know that God was up to something. I had a lunch meeting scheduled with a friend who had been preparing to ask me some very personal questions. God had arranged a collision in which I was one of the participants. It was to be a clash between my deep misery and God's eternal grace. I was about to be blindsided and struck blind by something God was about to do fresh and new in my life. Looking back, it was the best wreck of my life.

Sitting in a restaurant across the table from me, a friend from church asked, "How are you doing?"

"Fine," I registered. The response to the question was a little too scripted on my part to sound convincing.

"The church needs something from you right now," he continued. "You're the only one who can give the church a vision that turns this ship around. The staff and the church need focus. Reach inside yourself and tell me what you want that to be. Has God planted something in your heart that you're willing to give your life for? What matters most to you?"

The words, rather than having the usual effect of creating friction, had an appealing quality about them. These questions had been posed to me before, but either at the wrong time or in a way that caused deep frustration. I believed I'd been leading with vision; not only that but preaching it and oozing it out my ears. It was my carefully guarded fantasy. But the recurring questions of this nature were telling me the opposite was true. I needed to start listening and stop reacting.

On other occasions, what I often heard was, "Hey, Idiot, we're sinking, and you want us to rearrange chairs on the Titanic. Tell us what to do, or appoint someone who can!" No one actually said this to me, but my previous reactions to the "show us the vision" speeches sent back a flurry of terse replies.

Climbing out of the Pit

It was time to stop being defensive and start looking to the seeds God had planted long ago. The truth was I knew exactly what God had placed in my heart. He planted it there from the first day He called me into His service. In fact, at other churches I had led courageously from that core-calling of God upon my life.

But a problem had developed in me over time. Over the years, ministry had left me battered and sore. Whenever a pastor launches a vision, it initially creates degrees of conflict and chaos. One person put it this way: "Da vision creates division." Visionary language is so specific in nature that people must decide: are they for you or against you? Is this of God or not? It's the ultimate "fork-in-the-road" proposition laid out before the members of the church. The vision says, "Here is where this church is heading. Get on board! The ship is about to leave the harbor."

In each case, there are early adopters who love to see a new course charted. On average they make up approximately twenty-five percent of the church. Fifty percent live in spiritual Missouri. Their attitude is "show me." They require more proof that something is of God. The final twenty-five percent are ... well ... bless their hearts, against anything new. Church splits often happen during the vision-casting season in a church's lifecycle. However, the alternative is even less attractive. Without a vision, churches die a slow, painful death. The fire for God diminishes ever so slightly at first, dimming day by day, until that moment arrives when members run for the lifeboats and row to the new church on the other side of town.

As the pastor and primary vision-caster, this process can be physically, emotionally, and spiritually exhausting. I'm not whining; I'm just telling you how the cow ate the cabbage. In order for me to lead at this level and uncloak my skopós, I needed to regain the thing that had been left for dead.

God, in His infinite wisdom, was taking me through a personal journey of brokenness. All the frustration I referenced earlier had been carefully orchestrated by His hand. I'm convinced of it. People usually don't make changes until they receive enough to be *able* to change, learn enough that they *want* to change, or hurt enough that they *have* to change. Lucky me! I was in the last category, broken and hurting.

Brokenness can be a very beautiful experience. It's a moment when the God of the universe cracks through the shell of your stubbornness. He moves past all your layers of denial and puts His hand on the things that need to be healed or removed. Rather than running *away* from this kind of experience, we should run *to* it. The burdens that are lifted as a result are enormous. After it's over, we usually lament that we didn't do it sooner.

It's not a once-in-a-lifetime event, however. It's a seasonal thing, really. If life were static and stable, we could get a dose of God and be set for life. But things change. We are changing. The world and the people who live in it are caught in a vortex of swirling, churning change. Brokenness is God's strategy for preventing us from getting cynical and jaded about our life. Lean into it!

The Vision on Top

Okay, let me take you back to the restaurant. This was a meeting arranged by God. I'm not a hyper-Calvinist, but I do believe God plans these types of meetings long before we're born. He knows we'll need mid-course corrections and tune-ups along the way. This meeting was more like a transmission overhaul, slightly less costly than ripping out the engine and starting over. I was thankful for that.

So there at the table I took out my smart phone and typed in three things that would become the vision for our church. It was quick and decisive. Each of the three points appeared rhythmic and inseparable from the others, merging as one. They were inside me all along, waiting for that time when I had enough courage to let them escape from protective custody. After staring a moment at the screen of my phone, I read them to my friend.

- Delivering People
- Multiplying Disciples
- Building Bridges

Voices

When I told my story, you responded; train me well in your deep wisdom.
—Psalm 119:26 (The Message)

At some point in my early childhood, I fell in love with food. My mother and her family came from the deep-fried South. "If it can't be boiled in bacon grease," as Dad would say, "send it up North and let them eat it." We lived large on fried okra, chicken-fried steak, and mashed potatoes smothered in gravy. It didn't take long for me to learn the mysteries of physiology and physics, and in particular, the law of cause and effect.

My first lesson occurred during PE class at the beginning of seventh grade in Midland, Texas. Our coach instructed all the boys to stand in a single-file line. I arrived somewhere in the middle, wearing my super-cool Rod Laver tennis shoes, standard-issue white gym shorts, and a funky-smelling white T-shirt. At the head of the line was the trainer for San Jacinto Junior High School. Little did we know at the time that we were walking in the steps of a former student by the name of George W. Bush. Looking back, I wonder sometimes how he ever lived through what happened next.

One by one the trainer weighed and measured each of us on a rusty old balance-beam physician's scale. Then, in a rather dramatic fashion, he called out the name, weight, and height of each kid. The scene was a set-up for high drama of the first degree. Preteen boys will use any opportunity to humiliate another classmate. No doubt some of the world's most notorious thugs were born out of the embarrassment they experienced in a seventh-grade gym class.

"Baker ... 105 pounds, 5 feet even," the trainer shouted. His voice lingered as sounds echoed from the walls. An assistant registered the information on a Big Chief tablet as though it were being recorded for an upcoming auction.

"Young ... 119 pounds, 5 feet, 1 inch."

Snickers erupted from the crowd. "Porky" and other such slurs were commonplace.

"Johnson ... 85 pounds, 5 feet, 3 inches."

"Hey stick," someone yelled, "the girls weigh more than you!"

On and on it went until I was next. "Shupp ... 141 pounds, 5 feet, 1 inch. First one to crack 140! Good job, son."

Embarrassment started creeping over me as I heard the crowd of hecklers behind me. But it quickly subsided with his next statement. "Shupp," he said, "go see the football coach."

The next thing I remember was the opening game of the season against Goddard Junior High. I was a defensive lineman. The score was 0 to 42. We were the zeroes. Frustrations ran high. We were exhausted from chasing the running back into the end zone. Just perhaps, if we could score one touchdown, we could leave the game with our heads held high.

Close to the end of the game, Goddard's receiver fumbled the ball. It bounced wickedly, eluding all players on the field—except me. Somehow it came to rest at my feet. I looked ahead, and there was a clear shot into the end zone.

There are rare moments in life when someone is destined to achieve greatness. All that's required is the right opportunity and the appropriate action for the spark to ignite and set the world on fire. In such moments, time itself slows down. Temporal distortion seizes the senses. From the crowd, I could see the arms of moms and dads waving in unison. Through the quarter-sized hole in my helmet, the roar of the crowd reached my ears.

"Pick up the ball! Pick it up! Run!"

I looked at the ball. It was solitary, motionless. A wave of red and green jerseys began advancing on my position. In a surreal fashion, everything and everyone slowly faded out of my peripheral vision. I focused singularly on the ball. The sound of the crowd intensified.

"Pick it up. Run!"

My moment to shine had arrived. That dormant spark trapped somewhere deep within was about to blaze a glorious path to the goal line. Already I could see myself walking into school the next day. I envisioned cheerleaders surrounding my locker. Between classes and in the hallways, jocks were chanting my name out loud. I would tell the story repeatedly as often as I'm asked to relive it. I would be—

Suddenly, an offensive lineman fell on the ball. I had over-analyzed my moment. My chance for glory—vaporized. When the final whistle blew at the end of the game, there was a big donut on the scoreboard next to our school's name. Charlie Brown made a new friend that day.

<hr>

As I walked away from the lunch meeting at the restaurant, smartphone in hand, vision in mind, distant memories and insecurities began to creep over me. I held in my palm something that could change the momentum of the game. Where do I begin? Who do I enlist to get on the team with me? I knew I had to do one thing.

"Pick up the ball! Pick it up! *Run!*"

Just one thing prevented me from doing this: I must do something about the voices running through my mind.

Voices from Within

Several voices from within haunted me that day. One said, "The vision will flop—a big belly-buster off the high dive of imagination." Others followed: "You'll be exposed for the sightless wonder you are"; "The blind will lead the blind into a ditch"; "Don't embarrass yourself. Keep it to yourself."

I've heard these voices on many occasions throughout my life. Sadly, there are days they paralyze me from the brainstem up. And for one reason: I struggle with confidence.

People are normally surprised when I tell them I have wrestled with a lack of confidence all my life. "Are you kidding me?" they say. "You speak to more than 1,000 people each Sunday. You don't look scared." The truth is I've had this irritating "thorn in the flesh" ever since God drafted me to fight the good fight. And I was painfully aware that to carry the vision across the goal line, I needed the confidence to seize it and start running.

In my office I keep a replica of a famous oil painting by René Magritte titled "The Son of Man." Most likely you would recognize it once you laid eyes on it. The painting has appeared in several movies, most notably *The Thomas Crown Affair*, and even in popular sitcoms like *The Simpsons*. It's the picture of a man standing in a gray suit, white shirt underneath, a red tie, and a bowler hat. Beyond him is a cloudy sky that falls gently into the powder-blue sea.

The thing that makes the painting so memorable and riveting is the big green apple covering the man's face. It's the stunning focal point of the canvas. Most people are drawn into the picture with inquisitive thoughts. "What does it mean?" they ask.

Magritte said this about his masterpiece: "Everything you see hides something you do not." This is the key: The apple hides the face. The clouds hide the sky. The suit hides the man. "The Son of Man" teaches one thing about appearances: they hide what lies beneath.

Everyone has at least one big green apple to hide behind. I've been guilty of strolling through life with fruit on my face. What about you? My green apple is a cover-up for my weaknesses. It cloaks my "thorn in the flesh," the battleground where I exchange blows with the haunting voices, those midnight taunts that shout against my courage to lead. Whatever our great struggle may be, we have only two choices in dealing with it. In my case, I could look for a lasting solution. Or I could don my mask, walk alone, and hide my internal skirmish from the people I led.

Before you go shopping for a mask, consider this. Wearing a mask is like applying makeup to the soul. A little blush, a little rouge, outline this, bleach that, and *voilà*, nothing is wrong with us anymore. But alas, makeup only covers up flaws; it doesn't remove them. No matter how hard I've tried otherwise, I've never grown in confidence or exerted influence from behind a mask. I needed something more drastic, perhaps surgical in nature. I needed a facelift of the soul.

One day the solution nailed me to the wall. I discovered it in 1 John 3:19-21, where the apostle says,

> *This then is how we know that we belong to the truth,*
> *and how we set our hearts at rest in his presence*
> *whenever our hearts condemn us.*
> *For God is greater than our hearts, and he knows everything.*
> *Dear friends, if our hearts do not condemn us,*
> *we have confidence before God.*

So there it is, as plain as day. God is greater than the voices terrorizing our hearts. He knows everything about us, even the weaknesses we attempt to hide. Like a little child, we enter His presence with smudges on our face. Like a father, He wipes them from our cheek and smiles.

After reading this verse I knew there was only one thing left to do. I had no option but to take a courageous journey into His presence. I desperately needed a serious audience with God. So I set out on a voyage that carried me to a location deep within my own heart, that curious place called the temple of the Holy Spirit. There I met the Refiner standing beside a furnace. He asked if I wanted my heart purified from fear.

"Without question," I spoke.

In the crucible of His great love, He cast my fears into the fire. Deep within my heart He forged a new confidence. "Do not be afraid!" He said. The authority of those words shattered my stupor. Then I heard something echo from the halls of my memory. "Here is your second chance," He said. "Pick up the ball! Pick it up. Run!"

Here is where *you* enter my story. Most likely, you've fumbled one or two balls in the past as well. Or maybe you've left a few lying on the field. What every child of God needs to understand is this: God doesn't make junk. And neither will He cast you into the salvage yard after a few collisions. Your failures are never final. Never! And it doesn't matter what the voices inside you are saying. If they disagree with the truth of God's Word, they're lying to you. You're far too precious to God to be put on the shelf or thrown into the scrap pile. In fact, you're worth the most precious gift ever given—the life of God's own Son.

Believe it. Now run with it.

At the end of the day, I learned an incredible lesson in my Father's house: masks are not tolerated. Once you experience His indescribable love, you desire nothing less than to rip the disguise from your face. I threw mine to the ground and pulverized it beneath my feet. I carried the shards to Jesus and laid them at the foot of His Cross. It was then a miracle occurred. Those harsh, cynical voices slowly vanished. One by one they were taken captive and made obedient to the voice of God. My mind has found rest. I pray yours does too.

Perhaps it would be pleasant if this chapter ended here. Yes, it would be nice, but it wouldn't be honest. One hard-fought battle was finally over, but the war raged on. This was just a temporary ceasefire. I had other voices to face.

Voices from the Past

Thomas S. Jones, Jr., wrote the famous poem "Sometimes." I've spent years thinking about its meaning.

> *Across the fields of yesterday*
> *He sometimes comes to me.*
> *A little lad just back from play—*
> *The lad I used to be.*
> *And yet he smiles*
> *so wistfully*
> *Once he has crept within,*
> *I wonder if he hopes to see*
> *The man I might have been.*[2]

This poem provokes some intriguing questions. Are childhood memories simply events we think about from time to time? Or, more importantly, is our childhood still alive somewhere deep within us? Could there be a troubled child lingering within who still exerts influence over our present?

The main point of Jones' poem is that we live with voices from the past. You are your life story. No one simply walks away from the memories and experiences of their early days. Those events have shaped us in ways we dare not underestimate.

A second set of voices challenged me the day I walked out of the restaurant. They sounded something like this:

- "What makes you think you can carry the ball across the goal line this time?"

---

[2] Public domain.

- "How many times must you risk casting a forward-looking vision to a church when it's so much easier to keep repeating the past?"
- "Do you remember the pain the last time you did this?"
- "Are you ready to donate blood again?"

As I struggled with these questions, I had an image in my mind of Jacob wrestling with God at place called Mahanaim (see Gen. 32). He came to that contest with God as a result of wrestling with voices from the past. As a young man, he made a series of unfortunate blunders. He willingly deceived his father. Next, he swindled his older brother out of his birthright and his blessing. Then he cheated his father-in-law out of a chance to say farewell to his daughters and grandchildren. Jacob did all this to get what he wanted, simply because he didn't trust God to provide for him. One of the hardest lessons to learn is that we can't do God's will without God.

So these voices from the past mingled in Jacob's heart and caused panic. He'd burned too many bridges to get out of the swamp alive. I can almost hear Jacob thinking, "What to do? Here's a solution. I'll go box with God. He's the one I really have an issue with." So Jacob sent his demons into the ring to wrestle with an angel in disguise.

I heard a popular cliché a few years ago: "Your arms are too short to box with God." That's only partially true. Yes, your arms are shorter than God's, but you can box with God all day long. Many people do.

Jacob's fear and ours are simply an absence of faith, like darkness is an absence of light. When old voices create new fears, our issue is ultimately with God. This is something you will probably never hear a preacher say, but here it is anyway: God expects us to wrestle with Him. Most people are afraid to wrestle with God, so they run away like Jonah until they're swallowed by even bigger fears.

Running away has never gotten me very far from home. You and I keep bumping into God over the same issues because we don't deal with them in His presence. Say this next sentence with me out loud: "When I'm afraid, I take matters into my own hands because I don't trust God." Ultimately, this is what the fight is all about.

This one thing is true about wrestling with God: He won't lose. And neither will you, if you hang in there until He finishes with you. Therein lies the irony. God blessed Jacob at the end of His struggle. His name was changed from Jacob, which means "Heel Grabber" or "Cheater," to Israel, "The Prince Who Struggles with God." I get this crazy idea that God likes to step into the ring and spar a few rounds with His people. "You've wrestled with God and you've come through" (Gen. 32:28 The Message).

Voices from the Present

In sharing the vision with other people, I faced a third and final battle; this one was against the twin fears of failure and rejection. *What if they yawn?* I imagined. *What if they disagree?* Or worse still, *What if they gently smile back, nod with consent, and then walk away unmoved?*

Moses came to my mind here. Exodus 3 and 4 record an amazing dialogue between Moses and God. At issue was whether Moses would pick up the ball, run past the opposite team, and spike it in the end zone of the Promised Land. Would he tell Pharaoh that the Egyptian economy, fueled by slave-labor for centuries, was about to end? Would the sheepherder with a criminal past defy the most powerful man and army on earth?

Moses knew what was at stake here. So he asked God a series of questions:

• "Who am I?"
• "What is Your name?"
• "What if they don't believe me?"

- "What about my speech impediment?"
- "Why not send someone else?"

For Moses it came down to this: that moment we all face when a decision must be made. After we've analyzed all the options, thought about all the consequences, and asked all the tough questions, we must make our choice ... and make it count. We must choose to go with God, to stay the course. When the clock winds down and the buzzer sounds, we won't regret our decision.

A Final Thought

Now that we've identified all these voices, let's rid ourselves of spiritual schizophrenia. Here is a great truth. Life is best lived before an audience of One. God wants us to listen to but one voice: His! The other voices don't matter. They don't tell you anything important about yourself. It's the big guy standing in the corner of the construction site with the blueprints whose opinion matters most. God holds the blueprints on us. He scripted our DNA. You and I are "fearfully and wonderfully made" (Psa. 139:14).

I've always thought it amazing that our sense of balance is in the inner ear. Shouldn't it be in our feet? We might not fall over as much. Think about your sense of balance in a spiritual sense. There is a reason those other voices have such a stupefying effect on us. As we listen, they attack our spiritual equilibrium. Our peace gets destabilized. But if we want to rid ourselves of this spiritual vertigo, there is only one thing to do.

I've decided to host an eviction party. Here's how it works. I set the time, and I invite the Holy Spirit to attend. Since I'm His temple and He dwells in me, He never cancels. I read God's Word. I hear His voice. When peace arrives, we stomp and shout. Then we kick out all the vocal bums and squatters who don't own the temple. It's that simple.

Maybe you should host one too.

4

VISION

The most pathetic person in the world is someone who has sight,
but has no vision.
–Helen Keller

Growing up, I was the dumb kid.

It's more true than funny. I just didn't get the purpose of learning. By the third grade my teachers and parents were in a panic to discover why I wasn't learning to spell or read. I wasn't panicked. I really enjoyed the attention.

I knew how to shoot marbles and throw snowballs. I could see the pictures in comic books and figure out the storyline. When it came to math, what was there to count? I didn't have any money. I could tie my shoes faster than all the girls and race across the neighborhood with the guys. School didn't improve any of those important activities. In fact, it was a distraction.

I remember one day being escorted into a special room with the other "slow" learners. The teachers flashed words up on a screen and asked us to call them out when we knew what they were. It was high-tech for 1969. School had never been so much fun. It finally appealed to my competitive nature. I wanted to be the first one to shout out the word.

A few minutes into the exercise, I was getting my brains handed to me by the others in the room. I was in last place. For the first time in my life, winning was not about strength, agility, or speed. It was about intelligence. I didn't like the new rules.

Humiliated, I began to look around at the competition. I noticed something strange. The kids in the room had serious physical and mental disabilities. They were not the boys and girls I met on the playground at school, or the ones I played baseball with in the empty lots behind my home.

Wait a second, I thought. *Do they have me in this room because I'm mentally challenged?* Of course, I didn't know the phrase "mentally challenged" then. But I couldn't read, after all. I just remember thinking something like that, but on a more simple, if not illiterate, level.

Part of my problem was that my dad was in the military. I was in two or three different schools every year until the seventh grade. We moved around so much my learning environment was challenged. My brain was most likely fine. I don't remember eating any paint chips. One incident, however, would leave a lasting impression on me.

In the middle of my third-grade year, we moved yet again. My mom was determined I look presentable when I arrived at the new school. I had a military haircut, like my dad, and I'm not making this next part up. I wore a bowtie with a matching, dirt-brown vest. My pants were of the double-knit polyester variety. When my new teacher met me, she let out a squeal. It was a happy sound as best as I can remember.

"Ooh, come over here!" she said. "Look at you! Oh, just look at you! You are a handsome young man. You dress nicer than all the other boys and girls. Your mother has good taste in clothes."

I could already hear snickering in the classroom. Everyone else wore bell-bottomed jeans, tennis shoes, and psychedelic tie-dyed t-shirts. They were groovy. I looked like a bland, brown dork.

"Now you listen to me," she continued. "You are going to be my best student."

This is going pretty well, I thought to myself. *I think I can get what I want out of this woman.*

"Little darling, I am your new teacher," she gushed. "Let me have your records so I can see how smart you are."

And there it was. My short-lived dreams were gone. I swallowed hard. I knew what was coming next. With great reluctance, I handed over the manila folder for her scrutiny. She hummed softly as she slowly began digesting the report. I could see it in her eyes first. It slowly crept across her raised eyebrows as she read the transcript in stunned silence. It radiated across her temples and came to rest on her ears as they wiggled ever so slightly. All at once, her composure dropped like the Berlin Wall.

Then she spoke again. This time her voice was different. "You're not smart at all, are you?" she chastised. "You don't pay attention in class. Well, you won't cause me any trouble."

The next thing I remember was being whisked down the hallway to another classroom. She moved like a tank, decisive and with a mission to accomplish. She presented me before another teacher.

"Look at this young man," she said. "Doesn't he look smart?"

"Yes, he's absolutely adorable." She smiled.

"But take a look at his grades!"

It happened a second time. First in the eyes, then the eyebrows, finally it was all over her face. "How does he pass from one grade to the next?"

The conversation went back and forth from there. Finally we went back to my classroom. My new teacher presented me to the other students who were eager to know something about me, including why I dressed up like it was picture day. She told the entire class that no one should copy off my homework because they would most likely fail the third grade if they did. Mercifully, we soon moved again and I completed that school year in another town.

I remember dying of embarrassment that day. Slowly but surely I resolved to do better at school. At first, I figured out how to turn in passing grades. As the years passed, I became something of an academic zealot. Learning has become a lifelong goal and pursuit of mine. It's actually a passion and an enjoyment. Maybe some stories do have a happy ending after all.

The Learning Curve

As a result of my humble beginnings in the public education arena, I have spent a lot of time meditating on how people learn and why they change their behavior. Since I'm also a preacher, teacher, and leader, it's helpful to know these things. The first slide down the learning curve began with Adam and Eve. Only God knows what capacity and skill they forfeited when they ate the fruit and got the boot. Ever since that day, through sweat and toil, the human race has been soaking up the world with their brains and shaping it with their hands.

Education experts agree there are many different styles of learning. Two of the major styles are known as auditory and visual. Some people think primarily in terms of ideas. These are the auditory learners. Others view the world through the powerful images collected in their imagination. These are the visual learners. Most people have a combination of both styles, but lean significantly in one direction or another.

Learning is successful only when a behavioral change takes place. In other words, if you keep making the same mistakes, you'll keep getting the same results. In the third grade I decided to throw away my cloak of ignorance. I was sick of failure. Afterward, learning began at an accelerated pace. I paid attention, read and studied my assignments, memorized what was required, and did my homework—all because a third-grade teacher forced me to look in the mirror. However inappropriate her methodology might have been, I didn't like what I saw. So I changed.

The Power of Ideas and Images

Everything we hear and see presents us with an opportunity to learn and therefore change. Ideas we hear and images we see have the capacity to seize our emotions. When this happens, they stop renting space in our head and become the owners of the soul. If the ideas and images are radical or revolutionary in nature, they may crack the dams of stagnant thinking and unleash a torrent of human passion. Ideas and images shape the world like a potter molds clay—for good or for evil.

Hitler understood this fact, and he manipulated it for evil intent. *Mein Kampf*, Hitler's autobiographical Nazi rant, contained the ideas for his genocidal madness. The swastika was the menacing image that represented the Nazi ideology. The war and the Holocaust that followed nearly wrecked our planet. People of Jewish ancestry understand completely how ideas and images have shaped the world. If you ever doubt this fact, go talk to the curator of the National Holocaust Museum in Washington, DC.

Jesus mastered the power of ideas and images. His ideas are the most awe-inspiring and the most brilliant ever! The number of hospitals, orphanages, and universities founded in His name and by His teachings has no comparison. His impact is simply unrivaled in human history. Even more radical was the word-portrait He painted of His Father, "Abba." It was a tectonic shift in our understanding of the nature of God. Some of Jesus' most loved and memorable teachings are the stories He told. Art history is filled with paintings, tapestries, mosaics, frescoes, statues, and stained-glass portraits of the Prodigal Son caught in his "moment of truth." Jesus shaped the world with images and ideas.

New Ideas

I love the birth and discovery of a new idea. Ideas are friends. Ideas are like luminaries that invade the darkness of our ignorance. I am especially fascinated by the brilliant, big ideas that sharpen the understanding and propel the mind forward. The simplicity of a well-organized and clearly articulated thought has the power to unlock human potential like nothing else. Once we understand, we are free to conquer.

This is how we split the atom, walked on the moon, and hope one day to send a manned mission to Mars. Some of the biggest problems facing our planet today—like poverty, hunger, disease, and oppression—might be alleviated if we put our heads together and unleashed big ideas with brave hearts.

New Images

Likewise, I love the creative rendering of a new image, whether painted on canvas in an artist's studio or airbrushed in the imagination. Everyday images stir our dreams and elevate our spirits. The multi-colored pallet of an artist or the lens of a photographer can capture one dazzling moment and forever freeze it in time and space.

Such images can speak a thousand words in an instant. They hang in our homes and fill our museums. Images represent movements as large as nations. You may even feel this power yourself when your country's flag is raised at the Olympic Games. Images draw our attention like a magnet attracts steel. Once captivated we begin to reflect, and our imagination stirs into motion.

"Imagination," said Albert Einstein, "is more important than knowledge." Long before the Wright Brothers successfully engineered powered flight, Leonardo Davinci's imagination took off as he watched birds fly, and he created schematics for airplanes. God gave us our legs so we might walk. He gave us our imagination so we might fly.

God's Big Idea

It is no small wonder that God chose to reveal Himself with both ideas and images.

And the Word became flesh (John 1:14 NKJV).
We have heard…we have seen with our eyes (1 John 1:1 NKJV).

Logos is the Greek word for the English word "word." (Repeat that sentence out loud three times, and it might tangle your tongue.) Logos also means "idea." In Greek philosophy the logos was the guiding, governing principle of the cosmos. In Jewish philosophy the logos was the essence of divine wisdom. When we discuss big ideas, cosmic control and perfect wisdom are at the top of the list. So here you have Jesus, Logos, God's Son, the biggest idea ever to come out of heaven, matchless and unrivaled. But until we could see the Logos, it remained abstract and ethereal—the stuff philosophers and theologians love to talk about.

So God's really big Idea became flesh. Now we have the chance to see God in Jesus. We can watch how He acts, listen to His voice, and follow Him to dinner. Through the incarnation, the eternal "Logos" became temporal flesh, a baby wrapped in swaddling cloths. In Jesus, God paved the path to reveal Himself through our eyes and our ears.

The first disciples followed the Logos. He filled their ears with God's biggest ideas and thrilled their imaginations with wonder. "We saw Him, heard Him, and touched Him," John said (1 John 1:1). They saw Him in all His glory and then told the compelling story of what they witnessed. Everybody loves a compelling story wrapped in the creativity of fresh ideas, especially when it is joined with visual effects. This is why Jesus, the Logos, still has such magnetic appeal, even for today.

Thankfully, God has chosen to tell His story in both words and pictures.

In order to become part of the story, you need to hear it for yourself and see yourself in it. People don't become Christ-followers because they merely know the story of Jesus. They become Christ-followers when they *become part* of the story. Somewhere in my imagination—which by the way is not unhinged from reality—I am in a relationship with someone I have never seen physically. His name is Jesus. Is this real? Absolutely! He is more real to me than all the things I've ever held in my hands.

Imagination is not a substandard version of reality. Imagination is the very forerunner and creator of reality. When the Bible says God knew you before you were born, that means He imagined you into existence. You were created in God's image through God's imagination. Then the Creator made you creative by giving you an imagination. And it is in this place of imagination, a holy place, where God speaks to you and fills your mind with wonder and worship.

Visionary Leadership

Vision is born from the combination of divine imagination and bold ideas. Vision descends from heaven with the force of a blinding light and the voice of an archangel. The sound of it echoes through our imagination and expands our ideas about the future. It captures our convictions and drives our feet into action. It overcomes blindness and pushes back the darkness. Without vision, there is nothing left to do but perish.

Thankfully, God will not allow this to happen. His nature is to reveal. If God had not chosen to reveal Himself, we would be unaware of His existence. But He did, and we are. The Bible says He has set eternity in our hearts (see Eccles. 3:11). In our own way, each of us seeks to peer behind the curtain of heaven and see. And when just one person sees what God reveals, vision happens. Vision is a steamroller, an unstoppable force. It has an unrestricted capacity to create change on a revolutionary scale.

When a vision is born, a leader is born. He carries the vision from skin to core. If you cut a leader, you should expect him to bleed vision. The fusion of powerful images and ideas in the nucleus of a leader will result in a shockwave. Jump onboard, and you will have a blast. Stand in the way, and you will be blasted.

A leader is focused on the skopós with laser-like precision. It is the lens through which he sees the world. He is blind to nearly everything else that stands in his way. He is interested in acquiring followers. For them he will reveal the big ideas and paint pictures of what tomorrow will bring. The vision acts like a virus. In time the leader will be surrounded by an epidemic of contagious followers.

If leadership is your spiritual gift, do what the Bible says and "govern diligently." In other words, carry the vision forward. Pick up the ball and make a mad dash for the goal line. If you are not a leader, then don't become a vision orphan. Find somebody who knows the way, and follow. Neither be a vision antagonist. Find someone who is going where you want to go, and follow.

Vision Matters

The vision doesn't unlock doors; it tears them off their hinges. Vision gains access through the door to the Kingdom of God on earth. Step through to the other side. Beyond the threshold you will join the next great adventure. You will fly past old horizons and conquer long-standing frustrations. And finally, one day you will arrive at that place where the vision has carried you. There you will hear the words, "Take your shoes off. You are standing on holy ground."

God has placed in my heart a desire to unleash a vision that will change the world. I was once embarrassed to say this out loud. An inner voice told me, "James, you are crazy to think that big. Take smaller steps. Pull back on the reins." I no longer listen to that voice. It's a siren's song. It beckons us to live mediocre lives where imagination is dead and ideas are enemies.

There's but one motto now: "Sail on!"

Today I'm looking for people who want to live for *One Blinding Vision*. God created us for more than filling up space and competing for oxygen. For the remainder of your journey through this book, I will expose you to ideas and images that have shattered me and reshaped my thinking about the purpose of the Church. I refuse to go on this journey alone. I plan to gather some hungry hearts to take with me. Let me say up front that it would be my honor to have you as my traveling companion.

With ALL my heart, I believe this vision is worth your time. It's worth your best effort. Its worth is far greater than all your treasures piled high. It's more important than your hobbies and all your leisurely pursuits. It's to die for…and to live for. If you look at it long enough, you will go blind but not mad. It's the "one thing" to be consumed by if indeed you want your life to count by the measurement of eternity. It will outlast and outlive you.

So it comes down to this: If you share this vision with me, then we have no other choice but to believe it, breathe it, and bleed it. Why? Because Jesus did.

Will you?

If not, I know a third-grade elementary teacher who can help you learn the hard way.

PART 2: DELIVERING PEOPLE

So free we seem, so fettered we are!
~Robert Browning

PREFACE

Everybody yearns for freedom. Some have it; others don't.

For those of us who call Jesus Savior, we do so because He set us free. He delivered us from bondage. He destroyed the suffocating power of death and released the stranglehold it had on our lives. Jesus entered into our prison cell, took our punishment upon Himself, and paid our debts in full.

Why did He do this? Simple. "It is for freedom that Christ has set us free" (Gal. 5:1). Don't you love your freedom in Christ? I do. If I had a thousand lives to live, I'd give every one of them to Jesus Christ. My heart's desire is to engage Him in the daily routine of life. He is, and forever will be, my wonderful and magnificent Deliverer.

Ever since I first experienced this gift of freedom for myself, I have grown to love the word "deliverance." To be delivered from sin and death is an out-of-this-world, life-changing, and miraculous experience. And what's even better—it's for everybody. The Bible is very clear about this truth. God wants each person from every background to have a face-to-face encounter with the great Deliverer. God would desire for the whole world to confess, "He has delivered us from the power of darkness and conveyed us into the kingdom of the Son of His love" (Col. 1:13 NKJV).

Delivering People from Crisis

Jesus delivered people from two unique angles. First, He delivered them from crisis. A crisis may be defined as a critical situation or a turning point. It's that decisive moment when change is inevitable, either for better or for worse. Scores of people in the New Testament met Jesus during such a time—a time of personal crisis.

Leprosy, blindness, paralysis, sickness, disease, hunger, death, grief, poverty, abuse, moral failure, pride, loneliness, and desperation are the backdrop for many of the miracles performed by our Lord. Jesus jumped headfirst into the personal crises of thousands of people while He lived and moved among us. Many of the people He set free returned the favor by setting others free. They became healers themselves, a band of brothers and sisters who multiplied the ministry of the One they followed.

As we unpack what it means to deliver people from crisis, it's important to understand this reality: If you are in a crisis personally, please let *your* church or *a* church minister to you. Don't hide or run away out of a sense of shame. Don't allow your fear of exposure paralyze you. It may be your natural impulse, but I guarantee you it will only cause your situation to grow progressively worse over time.

On the other hand, if you have come out of a crisis, realize your story and experiences now belong to Jesus. They are now His resources to be used in helping others discover this same freedom for themselves. Never underestimate your personal worth and value in God's kingdom. The painful journey you have traveled can and will help others. God never wastes a tear.

Delivering People from Darkness

There was yet another angle in Jesus' deliverance ministry. He delivered people from darkness. Jesus could see the unseen world of evil forces. He was acutely aware of the presence of Satan and his demons. Our Lord saw straight through their evil initiatives to destroy God's plans and works. He experienced firsthand how sinister powers plotted to wreck human hearts.

Jesus not only talked about the power of temptation to lure people into a trap; He experienced it for Himself. While He never fell into sin after being tempted personally, everyone surrounding Him did. Even after His own disciples witnessed firsthand the ravages of demon-possession, Satan was still able to infiltrate their group. Jesus took this threat so seriously that He once said to Peter, "Get behind me, Satan!" (Matt. 16:23).

Consider that this rebuke happened just after Jesus gave Peter the keys to the kingdom of heaven. Keys represent access, ownership, and authority. Jesus spelled this out to Peter when He said, "Whatever you bind on earth will be bound in heaven, and whatever you loose on earth will be loosed in heaven" (v. 19).

Satan attempted to infiltrate Peter's life because he detested the access and authority Jesus gave His disciple. In fact, the devil is still doing the same thing today. He wants to drive a hard wedge between us and the Savior who loves us. Satan is forever jealous of our access to the kingdom of heaven, and he envies our inheritance in it. He despises the authority we have over his domain, and he's desperate to thwart our mission. He's a pickpocket and a thief who wants to steal our keys. Nothing would make him happier than to prevent us from unlocking the prison doors and setting the captives free.

If we do not vanquish Satan on the battlefield, we may one day become his victims. Unfortunately, Peter fell for a brief period of time. But thank God, he later recovered, placed the devil under his feet, and did some serious damage to Satan's schemes.

Judas had a completely different story, however. What we read in Luke 22:3 is tragic: "Then Satan entered Judas, called Iscariot, one of the Twelve." Consider that it took only ten words for the Bible to describe how Judas lost his soul. This fact should have a chilling effect on everyone who reads the story of his sad demise.

Have you ever noticed this startling contrast? Peter and Judas both followed the same Rabbi. They heard the same teachings. They saw the same miracles. They experienced the same temptations. The results, on the other hand, were completely different. After betraying Jesus, Judas hanged himself. Next, "he fell headlong, his body burst open and all his intestines spilled out" (Acts 1:18). Then it was Peter's turn. After denying Jesus three times, he became the first Christian preacher and led three-thousand people to faith in his Lord. I've never known a sharper distinction to exist between two men!

When engaging in spiritual warfare, the most important thing to consider is this: Jesus gave His disciples what they needed to overcome the evil one. Luke 9:1 says, "When Jesus had called the Twelve together, he gave them power and authority to drive out all demons and to cure diseases." I don't believe Jesus ever rescinded this power. Therefore, He hasn't removed it from the arsenal of His Church. Nor do I believe Satan has lost interest in us, or for that matter, in our mission. All of this is as real today as it was yesterday.

Personally, I'm tired of seeing our territory invaded. I'm sick of retreating. The devil thinks he can casually walk into our homes and rampage through our churches unchallenged. He invades the minds of the people we love and then robs them of their greatest gifts. He has gone after our spouses, our children, and our friends. Some are now trapped in his prison. He walks in and out of our camp, often unnoticed and undisturbed.

Enough! Let's draw a line in the sand and say, "Satan, you will not cross this line. Stop here and move no farther! By the authority of God and the power of the blood of our risen Lord, I forbid you to move one step closer." Rattle his cage for a change. Let the gates of Hades tremble before the steady march of your feet. It's time to take back what has been stolen from us. So put on your armor. Pick up the sword of the Spirit, and advance the cause of Christ.

I didn't start this fight and neither did you. But if we must fight, let's fight to win. Victory—for the glory of God!

A COMPASSION CRUSADE

The LORD answered me: "Write down the vision; write it clearly
on clay tablets so whoever reads it can run to tell others.
It is not yet time for the message to come true,
but that time is coming soon;
the message will come true. It may seem like a long time,
but be patient and wait for it, because it will surely come;
it will not be delayed."
(Habakkuk 2:2-3 NCV)

If a meteorite survives the impact with the earth's atmosphere, it will leave a crater behind. If a vision slams into the atmosphere of a church, it will leave an impression on the hearts of Christ-followers. I remember the day a bright shooting star from heaven's throne slammed into my heart. I hope to write about it clearly enough that "whoever reads it can run to tell others."

From the sixth grade until I married, our family lived in a 14' x 80' Lancer mobile home at the end of a dirt road in Midland, Texas. While many of my friends lived in houses, I felt myself fortunate to live on wheels. The blessings came in many forms. I had quarter horses to ride, a pellet gun to shoot, open fields without fences to rampage, and all the carefree time in the world to spend outdoors.

"Those were the good ol' days," I tell my two sons. They usually stare back in bewilderment. It's hard for them to imagine a day without surfing the Web and sending out hundreds of text messages to their friends.

My favorite childhood dog was a half-breed mutt I named Skipper. He was a mixture of Border Collie and some other type of shepherd. Like most dogs at that time, he roamed freely throughout the sparsely populated area where we lived. Frequently he dragged things home that caught his fancy. Toys, tools, shoes, bones, and a variety of "girlfriends" all ended up in our front yard.

"One day," as my dad would say, "he got the taste of real chicken in his belly." Skipper was so happy the first time he dragged home a fresh kill. If dogs could smile, he was doing it. He was covered in feathers and pride. In a gesture of kindness and loyalty, he carried the dead chicken in his mouth and laid it at my feet. I accepted his offering and praised him for what I thought was a job well done.

Dad, however, wasn't so pleased. "That dog has chicken lust," he said ominously. "You've got to beat him within an inch of his life with that chicken or his lust will kill him."

I loved my dog very much, as little boys often do. "Dad," I pleaded, "don't make me hurt Skipper." The words tightened my throat and stung my ears. I did the best I could to fight back the tears.

But Dad didn't give me a choice, "Either smack him with that chicken or kiss him goodbye."

With tear-soaked eyes and agony in my heart, I grabbed the dead bird by its drumsticks, held Skipper by his collar, and delivered him a beating that I hoped would cure his chicken addiction. Throughout the entire ordeal I bawled like a little girl. Feathers flew everywhere. "Skipper," I said, "I'm sorry. I don't want to lose you. But you have a problem."

Sadly, Skipper never recovered from his addiction. The consequences of getting caught and punished were not severe enough to inspire a change.

His all-consuming pleasure led him too far down the wrong path. One day Skipper never made it back home.

It was during my freshman year at Texas Tech University that Skipper's life ended tragically. He met his end at the hands of a chicken. Perhaps I should clarify: at the hands of a chicken farmer who fed my dog a poisoned bird. Skipper's lust had finally caught up with him. His addiction led to his demise. To this day I have knots in my gut just thinking about it.

Man and man's best friend share many things in common.

Years ago I had a friend who fought an addiction to alcohol. During a season of tremendous heartache, he leaned on the one thing that had taken care of his pain before—not God but beer. In a drunken stupor one evening, he stepped in front of a moving car. That was his last night on earth. When I heard of his death shortly thereafter, something inside me snapped.

The Snapping Moment

- Beneath the South Indian Ocean, on December 26, 2004, the tectonic plates shifted violently. In just one moment a force was unleashed that caused the earth to wobble on its rotating axis. The waves that thrashed the coastline for thousands of miles resulted in a staggering loss of life, all because something snapped.

- The Markham Ice Shelf extended off the coast of Canada. Geologists who studied it thought it to be 4,500 years old. At nineteen square miles, it was large enough to cover Manhattan. Then one September day in 2008, weakened by the forces of nature over decades, it snapped. The ice shelf drifted away to melt in the Arctic Ocean.

- To this day his real identity is unknown. The people who saw what he did on June 5, 1989, have given him a name. In Beijing,

China, an anonymous bystander observed a column of four tanks advancing on a massive crowd of students who were protesting in Tiananmen Square. "Tank Man," as he is called today, got his name for what happened next. Something inside him snapped. He stepped into the middle of the street, stood motionless, and became a human roadblock. The photographers also snapped— pictures, that is. These photos of one heroic man, standing between the armored vehicles and the ill-fated protesters, crossed the globe.

- On December 1, 1955, Rosa Parks climbed onto a bus in Montgomery, Alabama. Exhausted and with weary feet, she sat down in a front seat. The bus driver, James Blake, commanded her to take a seat at the back of the bus. Something snapped, and a movement was born.

- Mother Teresa walked through the streets of India. Looking through the slums to the piles of trash within, she saw a leper. She heard the cry of an abandoned infant. She watched the children playing among the piles of refuse instead of attending school. Something snapped.

As Jesus traveled through Jericho on His way to the Cross, a blind beggar by the name of Bartimaeus called out His name (see Mark 10:46-52). Bartimaeus didn't plead for money or for his eyesight to be restored. He simply begged Jesus for mercy. Some of the bystanders in the thick crowd were clearly agitated by this request. They ordered the pauper to be silent and allow Jesus to pass by without interruption.

Why such insensitivity to this poor man's suffering? How could these people be so stingy with Jesus' mercy? Perhaps they imagined Jesus was too busy. Or they thought He had more important things to do than camp out with a dusty old blind man.

Thankfully, Bartimaeus didn't stand down. He cried out to Jesus once again. This last plea for mercy penetrated the Lord's sensitive ears. Then something snapped. Jesus stopped. For one spectacular moment He suspended His journey to the Cross. And in the next, Bartimaeus was ushered into Jesus' presence.

Jesus asked the blind beggar the question He asks the whole world: "What do you want Me to do for you?"

"I want to see," he answered. Wonder of all wonders, a blind man received his sight.

Jesus delivered Bartimaeus from his crisis. A beggar became a believer. From that day forward he no longer sat in the dust. He no longer listened to the hurried patter of feet trailing off in the distance as life passed him by. The rattling sound of loose change hitting the bottom of his empty beggar's cup soon became a distant memory.

Bartimaeus was delivered from darkness. Now he had vision. What is the first thing you would expect a blind man to do with his new eyes? Travel, take a sightseeing tour across the Holy Land, or soak up the sights on the beach of the Mediterranean? Bartimaeus did the one thing that must have stunned the audience observing him that day: He followed Jesus to the Cross. Roll the credits.

I love it when Jesus snaps!

Jesus' Ministry

Jesus did more than speak nice words and moderately improve the lives of the people He encountered. Jesus delivered people. In fact, He was attracted to people who needed deliverance. If we possessed "before and after photos" of the men and women who crossed His path, we would be shocked by the difference. He didn't just change them; He transformed them.

If you haven't done so already, take a look for yourself. When you have idle time on some lazy day, go sit on the dock and dip a big toe into the shallow end of one of the four Gospels. Underneath you'll discover an ocean teeming with hurt and suffering people, a virtual menagerie of outcast members of society. Jesus attracted broken human beings like bait lures hungry fish. He wasn't embarrassed to keep company with them, and they swarmed to His side.

In Jesus' biography, you meet diseased lepers, the crippled, the blind, the deaf, and the dying. You encounter the demon-possessed, the prostitutes, and grieving parents. You come face to face with chronic illnesses and long-term suffering. You meet the prideful, the shamed, the distracted, and the self-sufficient. By far, my favorite stories in the Gospels are the ones where Jesus performed miracles of deliverance.

Have you ever noticed that most people run *away* from human tragedy? It's rare to see someone running *towards* suffering. Like so many others, I watched the drama of 9/11 unfold on television that dreadful Tuesday morning. I'll never forget the firefighters who charged into the Towers to save people they didn't know, risking and then sacrificing their own lives in the process. Americans of every color, creed, and class stood as one that day. Collectively, our hearts were stirred with pain and bewilderment. While some ran for their lives, we gasped as others ran to their deaths. And we have to ask ourselves, "What compelled the firefighters to rush into the buildings and up those stairs?"

Compassion

I believe I know the answer. If there is just one thing that binds the human race together and propels us forward like nothing else, it is compassion. Without a doubt, the firefighters had it that day. With axes and medical kits in hand, wearing fire-retardant suits and oxygen tanks, they lunged toward the danger. Each step was taken with an unwavering resolve to save people from certain death.

When it comes to compassion, no one felt it or lived it more intensely than Jesus. He breathed it, and He bled it. Take a long look at the last day of His life. Without compassion Jesus never would have touched the Cross. He could have called an army of angels to rescue Him. He could have refused to bear our sins. He could have annihilated His executioners. Instead, He took the place of a criminal. He saved a thief. He asked God to forgive the people who did Him evil. He entered the twin towers of death and the grave to pay for our sins. He laid down His sinless life. And now He offers to deliver us. Remove compassion from the equation, and there would be no mercy, no grace, no love, and no salvation.

One of my favorite verses is found in Matthew 9:36: "When he saw the crowds, he had compassion on them, because they were harassed and helpless, like sheep without a shepherd." It wasn't a one-time lump in His throat that caused Him to feel this way. We see this repeatedly throughout Jesus' life.

In Matthew 14:14 we read, "He had compassion on them and healed their sick." In Matthew 15:32 we see Him say, "I have compassion for these people." Matthew 20:34 records that when Jesus encountered two blind men, He "...had compassion on them and touched their eyes." After meeting an outcast leper (see Mark 1:41), Jesus did an unimaginably risky—and even unheard of—thing. Mark writes, "Filled with compassion, Jesus reached out his hand and touched the man."

Do you remember the familiar story of the son who rebelled against his father, took the money, and ran away? Have you ever asked yourself the question, "When the prodigal came crawling back home, why didn't the father scorch him with verbal napalm?" The kid's personal and moral failures were catastrophic.

Although the father had an excellent opportunity to rub salt in an open wound, he didn't say, "I knew all along you'd fall flat on your face." Neither did he say, "Maybe next time you'll listen when I try to give you advice." Or my favorite: "I'd offer you something to eat, but it looks like you're already choking on your own pride." Instead, Luke 15:20 reads, "But while he was still a long way off, his father saw him and was filled with compassion for him; he ran to his son, threw his arms around him and kissed him."

What an amazing picture of compassion! Compassion is like the "welcome home" kiss of a father on the cheek of a brokenhearted son. It's undeserved but freely given. Everybody on the planet wants a father like that. In essence Jesus said, "That's My Father. And He wants to be yours too."

Jesus understood how love-starved and shattered people really are. Like no other person before or since, He unleashed generous amounts of compassion. He opened the valve to heaven's floodgates. He soaked the parched valleys and the dried-up souls below with "living water." The people who experienced His compassion did not do so on the basis of their own merits. All they were required to do was step into the rapids and be swept away. It reminds me of an old phrase I used to hear growing up in church: "Hallelujah! What a Savior!"

The word "compassion" has an interesting meaning in the biblical sense. It's a word that describes what happens to a person when their intestines are tied up in emotional knots. Compassion is a pain that settles deep in the gut. It's when you experience something that causes you to say, "That tears me apart inside." It may happen suddenly, depending on the cause. Or it may be a slow grind, an agonizing ache that resonates to the core.

But it's more than a feeling. Compassion must break free from its emotional prison. In fact, you have no choice but to make a choice. It's a coiled spring that cannot be compressed any farther. Set it free, or it will punch a hole straight through you.

The Challenges

So what are we waiting for? What keeps us from slamming the throttle to the firewall and launching our compassion to circle the globe? Didn't Jesus model it? Yes! Isn't the world dying for lack of it? Undeniably! Isn't our mandate to unleash it? Absolutely!

In order to unleash your compassion, you need to know what wrecks your world and messes up your insides. You must feel the pain—enough pain that something inside you snaps. Once you understand that, you've identified your passion. Now you're ready to join Jesus in ministry.

Once you get started, you'll have to overcome the compassion assassins. The first is to be overwhelmed by the sheer size of the problem and the amount of needs that go unmet. Notice this didn't stop Jesus. He didn't heal every blind man. He didn't cleanse every leper. When He died, there were still demon-possessed men and women terrorizing the countryside. He did all that heaven allowed, and it was enough.

The second assassin is to allow other people to discourage you. The earth is populated with critics. Self-righteous condemnation is in no short supply. Some people, bless their hearts, are jaded by cynicism. Jesus faced toxic people and their "stinking thinking" every day. He dealt with them through His convictions. Jesus knew what God wanted Him to do. He didn't let other people define His Father's will for Him. Rarely will God tell someone else more about His plan for your life than He tells you. You would have to be a hardcore, hardheaded stump for God to keep you in the dark.

The last compassion assassin is numbness. Sometimes it's easier to crawl into a cocoon and shelter your eyes from all the suffering. Frankly, it's delusional to believe you can become comfortably numb. You'll find yourself boxed in by walls built with your own hands. And one day, you'll find yourself in need of the very compassion you've avoided giving others. Take a lesson from others who've done this before: It doesn't work.

The Secret Ingredient

The world is filled with salt. Heavy concentrations exist in our oceans and in many of our lakes and seas. Salt is found in mines and rocks, in dried-up riverbeds, and in deep wells. We also have salt in our blood and in our tears.

Jesus said His followers are "the salt of the earth" (see Matt. 5:13). I've often considered this statement to be one of His greatest compliments. So what does it mean? Simply this: We live in a tasteless society. Sprinkle a few Christians around here and there, and *voilà*, life has more flavor. Jesus is saying we have the capacity to add seasoning to this bland and boring world.

According to Jesus, you and I are the secret ingredient missing from the main course. The Master Chef has chosen us for a special purpose. As you would imagine, it isn't to gather in the shaker and sit comfortably on the shelf. The shaker must be turned upside down and shaken violently if it is to be of any use at all. As He empties our lives from the saltshaker, we're poured out onto the face of the earth. We find ourselves coming into contact with the open wounds of broken people. Unlike real salt, this is a good thing.

Here's how I spell "salt."

> **S**ee people the way Jesus saw them.
> **A**ccept people the way Jesus accepted them.
> **L**ove people the way Jesus loved them.
> **T**ouch people the way Jesus touched them.

S: You must *see* people—really see them—the same way Jesus looked at them with His own eyes. He could see things no one else was even looking for. What eyes He had! Observe how He saw straight through the shattered dreams and the shriveled-up hope of the people He encountered. He even peered into the darkness of madness and demon-possession. He looked with compassion at the people who were crushed and bruised. Today, we're the Body of Christ. Will someone reading this take up the challenge of seeing with His eyes?

A: You must *accept* people—regardless of how problematic and awkward the relationship might be—the way Jesus accepted people. He embraced people in His arms. And what arms He had! Jesus was called "a friend to sinners." He made a clean break with the traditional taboos and accepted invitations to eat in their homes. He went to their parties, attended their weddings, and gathered them into His core group of followers. Prostitutes, tax-gatherers, political rebels, and thieves found their way into His company. We are His Body. Will someone reading this be brave enough to embrace another hurting human being in Christ's arms?

L: You must *love* people—regardless of how unlovable or undeserving of love they may be—the way Jesus loved people. What a heart Jesus had! He loved everyone, without exception or exclusion. His love extends across the whole world. He loves every continent, every nation, every city, and every person living in every home. He even loves those without homes and commanded us to do the same. Today we need someone to be the heart of Christ. Is yours beating faster right now? I dare you to let your heart beat in tandem with His.

T: You must *touch* people—really get up close and personal—the way Jesus touched people. What hands Jesus had! He touched a leper. No one did that. The fear of contracting leprosy was huge. But Jesus didn't even flinch. He touched the eyes of the blind, the ears of the deaf, and the mouths of the mute. One day He touched me. I've never been the same. We're in desperate need of more people to be the hands of Jesus.

A Compassion Crusade

As I gaze upon my Savior, I see eyes filled with compassion, connected to a heart completely accepting, producing a love never-ending, extended by hands forever reaching. Isn't it time for the Church to rise up from the ashes and live once again as Jesus lived? If we desire to deliver the world, we must stop long enough to see the people who are in need of deliverance. We must accept them the way Jesus accepted us—warts and all. It might look messy and chaotic from the outside, but it will look no different from Jesus' ministry. We must stop condemning people before we've even begun to love them. We must touch their fears and hurts with the gospel of outrageous and unparalleled love.

Someone might say, "That doesn't sound very tough on sin." The only people I can find Jesus slamming against the wall for their behavior were already religious to begin with. In other words, Jesus is tough on my sin, and I'll leave it up to Him to be tough on other people's sin. I know the difference between right and wrong, and I fail to live up to my own standards, let alone God's.

Sometimes we say, "Love the sinner and hate the sin." We need to correct that statement and say, "Love the sinner and hate your own sin." I have enough sin to hate for a lifetime. I'm not going to waste my time anymore hating everybody else's sin. My biggest problem is with me, no one else.

Jesus called us to be fishers of men. We catch the fish; Jesus cleans them. Reality check! We will never see any fish cleaned until we start catching the fish to begin with. Many ministries fail because they spend all their time just shouting at the fish. It's the job of the Holy Spirit to convict people, not ours. We must preach the word and speak the truth as we are commanded. But for God's sake, we must not do it without love. The loveless truth is a half-truth. And a half-truth is no better than a lie.

Something inside me snapped one day when I heard that people who live outside our faith view us as hypocritical, judgmental, self-absorbed, and unloving. If only ten percent of this is true, we should repent in dust and ashes before the throne of God. Judgment begins inside, not outside the house of God.

We must recapture an outrageous compassion for the people who are separated from the Father's love. Too many of us live like there is no hell to come. I believe there is, and it tears me up inside. What will it take for the local church, once a lighthouse for shipwrecked souls, to recapture a love for evangelism? Must the number of baptisms go down every year in the major denominations in America? Are we turning a blind eye and a deaf ear to the cries of people around us? Have we lost the capacity to feel?

If you don't feel the burning desire to bring people with you into heaven, find something you can do. Find a place you can go then gather some sharp instrument to prick your heart until it bleeds again. Our time is limited. Like Jesus said, we "must work the works of Him who sent Me while it is day; the night is coming when no one can work" (John 9:4 NKJV).

It's perfectly acceptable to be blind if you were never given eyes to see. But to have physical sight only to suffer from spiritual blindness is the greatest tragedy of all. No one is so blind as the one who refuses to see. We cannot afford to carry on our visionless business as usual. Many churches have become insulated caverns of self-absorbed study and endless debate over style and preference concerns. Shame on us! We argue and condemn one another, then wonder why the world isn't interested in becoming like us. If there is so little compassion and understanding inside our churches, then compassion and understanding will never break free to those who live outside. Revival happens when the church gets turned inside out. It's the only cure when things are upside down.

One Blinding Vision is needed. It starts with a burning desire to deliver people. It's empowered by a compassion born from Jesus' own heart. When our gut agonizes over the pain created from holding it in, we're ready to unleash a compassion crusade. I'm convinced it's the only type of crusade ever launched that doesn't produce more atheists than believers.

Let's turn the mother ship around and get back into the real battle. Let's stop shooting our own wounded and re-enter the war against the dark, unseen forces that enslave humanity's mind and will. If there were only one great cause for which to stand up and fight until our dying breath, this one is it. This battleground is already drenched with our Savior's blood. The apostles and the early martyrs spilled their blood there as well. This is holy ground.

Nothing you give to the conflict will go unrecognized by God. One day you will stand before Him in high adoration and praise. The angels of heaven and the Father of lights Himself will applaud your selfless sacrifice. And God will reward you for fighting the good fight, finishing the race, and keeping the faith. That day, my friend, will be the day to remember throughout all eternity. Amen.

2

My Story

"But you, O Sovereign LORD, deal well with
me for your name's sake; out of the goodness
of your love, deliver me."
(Psalm 109:21)

My mother lived her entire childhood in the same small town in Tennessee. Her teenage boyfriend was a young man, tall, popular at school, but prone to reckless behavior. One evening he arrived in his truck to take her out for a date. As they chatted about the evening and their plans that night, it didn't take her long to discover he'd been drinking.

Conceived in Crisis

As I've heard my mom tell the story, there was something strange about his behavior that night. It was as though he had already determined beforehand what he wanted. He had a singular focus as he bypassed all the familiar places where they hung out together. With a quick turn of the steering wheel he parked the vehicle in a secluded place. Then he raped her. She was fifteen.

She was shattered, embarrassed by what he did, and determined never to see him again. To make matters worse, her mother and father were going through a bitter separation and divorce. Her dad was a philanderer, though her mother clung to the faint hope that the marriage would survive. Compounding all of these problems was the recent discovery of breast cancer. Her mom was scheduled for surgery.

My mom was sent out of state to spend a few weeks with her aunt and uncle. While there she grew sick and was taken to see a doctor. After a brief examination the doctor informed her she was pregnant. With those words the trajectory of her life changed.

"Barbara," the doctor said, "I can take care of this for you. You don't need to go back to school and suffer the shame of carrying a child. This will ruin your life. Don't you want to attend your prom? You need to graduate from high school and be free from this burden."

The doctor walked swiftly over to a cabinet and removed some surgical instruments from shelves. His motions portrayed a certain air of confidence. He was focused and certain he knew what was best for her. As on many similar occasions, he probably imagined his actions were noble. Indeed, they must be ethical as well. Who could argue against the necessity of this minor surgical procedure? Was it not an act of medical heroism to rescue a young girl's future?

The doctor was stunned by what happened next. My mom began to weep. The doctor sought to calm her, but nothing he said closed the floodgate of emotions that flowed uninterrupted. He gave her a shot to numb the emotional pain; it didn't help. As she continued sobbing, the doctor called for her aunt and uncle to enter the examination room. He explained the situation and asked them to help her understand what must be done. They concurred. Abortion was the only sensible option.

She stood to her feet and abruptly moved to the corner of the room. Then she withered into the fetal position. The room fell silent.

Born into Crisis

Twenty-seven years later I sat in my office at the First Baptist Church in Allen, Oklahoma, and heard my mom tell me this story for the very first time. She cried like it happened yesterday. I don't know what the expression was on my face. All I remember is what I was thinking at that moment: *Did she give birth? Why has she never shared this with me before? Does this mean I have an older brother?*

I felt a deep wave of compassion come over me as she continued the story. Her voice softened as she spoke. "I didn't know how I was going to get through that moment. All I knew was my mom and dad were not there to help me make a decision. I was alone, and everyone was telling me to stop this pregnancy."

She paused for a moment, and her expression changed. With the confidence I had seen her exhibit over so many years during my childhood, she said, "I heard a voice from someone who wasn't in the room." She paused again. "I'd never heard that voice before, but I still remember every word. Sometimes when I look at you, son, I can still hear it." Then she conveyed what she heard that day. The voice said, "Stop him! This one belongs to Me."

Her next words sent shivers down my spine. "Son, you are that child."

Living through Crisis

The years that followed were chaotic and challenging for my mom. She left her hometown and married her brother's best friend. She hardly knew him, but he promised to love her and raise me as his own child. She was barely sixteen when she married. I was born shortly thereafter.

Sadly, her new husband, the man I believed to be my biological father for twenty-seven years, was a binging alcoholic and a chronic gambler. He was a violent man when he drank, and detached when he didn't. He chased lady luck with reckless abandon and to no avail. I remember accompanying him on one of his frequent trips to the bar when I was just four years old. He handed me a roll of coins and taught me how to play the slot machines.

He hated God, if language is any indication, but he confessed to be an atheist. One day I asked him about God. He said, "All you need to know is that I'm your god!" My other memories are centered in the fact that he was seldom home. He left when I was ten, and I never saw him again. It was what he wanted. He eluded my efforts to see him until the day he died.

For the first decade of my life we did not go to church. The voice my mother heard shortly after my conception faded over time. God seemed distant and detached from our daily struggle to keep out of the shelters and off the streets. I can remember holding my mother's hand one day as we knocked on doors. We'd run out of food and were asking the neighbors if they had any to spare. We pan-handled a couple cans of beans to get us through the next few days. I didn't know it at the time, but I must have looked hungry. The generosity of others carried us through the difficult times.

If I could change one thing about my childhood, it would be that some church filled with Christ-followers had come after us. In our crisis, what we needed more than anything else was Jesus. He had the plan and the answers to get us out of the pit. Unfortunately, we weren't on anybody's radar. As a kid I remember sitting in the backseat of our car as we drove by many different churches. I was curious. I had no idea what happened inside those buildings. Then again, they didn't know what was happening inside me either.

In spite of all this, I loved being a kid. I had no idea we were different from anyone else or that I had a cliffhanger start on life. Somewhere around three-and-a-half years of age, I met Elvis Presley outside the gates of Graceland. He actually picked me up and held me in his arms. Later, we were invited to tour his house. Somehow I kept this memory alive in my head, even though it seemed like an average day at the time.

From such humble beginnings, I have been given so many blessings. After my first father left, my mom married a godly man. He took us to church, and we all came to faith in Jesus Christ. I'm so very glad to be alive, especially after coming face to face with the story of my conception. God has given me a beautiful wife, two incredible sons, and a calling to serve His Church. I call this irrefutable evidence of His amazing grace. Nothing I've done or experienced qualified me for His generous outpouring from heaven's throne. Our Father simply loves to give good gifts to His children.

We're all marked by our past. My past has had one great influence over my life as I press toward the future. It causes me to empathize with the heartache many people endure on a daily basis. Although I wouldn't change this reality, it carries a heavy price tag. I'm wrecked on the inside when I see misfortune and suffering. I can honestly say I know what it's like, and I feel compelled to do something about it.

Called to Crisis

Ever since I became a follower of Christ, I've never stopped loving Him. I had other issues, however. I voiced one big objection to God when I left home for college. "I have issues with Your church," I said. With Mom and Dad no longer around to enforce attendance, I didn't darken the door of a church my entire freshman year

Even though I found salvation through Jesus Christ in a church, frankly the experience of attending one often sucked the joy clean out of my head. I withered under condemning sermons and judgmental members. My opinion at the time was that the whole institution of organized religion lacked relevance. I desperately desired to follow Jesus. I just didn't think it necessary to do it by sitting in a pew.

Then something horrible happened to my critical attitude. The God of heaven called me to preach the gospel and lead a local church. How ironic was that? There were so many compliant, happy people He could have appointed for the assignment. *Why me?* I wondered.

At a pastor's conference years ago, I heard Warren Wiersbe make a statement that cleared away the fog. He explained why God's M.O. seems so crazy to us at times. "When God has a work to be done, He calls a worker," he said. "Then God goes to work on the worker so that the worker can do the work." I was a piece of work, without question. In fact, as the children's song goes, "He's still working on me."

After a brief period of bewilderment over God's calling, I signed up. It made more sense than to run away. I didn't want Jonah's fate to catch up to me.

It wasn't long before I began leading a small church in north Texas. I had visions of shaking up Christianity, something on the scale of another Great Reformation. I wanted to build the kind of church that would have rescued my family when I was a child and maintained my interest as a teenager. I was filled with fresh dreams and unlimited amounts of idealism. I was ready to give everything I had for the cause of Christ. A pound of flesh or a pint of blood would have been the lower limits of what I was prepared to sacrifice. I was dead serious about building a church out of people who had been rescued and delivered from crisis. I thought of a motto somewhat reminiscent of the words by Emma Lazarus on the statue of Liberty:

> *Give me all the people no other church wants,*
> *and we'll turn them into the kind of people*
> *every other church would die for.*

But as the years progressed, I found myself leading the same type of churches I'd fought hard to stay awake in. Old frustrations resurfaced. As a new leader, I encountered attitudes among some church members that frustrated me and deeply challenged my ability to lead. It seemed nearly impossible to make progress or engineer lasting change. I'm convinced that some of the most painful battles ever fought are waged on the frontlines of resuscitating dead churches. And for one simple reason: Many people have conflicting views over the nature and the function of the Church of Jesus Christ. It's all wrapped up in the mysterious question "Why does the Church exist?"

Why Does the Church Exist?

The answer to this question answers not only why the worldwide Church exists, but it will also drive everything the local church does and what it looks like to the outside world. It determines how the money is spent and what ministries the people set out to accomplish. It's the looking glass through which church members evaluate their own success and failure. But even more important, the answer to this question determines what God thinks about that church. He makes the final call on whether or not a church exists for the right reasons.

Most Christians want to be part of a church that has a strong identity and understanding of why it exists. In fact, it's at the epicenter of their decision-making criteria when they go church-shopping. When most people plant their life in a new church home, it's because they agree with the answer to the question of why the local church exists. Personal convictions drive the choice.

If we're not careful, however, we'll select a church much like we shop for our clothes. If it fits our personality and looks good from the outside, then mission accomplished. All that remains is to pull out the plastic and pay for the purchase. But just as clothes don't make the man or the woman, neither do outward appearances guarantee that a particular church exists for the right reasons. Answer the question incorrectly, and it's entirely possible to experience a wardrobe malfunction.

Many people believe the local church exists for its members, or more simply stated, "for me." This is absolutely and entirely incorrect. Paul wrote clearly in 1 Corinthians 12:27, "Now you are the body of Christ, and each one of you is a part of it." Neither the worldwide Church or the local church exists for us, but rather through us and because of us. We are the visible Church in the fallen world. We are the body of Christ and the temple of the Spirit of God. It would be tragic and self-serving if the Church existed merely for our benefit and pleasure alone.

So why then does the Church exist? It exists for the purpose of completing the ministry of our ascended Lord. Simply put, we're His only hands and feet, His only eyes and ears. We're all that remains of His physical presence on the earth. The Church exists to be Jesus to the lost world, and we do that through the local church where God has planted us.

I've heard it said often enough, "You're the only Jesus some people may ever see." The definition of the Church in the New Testament is "the ones who have been called out." This is exactly what happened to us when we first responded to His voice. We were drawn out of our upside-down world and turned right-side up by God's grace. We were saved and changed by the love of Jesus Christ. Now we're citizens of a distant land. Our worldview has been transformed into a different view. Today we see things according to God's perspective and live accordingly. But Jesus made it very clear that while we have been called out, we also have been called to go back in and finish His work.

What Is His Work?

The next question is obvious. "What *is* His work?" Here's where things get sticky. Many Christians have a view of church that can be simply described as "Me Church." They want the time they spend at church to fill their spiritual gas tanks enough to bring them back into the parking lot next Sunday. If you happen to be a hired pastor or a leader, you'd better "top off" those tanks lest they run out of gas and end up in some other church's parking lot. The pressure to build a church according to this model is intense. And it may very well kill it one day.

The reason I had grown so frustrated early on is that I fell into the same trap many other ministers stumble into. Most of my time was spent servicing the needs of the insiders. I planned worship services, prepared sermons, ran programs, and raised funds to keep the offering plates spinning. Most attempts to break free from this box were like trying to kiss a buzz saw. Every time I tried to rally the troops to take a hill for Jesus, we stumbled awkwardly just trying to make it out the front door. "At least we tried," we mumbled. Then we retreated once again to our fantasy world.

Even worse, everyone seemed to have an opinion about what the focus of the church was supposed to be. "We need to teach Bible prophecy," I would hear. "The world needs to know the end is near." Others would tell me, "Preacher, just let the people know who they are in Christ. That will solve all our problems." The advice kept coming. "We need to win this next election, or it's lights out for America." My favorite solution to the world's problems came from one person who said, "You need to preach more Calvinism, and we need to sing more old hymns about the doctrines of grace."

All of this seemed so hollow. Looking back, my frustration was over the fact that most people kept missing the main point. Why weren't we more concerned about rescuing people in crisis and offering them deliverance in the name of Jesus Christ? Ever since I was made aware of the circumstances of my conception and birth, I cannot get one frozen image out of my mind: the picture of my fifteen-year-old mom curled up in a little ball in the corner of an examination room. As she lay weeping, there was nothing I could do to help her that day. Sometimes I wonder if, in the holy place where we are "fearfully and wonderfully made" by the hand if God, I felt something too. Did God plant a small seed in my tiny heart that has grown over the years?

I have no other way to explain what I feel inside. Just the sight of bitter tears and the sound of brokenhearted cries shift my feet into high gear. What's even worse is that I ache when the body of Christ misses the opportunity to wrap its arms around their suffering. It sends a high-voltage jolt through my system.

Do you feel it too?

3

His Story

Alexander, Caesar, Charlemagne, and I have founded empires.
But on what did we rest the creations of our genius?
Upon force. Jesus Christ founded his empire upon love;
and at this hour millions of men would die for him.
–Napoleon Bonaparte

One day Jesus was busy healing the sick and teaching some pretty amazing stuff. The champions of the status quo noticed Jesus had broken with an important tradition. It appeared that neither He nor His disciples fasted, at least not in the eyes of the public. The Pharisees fasted. They were the masters of sucking in their guts and tightening their belts for God. Even the disciples of John the Baptist fasted. "But Your disciples do not fast," they said (see Matt. 9:14, Mark 2:18).

A Groom, a Patch, and Wine

Here's a little side note: Jesus fasted once for forty days straight. He could have buried them with His fasting prowess. He even conquered the temptation to turn rocks into bread as He teetered on the brink of starvation. How laughable it must have seemed to Jesus that they would question His commitment to fast. He fasted regularly; He just didn't brag about it like everyone else.

At the heart of their inquiry was the notion that Jesus had parted company with the old guard. He was different, and they could see it clearly. They wanted an explanation in order to critique His choices, perhaps even humiliate Him in the eyes of His followers. I love the fact that Jesus didn't flinch or change the direction of His focus to please the critics.

He indulged their inquiry about fasting. But Jesus did it in a way that defused the verbal hand grenade they had just tossed at His feet. On many occasions Jesus confronted baseless convictions and stubborn ideas with curve balls. He loved the indirect approach. He regaled them with a picture painted in words, an illustration for the imagination. The answer to their question lay in understanding simple things like weddings, cloth patches, and wine. Most people would have been sucked into His creative style of communication and disarmed by its apparent harmlessness. It reminds me of how much fun it is to hold a cute little kitten in your hands. It would be entirely pleasurable were it not for those sharp little claws that snag you so unexpectedly.

Here's the essence of what Jesus said in Matthew 9: when people are invited to a wedding feast, they come with the expectation of celebrating. They enjoy being a guest in the presence of the groom and having fun with the rest of the wedding party. It is a day of festivity. So why would someone show up to a banquet, filled with fine cuisine and a spirit of celebration, as though they were attending a funeral? Jesus drives this point hard. Don't confuse times of celebration with sorrow! Why is it that "spiritual people" must look like they're never having any fun?

Jesus then shifted the focus to clothes. Here's something we can all relate to. You have a nice piece of clothing you love wearing. It's comfortable, and you look good in it. Then you brush up against a nail or a jagged piece of furniture, and it rips. Rats! Now you have a choice to make. You can throw it away. You can keep wearing it with a big hole that exposes a portion of your body. Or you may choose to sew a patch on the garment. Now if you choose to do the latter, you'd never put a new piece of cloth on an old piece of clothing. As the new cloth shrinks over time, it tears a larger hole in your clothes. You're right back where you started, only worse off and more exposed.

The point Jesus was making is this: when you call attention to yourself by fasting in public, you are only seeking the praise of men. Jesus said, "When you fast, do not look somber as the hypocrites do, for they disfigure their faces to show men they are fasting. I tell you the truth, they have received their reward in full" (Matt. 6:16). In other words, showcasing self-righteousness is a sham. It doesn't prove how devout you are or how genuinely spiritual your lifestyle may be. This type of fake, pious maneuvering doesn't fix the big rip in the worn-out clothing of religion. It's the same tired approach that doesn't work, will never work, and ultimately fails to inspire others to follow our God. So stop putting the wrong patch job on what's wrong about our worship and service to God. Just fix it!

At last Jesus came to the third and perhaps the most powerful illustration of all. Consider what happens when a person puts wine into a wineskin. As the wine ferments, it releases gasses that cause the wineskin to expand. If the wineskin is old and stressed, it's foolish to fill it with new wine. It will explode. The wine and the wineskin will be ruined. All your effort to prepare for the day you would enjoy this pleasure is wasted. New wine belongs in new wineskins.

Perhaps the hardest thing to do is to put something new into something old. It's a peculiar trait of human nature to hang onto our old ideas, our old preferences, and our old ways. As we age, we face the great risk of losing our elasticity. We may become inflexible and resistant to change. It's hard to adapt once we allow ourselves to become old wineskins. We just sit around and whine about the new wine.

The ministry of Jesus Christ was like a taste of new wine. He didn't view the God of heaven as detached and unapproachable or hidden behind some dark and ominous cloud up above. God didn't sneer at humanity as they crawled in the dust below. Jesus called God "Father." And with spectacular flare He poured out the new wine of God's grace. Jesus was a generous host. On many occasions He brought a hush over the banquet celebration. As all eyes focused on Him, He offered a toast to God's spectacular glory.

Jesus understood that the old wineskins, filled with the dead traditions of men, would never tolerate such an encounter with grace. They required men and women to inch their way into God's presence. Jesus blazed a new trail and lifted the traveling burdens they placed on the backs of humanity.

No longer would it be necessary for a man or a woman to starve their way into heaven. No longer would people be expected to earn the right to become a child of God. He swung the gates of heaven open wide for anyone who dared to believe in Him and follow Him across the threshold. The sinners, the physically diseased and disabled, the people swallowed up by misery and misfortune, loved Him for this taste of new wine.

The old wineskins, however, spewed bitter wine at Him throughout His entire three-year ministry. Perhaps it's an irony that He once fasted publicly for all to see. It happened as He hung on the Cross. During those final moments of His earthly life, Jesus cried out, "I thirst." So the old wineskins rushed to give Him the only thing they had to offer the battered Son of God. It was the only thing they had ever given anyone for centuries. They offered Him their vinegar, their old soured wine. After He took their medicine on the Cross, He died. And it was finished.

Jesus drank the bitter wine so we wouldn't have to drink it for ourselves. If you haven't expressed thanks today for His gift to you, why not pause right now and do so? Tell Him how wonderfully blessed you are. If you've never received the gift of salvation that He offers, don't read another word until you've given Him your life. You must try this new wine.

Taste and see that the LORD *is good; blessed is the*
man who takes refuge in him (Psa. 34:8).

Jesus Pours out New Wine

Thankfully, Jesus didn't propose to change religion into a "new and improved" version of itself. He didn't offer an old product in a new box. He threatened to blow it up entirely. His walk with God was nothing short of revolutionary. Jesus stepped into our human maze and fulfilled the entire system of the Old Testament law. He dismantled the suffocating traditions of men that sucked the life and joy from our hearts. He exposed the sinister plot of evil forces to damn our souls. Absolute forgiveness and peace with God are His legacy and our inheritance.

When Jesus finished His teaching about weddings, patches, and wineskins, something amazing happened. It further illustrated the truth of what He had been teaching. In rapid succession, one crisis after another presented itself to Jesus. Enter Jairus, ruler of the local synagogue, a grief-stricken father who had just left his dying daughter's bedside. He has but one hope. He must somehow persuade the miracle worker to prove His reputation against the greatest challenge of all. So he pleaded with Jesus, "Come and put your hand on her, and she will live" (Matt. 9:18).

On the journey to Jairus' home, a woman who suffered with a bleeding problem for twelve years brushed her finger against the outer edges of Jesus' clothes. She was afraid and ashamed. Because of her illness, everyone considered her unclean. Today we might say, "Don't get too close," or "Keep a safe distance!" She couldn't touch or be touched. She was no better off than a leper in the eyes of the public. Her medical bills had already wiped out her life savings. This was perhaps the last desperate act of a dying woman. She had nothing and no one—until she found Jesus. Her trembling touch combined with one courageous act of faith brought healing to her body. Disease and sickness were handed a fatal blow that day.

From there, Jesus resumed His flight with the anguished father. At the house they encountered a circus of mourners parading around the lifeless girl's bedside. It's hard to imagine, but it was the crazy custom of that day. All eyes were upon Jesus, though, as He gazed upon her quiet and innocent face. He viewed death from the perspective of someone who had lived where people go after they die. Jesus said, "'The girl is not dead but asleep.' But they laughed at him" (Matt. 9:24). How cruel was that? But how sweet it must have been to see Jesus take the hand of that little child and pull her back into the land of the living. With these words in Luke 8:54—"My child, get up!"— death was delivered a knockout punch that day.

As if this weren't enough commotion for one day, while He was leaving the house, two blind men followed Him. I've often wondered how they were able to do that. Nevertheless, they were extremely motivated by what Jesus had just done for a dead child and her grieving parents. News traveled fast, even in first-century Capernaum. I'm sure the blind men reasoned, "If a home shrouded in grief could be transformed into a dwelling place of celebration, it would be a small thing for Jesus to remove the shroud from our eyes. We want to see!" What a sight it must have been when Jesus touched their eyes with His calloused carpenter's hands. His touch, combined with their faith, reopened the windows of the world to their senses. They stood there dumbfounded as Jesus lectured them about keeping what He had just done a secret. Already the press of people had begun to restrict His freedom of movement. Their previous blindness must have retreated to their ears because they did the exact opposite of what Jesus requested. But don't miss this truth: the Light of the world invaded darkness that day.

There was no time for rest, not even for the weary. As the day slowly retired, there was one more person for Jesus to transform. Perhaps even greater than death itself, the most feared of all conditions in this ancient land was demon-possession. This was the living death. They saved the most difficult case for last. With an economy of words—noticeably different from Hollywood-style sensationalism—Matthew stated that Jesus performed an exorcism. The evangelist made no mention of spinning heads or foaming at the mouth. There was only one sign that this man had been delivered from his demons. Ever since they had seized control, He had been mute. He had lived in silence…but now he spoke. The crowd was amazed at what Jesus did. They said, "Nothing like this has ever been seen in Israel" (Matt. 9:33). Hell was delivered a mortal wound that day.

This reminds me of a statement Jesus once made about the effects of His ministry. "The blind receive sight, the lame walk, those who have leprosy are cured, the deaf hear, the dead are raised, and the good news is preached to the poor" (11:5). It was just another day at the office. Jesus loved what He did because it was what the Father sent Him to do.

A "New Wine" Church

Matthew chapter nine comes to an end as Jesus says, "The harvest is plentiful but the workers are few. Ask the Lord of the harvest, therefore, to send out workers into his harvest field" (9:37-38). This was reality for Jesus. He wanted to send workers into the sprawling fields of human suffering and crisis. Even though the religious leaders of the day were surrounded by many great opportunities and needs, they had succumbed to physical and spiritual blindness. Tragically, all their emotional energy was wasted on the attempt to discredit Jesus: "Why don't you and your disciples fast?" Jesus, on the other hand, was bothered that people lacked compassion for those in crisis and lacked the inspiration to minister to their hurts.

The religionists loved their rules, but they had no relationship with the Rule-Giver. It must have pricked their conscience when He turned to them and said, "It is not the healthy who need a doctor, but the sick. …For I have not come to call the righteous, but sinners" (vv. 12-13). Jesus viewed

His ministry activity as a type of spiritual triage. The healthy were in no immediate need of a doctor. Jesus wanted His disciples to step out of the old ways of thinking, discard the old wineskins of stale religion, and love broken, sick people, like He did. He wanted to establish nothing less than a groundbreaking, religion-busting, earth-transforming revolution. This is what Jesus meant by "new wine" in "new wineskins."

Imagine a church that allowed itself to be transformed into a new wineskin. A fresh, new wine could be poured into her. Our Lord would be so pleased. The beauty of His Bride—His church—would shine with breathtaking effect. What's even better is that she would be filled with the joy of His indwelling presence. The power of His ministry through that church would shake the foundations of hell itself. Imagine the people who would be positively changed and delivered. We have a great opportunity to free people from the crises that paralyze their lives. Imagine them filling our hallways and pews, giving testimonies of the miracles they've experienced.

So let's either be that kind of church together…or go start one that is. Life is too short to miss this.

4

OVERCOMING THE CHALLENGES

When it is a question of God's almighty Spirit, never say, "I can't."
–Oswald Chambers

One early summer evening, just before a spectacular west Texas sunset, I was out walking on one of the dirt roads near my home. I was the tender age of nineteen. I remember praying to God, "What do You want me to do with my life?" Little did I know He was prepared to answer that question in a compelling way! I was about to enter into a defining moment that would determine the direction of my life.

As the sun neared the horizon that evening, I marveled at a spectacular cumulonimbus cloud suspended in the sky. It was isolated, towering, growing toward the jet stream. I felt the power and the beauty of nature in my senses. Then God spoke to my heart: *Look at My cloud. Do you see it?*

"Yes, Lord. It is magnificent. Bravo!"

Do you see the plane circling the storm?

"Yes, Lord."

As I talked with God, He filled my mind with ideas and impressions. His communication with me that evening was not limited to the type of conversation one normally experiences in an exchange with another person. He spoke in my soul rather than in my ears. In fact, these words have had incredible staying power over the years. I revisit them frequently.

He continued. *That plane represents the height of man's technological achievements.*

The plane itself was dwarfed by the thunderstorm. To this day I'm not sure what type of aircraft it was, perhaps a 737 or another type of passenger jet. In all likelihood, the pilot had requested a course change to avoid this isolated thunderstorm. A mere flirtation with the convective forces off the wingtip might have spelled disaster.

The impressions from God resumed in my mind. *For centuries man dreamed of taking flight, worked diligently to advance his knowledge of physics, and sought to master these forces at will. The plane flies not because man invented something new. He merely harnessed a few of the fundamental principles contained within the laws by which I direct the universe. By comparison, My cloud is suspended effortlessly above the earth.*

At that moment the cloud began a transformation. As the sun set, I saw a metamorphosis in the spectrum of colors reflecting from the cloud. Red, deep purple, yellow, and orange all filled the sky. Increasingly visible were the flashes of lightning from within the cloud, momentarily erasing the color palette with intense bursts of white light. I wondered if anyone else had stopped what they were doing to marvel at this presentation of force and beauty.

James, God said, *nothing compares to Me. My power and beauty are without parallel. With one blast of turbulent air from this cloud, the airplane would be sent careening to the ground. Of all the achievements of man, has he found a way to duplicate this cloud? It's enormous, and yet with all of man's arrogance, he cannot compare himself or his accomplishments to My glory.*

Just as I made this cloud, I made you. I had a plan for you before you were born. I designed you to be a preacher. I am now calling you to be a preacher. Many people are lost on a broad road that leads to destruction. Call out to them. Lead them to see Me as you see Me now. Rescue them. I will use you to turn people to Me. Go! Leave. Prepare yourself to serve Me.

I've spent more than thirty years reflecting on what He said to me that evening. It was the beginning of a very intimate journey with God, through the years sustained by faith, strengthened by the unshakeable experience of an undeniable encounter with my Creator. I'm still in awe over His choice of me individually. I never would have chosen me for this assignment. I've seen in others gifts and personality traits that far exceed my own. I've often wondered, *Why, God, did you choose me and not them?*

My greatest challenges were yet to come, however. I had no idea how to begin. Should I go to college and study the Bible? If so, which college should I attend? Where would the money come from? The most frightening thought was, *People will think you're crazy if you tell this story out loud.*

What to do?

A few weeks later I found myself sitting in church, listening to a guest preacher. The sermon caught my attention because of the subject matter. The minister grew increasingly excited as he talked about the wonders of creation, the stars in the heavens, the distance between the galaxies, and the mysteries of life on earth. Given the similarity and the magnitude of recent events in my own life, I was captivated by his message.

It would have been a normal Sunday morning service except for what happened at the end. After the invitation for people to come forward in response to the message, after the offering plates were passed, and even after the final prayer was offered, he stopped everyone from making a hasty retreat to the parking lot. "Excuse me," he said. The audience stopped abruptly. "I almost forgot. I'm the dean of admissions at Hardin-Simmons University. If anyone here has been called to enter the ministry or desires to attend one of our Baptist colleges, please come see me."

I didn't walk; I *ran* down the aisle. I told him my crazy story about the cloud and the plane. He didn't think I was nuts. As for me, this was the biggest confirmation that I hadn't flown over the cuckoo's nest. "Son," he said, "I'll give you a call tomorrow. We'll see about getting you enrolled for the fall semester."

With the kind of speed that would impress even a West Texas jackrabbit, I was enrolled at the university. Tuition and expenses were all but completely covered. After I arrived on campus, I paid a visit to the dean to thank him personally. As I entered his office, I saw the most beautiful girl I'd ever laid my eyes upon. She was the dean's student secretary. Two years later, I marched that girl down the aisle and married her.

I may not know much, but of this one thing I am certain: Expect God to challenge you with a big agenda that can be accomplished only by placing all your faith in Him. He does this for one simple reason: during these seasons we learn that God is absolutely trustworthy. Anytime He asks you to do something, He will provide both the resources and abilities for you to succeed. My experience tells me this: God opens big doors.

Open Doors

God loves to open doors. I believe it's one of His many specialties. And He's been doing it ever since creation. God maintained an open door to Paradise for Adam and Eve. God promised an open door to the land "flowing with milk and honey" for the children of Israel. Jonah was given an open-door invitation to travel to Nineveh and preach. The rich young ruler was shown the open door to eternal life.

Sadly in each of these cases, the door was slammed shut in their faces. Adam and Eve were kicked out of Eden. The first generation of Hebrew slaves coming out of Egypt died in the wilderness. Jonah went fishing for trouble and used himself for bait. The rich young ruler simply turned around and walked the other away.

This can happen to Christians and to their churches as well. The church of Laodicea mentioned in the book of Revelation had a closed-door policy. If they had a vision statement, it might have read "All Things in Moderation." Their organizational values suffered from Goldilocks' Syndrome: they were not too hot and not too cold. They were just right. Or so they thought.

Jesus had a different diagnosis. They weren't completely dead, but they weren't entirely alive either. They were comfortably caught somewhere in between. Neither hot nor cold, they were happily "lukewarm." It nauseated and disgusted Jesus. It made Him so sick to His stomach that He said, "I am about to spit you out of my mouth" (Rev. 3:16). The Greek word for "spit" used here is even more intense. It's the word for "vomit." I'm sure that would make for an awkward worship experience. We shouldn't look to Jesus for gentle and tame speech when something is crawling under His skin.

The intriguing thing about this Laodicean church is the one thing they were missing. Jesus clearly diagnosed the problem when He said to them, "Here I am! I stand at the door and knock. If anyone hears my voice and opens the door, I will come in and eat with him, and he with me" (v. 20). Imagine that! Jesus was an outsider in His own church. What's worse is they either didn't seem to know, or if they did, they didn't really care.

Do people know when Jesus is missing in church? When He was twelve years old, His parents left Him in Jerusalem for three days before they discovered He was absent. If CPS existed in those days, Jesus would have been snatched from Mary and Joseph and placed in a foster home. In any case, if His own parents didn't know He was missing, how much more difficult is it for a church to realize that Jesus didn't show up for worship last Sunday?

He's always in the vicinity, however. Sometimes Jesus is knocking on the outside door, hoping someone will hear His voice and let Him in. But we would never need to let Him in if we didn't so often shut Him out. I get the picture that Jesus was calling out to anybody in the church of Laodicea to open the door. One person could have stood up, run to the back of the church, unlocked the door from the inside, and embraced the One the Bible calls "the Head" of the Church. Ironic, isn't it? Just one person can be the individual who brings Jesus to church with them. Are you that kind of person? I ask myself this question all the time.

Two Doors

Do you have the courage to walk through an open door? The increasing need for crisis ministry is one of the great challenges the Church of Jesus Christ faces today. It's messy, hard work. The people aren't always grateful and sometimes abuse the good will of the people who help them. Jesus once healed ten lepers; only one came back and thanked Him for what He did. This same ratio may hold true today as well. One out of every ten doesn't sound like success, does it? But it all depends on how you define success.

Jesus defined it this way: In Matthew chapter 25 He tells of a day when believers and unbelievers alike will stand before Him in judgment. At that time, He will separate the two groups from each other. Some will be shown an open door to eternal life. Those remaining will be presented with an open door to eternal punishment. The criterion used for entering heaven is simply stated as things done "for the least of these." The least are defined as those who were hungry, thirsty, strangers, naked, sick, and imprisoned. Jesus says,

> *"Come, you who are blessed by my Father; take your inheritance, the kingdom prepared for you since the creation of the world. For I was hungry and you gave me something to eat, I was thirsty and you gave me something to drink, I was a stranger and you invited me in, I needed clothes and you clothed me, I was sick and you looked after me, I was in prison and you came to visit me"* (Matt. 25:34-36).

Then believers will ask Jesus when He appeared to them in such manner. His answer: "I tell you the truth, whatever you did for one of the least of these brothers of mine, you did for me" (v. 40).

Jesus did not advocate "climbing a stairway to heaven." Good deeds are not the price of admission to journey past the gates of pearl. The Bible says, "All have sinned and fallen short of the glory of God" (Rom. 3:23). Jesus paid the price in full by shedding His blood on a hill called Calvary. Thank God! It would cramp my brain to figure out why Jesus even needed to go to the Cross if His sacrifice were insufficient to save us to the uttermost.

What Jesus clearly means is this: any true disciple of His will seek Him, follow Him, and do the things He did. It's really that simple.

Lately I've had to ask myself a very painful question: how can I consider myself a committed follower of Christ if I'm not diving headfirst into the hurt surrounding me? Jesus said we must consider the needs of the hungry—the malnourished. Our hearts should break for the thirsting masses that have no access to clean drinking water. We can no longer ignore the lonely stranger living among us. Many in our world suffer from overexposure and sickness. When was the last time any of us ministered to someone in prison? Recently I've been asking God to show me how I can do more in these areas personally. Jesus didn't leave any of us any wiggle room when He said, "If you love me, you will obey what I command" (John 14:15).

And yet, few things excite me more than the opportunity to raise a flag and march into battle over this issue. I get charged up just thinking about recapturing the original vision Jesus had for His followers. In my mind I can see committed Christ-followers from every class, color, and creed delivering people in crisis. Can anything be more important than hearing the sound and feeling the impact of Jesus' original heartbeat? We're the generation called to do some serious damage to the problem of suffering in our world. Don't call this the social gospel. Simply call it being Jesus' hands and feet.

So how do we start, and what will it take? In order to do this, we must yearn for a fresh outpouring of the Holy Spirit. We need a taste of new wine. Only Jesus can correct our "old-wineskin" thinking. Only He can transform our "old-wineskin" churches and enable us to see the world through His eyes. Our minds need renewing, and our hearts need convicting. This is our great challenge. Every Christ-follower in every church, on every block, in every city around the world can be part of this new movement. Without delay, let's do away with the major issue that keeps holding us back.

Old-Wineskin Thinking

Old-wineskin thinking is not a symptom of age. It doesn't have anything to do with being old, middle-aged, or even young for that matter. It may infect any mind at any time and over any issue.

What is it? I define it as a single-minded loyalty to the traditions of men. It carries with it a fear that change is compromise and that our mission is to wage war against popular culture. The "new wine" or the new ideas about church structure, ministries, and how we communicate our message are held in suspicion and contempt. Old-wineskin thinking neglects to understand that every tradition was once born out of a new idea itself, that our priceless old bottles of burgundy were once juicy grapes in someone else's vineyard.

Churches and believers may fall prey to old-wineskin thinking. It's easy to feel threatened by new wine, especially if you happen to be an old wineskin. It's painful to embrace something that has the capacity to stretch your core from the inside out.

For years I've listened to people, young and old, lament changes that take place within the church. Often it really didn't matter whether the change was good or bad, whether it produced fruit, or even led people into a relationship with Jesus Christ. After it hit the front page of the gossip column, the snowball effect took control.

Occasionally people skip the lamenting phase altogether. They jump headfirst into a full-fledged holy war. The change functions as a type of Mason-Dixon line—traditionalists on one side, innovators on the other. Some will champion the cause of complete prohibition with regard to the new wine. Others want to mass-produce it and throw a party.

I must admit I often struggle with introducing new wine into a congregation. It's risky! Some people easily develop a bad case of heartburn when they taste it. From my own experience, I've seen great changes produce bad results. Even when I believed with all my heart that the change originated with God and He was willing to bless it, I've been disappointed in the end. If enough people curse the presence of new wine, it will grieve God's Holy Spirit. Years of forward momentum can be erased by the thoughtless overreaction to change.

Please remember this: No matter how passionate we are against a new idea, a new direction, or a new ministry, it doesn't give us the right to behave in a way Christ would not. But it works both ways. The new-wineskin thinkers need not torment the old wineskins. God's word is clear: "If it is possible, as far as it depends on you, live at peace with everyone" (Rom. 12:18). We may even learn to sip the new wine in each other's company. God will open the doors for any church to stand united...but He can also slam them in our faces in order to discipline us.

The Art of Pouring New Wine

How should change be introduced among God's people? Before the wineglasses of ministry receive new drink, the wine must first pass the taste test. We must thoroughly test every new endeavor by the Word of God and taste for the presence of the Spirit of Christ. We must use the spiritual gift of discernment to determine whether we are in the sweet spot of God's perfect timing. Once we discover we have captured God's heart on the matter, it's time to pop the corks and start the party.

Allow leaders to take risks, if your will and conscience allow you. The best leaders will fill your wineskin with God's sweetest nectar. You will be intoxicated by the joy of heaven. That's why the Bible says, "Do not get drunk on wine, which leads to debauchery. Instead, be filled with the Spirit" (Eph. 5:18). Trust your leader. He's the toastmaster of your local church. If not, then perhaps it's time for you to find a new leader—one you'd be willing to follow in an uphill assault on hell with a water pistol.

Even if a person or a group fights against the outpouring of new wine, releasing it is still the right thing to do. Never think the presence of opposition equals failure or the lack of it means success. It's also important to realize the majority opinion may sometimes be in error. Barabbas won the popular vote on the day Jesus carried the Cross to Golgotha. God's will doesn't change because someone conducts a poll. Who cares what the majority thinks? Go with God. What He thinks matters most—always!

The presence of new wine will cause a degree of conflict. Be ready! The open doors created by its presence may seem more like tunnels of torture. The New Testament doesn't hide this truth. Just look at the number of head-on collisions and fender-benders that occurred in Jesus' ministry and in the early Church. Paul and Barnabas, two great men, had a bitter dispute over whether or not to take John Mark on their next missionary journey. The church of Corinth was a mess. Paul nearly came to blows with Peter over the way he treated the Gentiles. Perhaps they all needed to chill and taste the new wine together. Every once in a while, a church needs to schedule a Spirit-filled happy hour.

It's an undisputed fact that change is one of the many consistencies running throughout the whole course of Church history. In every century we see the effects of new wine poured into the Church. The Church of Jesus Christ today looks different than it did in the first century and in every century that followed. If we keep trying to make the Church fit the mold of last century's great ideas, we'll miss the new thing God wants to do today. Jesus never wanted His Bride to become an old, wrinkled wineskin. He never wanted us to lack inspiration or willingness to try something new for God's glory.

A taste of new wine will bring progress. In a vibrant church, old ministries can be laid to rest and new ones started. Old wineskins can become new again. From His throne in heaven God said, "Behold, I make all things new" (Rev. 21:5 NKJV). Sacred cows can be buried without causing damage and pain to our churches. Praise God! Every cow has a lifespan. We don't need to keep reincarnating them like the Hindus. We can conduct happy funerals and thank God for the wonderful memories. I don't believe we have another option.

The worst kind of failure is success...success at the wrong thing. It's really okay to sacrifice some of the good things in order to do the best things even better. It is often said that *the good* is the enemy of *the great*, and I believe it. No, I've done more than that. I've lived it. To meet the new wave of challenges in our culture, we must focus our efforts on the few things that make the most difference. And may God help us discard the many things that keep us from attaining the skopós—the goal.

I propose a toast. To the Christians in churches everywhere who want the new wine to transform our culture: cheers! May your ministries to people in crisis never cease. Time is short. The end may be near. But remember this: it was said of the first miracle of our Lord, when He changed ordinary water into wine, "You have saved the best wine for now" (John 2:10 GW).

Spread the New Wine

So are you ready to pour out the new wine? Let's be painfully specific. The new wine of crisis ministry will have a difficult time fitting into the old wineskins of traditional church. The old wineskins are built around a ministry strategy that says, "Come and hear!" The new wineskins have a different emphasis all together: "Go and tell!" The former is an invention of the modern Church. The later was Jesus' heartbeat.

A church that gathers to worship but never scatters to deliver people ultimately splinters and withers. What if church were a launching pad as well as a gathering pad? We have perfected the "come and hear" model of ministry, but we need a new model if we're ever to succeed in delivering people from crisis. We need a "go and deliver" model. For a long time I've had this burning desire to transform our churches into a place where we do as much outreach as in-reach. Both are necessary. Neither can be neglected.

It's hard to top the excitement that comes from reaching out to those in crisis. When people have been delivered and placed on the guest list of our banquet celebration, they add an extra dimension to worship and preaching. I get fired up on stage when I see people who have just experienced a miracle. I find I preach better when I'm looking into the eyes of someone whose world has just been turned right-side up. The same holds true for corporate worship. Something happens within a room when we hear someone praising God for the deliverance they experienced moments ago.

Jesus collected people He'd delivered from crises. He wants us to follow Him and do what He did. He said, "Anyone who has faith in me will do what I have been doing. He will do even greater things than these, because I am going to the Father" (John 14:12). It's true. A crisis is really an opportunity in disguise. It provides the body of Christ with a shining moment, a unique opportunity to be caught in the Son's gravitational force. Why aren't we knocking each other over to get to a crisis wherever one emerges?

Today some parents were told their teenage daughter is pregnant. Somewhere a young man just discovered his cancer has spread to his brain. He wonders how his wife will be able to raise their children on her own.

In a small business, a single mother closes the door to the HR office. She's holding a severance check in her hands. Tonight an emergency-room nurse will call a home phone number looking for the parents of a teenage boy they failed to resuscitate. Late this morning a man kissed his wife as he's done each day for the last fifty-two years. As he walks away, the funeral director closes the casket. He must now make the journey home and face the emptiness.

A crisis is messy by its very nature. If you become involved, you may very well have someone blow his or her frustrations all over you. I have a friend who is a fireman and a paramedic. He said to me once that when he arrives on the scene of an emergency, the people he meets are dealing with one of the top five worst days of their entire lives. Sometimes they yell and curse at the rescue team. Other times they gaze helplessly through shock-filled eyes. "It's a surreal and unique moment," he said, "when people are living real time in the presence of a tragedy."

To be pulled into someone else's crisis is to be interrupted. I have a calendar on my computer that syncs with my assistant via a network. One day it went haywire. My calendar was infected with a rogue file that multiplied the number of events on my schedule. I never figured out why it malfunctioned, but it took a week to clear up my life.

There are days when traumatic events break through the firewall and interrupt our predictable schedules. Wouldn't it be nice if we could schedule meltdowns for a convenient time? It's never worked that way for me. In fact, it didn't happen that way for Jesus either. Some of the greatest miracles He performed happened as a result of interruptions. But Jesus built enough margin into His schedule to meet the demands as they arose. Here's the big question: What prevents us from doing this? For most of us it comes down to time, how we schedule it, and perhaps even how we selfishly guard it.

R. James Shupp

Lessons from the Dodo

Have you ever wondered what happened to the dodo bird? Until the late seventeenth century, it enjoyed a sheltered life on the island of Mauritius in the Indian Ocean. Weighing in at nearly fifty pounds, the dodo was both clumsy and flightless. But the big bird thrived in its natural environment. Free from any predators, it flourished among the class of feathered creatures.

Then things changed, as they always do. The beginning of the end was first signaled by the arrival of Dutch and Portuguese merchant ships. Along with their costly cargo, the massive hulls of those vessels were infested with rats. To alleviate this annoying problem, the ship's captains unleashed an ample number of cats to patrol the payload. Also riding on the ships were a large number of hungry sailors and the pigs they loved to eat. The food chain was rather simple during those long voyages. The cats ate the rats, and the people ate the pigs.

But when the ships arrived in the dodo's domain, a new link was added to the chain. The cats, rats, people, and pigs acquired a new taste for the defenseless dodo and their enormous eggs. According to early eyewitness accounts, the earthbound birds had no fear of their new visitors. Disaster was swift. The story of the dodo's demise is a classic case-study of the failure to adapt in a rapidly changing environment.

I wonder what the dodos were thinking when they saw those first sails on the horizon? Those overgrown birds probably didn't have many noble thoughts. But if they did, what might they have been?

"Look!" I imagine one dodo saying to another. "A vessel on the ocean is coming our way. Those milky white sails are so pretty. I wonder what this means?"

"I see it too. What is it?"

Well, now we know. According to the paleontologists, those ships were the harbingers of extinction. Today the dodo bird has become an iconic symbol of anything that has become outmoded or obsolete. Its complete disappearance has given us timeless phrases, such as: "Gone the way of the dodo" and "dead as a dodo." And the word itself has entered our vocabulary as an unflattering synonym for "slow reacting," "sap," and "dimwitted."

So what about old-wineskin churches? Can they survive?

Ominous Signs

I'm sure you've seen the ominous signs on the horizon for the church in America. Almost daily our critics slam us in the news media. They shine glaring spotlights on our weaknesses and swarm in parades around our blind spots. Though we are constantly accused of neglecting the big problems facing this generation, we are seldom noticed for the contributions we make to society.

Making matters worse, many famous ministers have been exposed as hypocrites, preaching in public against the very things they do in private. The mosaic or millennial generation is disappearing from our pews—disillusioned and vowing never to return. And there's often as much conflict inside our church walls as outside.

We need more brokenness in the Body of Christ. We should be deeply grieved over these realities. If we don't wake up and repent, our churches will become museums filled with the bleached bones of bygone believers. We must adapt or we will not survive.

Perhaps the biggest question is whether or not Jesus will let any church survive if it doesn't carry His mission forward. Our buried bones need to rise up from death's valley and do church the way Jesus commanded. We need to unleash our compassion on people who are in the throes of crises.

Personally, what are you doing for the poor and the oppressed or the sick and the diseased? Have you done something to reach out to the widows and orphans? Are you looking to help those who are in bondage to addictions or imprisoned behind bars? When was the last time you visited a nursing home to love someone who's dying? What about the child who doesn't have a father? Are you willing to be a role model?

If any of these questions make you uncomfortable, good. They should. Personally speaking, they haunt me daily. The real issue here is not our personal comfort. This is about our undying, unconditional obedience to be the real Church. It's about our survival. Nothing less!

You and I can't do everything…but we must do something.

MY BROTHER, MY NEIGHBOR

Jesus belonged to the race of prophets. He saw with open eyes the mystery of the soul. One man was true to what is in you and me. He, as I think, is the only soul in history who has appreciated the worth of man.
–Ralph Waldo Emerson

One of the favorite pastimes of young men and women studying for vocational ministry is debating the interpretation of Scripture. I'll never forget an argument I had with a girl at Hardin-Simmons University. I was a cocky undergraduate enrolled in the school of theology. She was a formidable opponent by virtue of the fact that she was raised in a pastor's home. Our dispute centered on the curious question Cain asked God, referenced in Genesis 4:9.

Am I My Brother's Keeper?

The question itself was born out of a very familiar back-story. Cain was jealous of his brother, Abel, and what he perceived to be God's personal favoritism. Jealousy turned to anger, anger to rage, and rage to murder. After the dust settled, Cain was the last man standing. Abel's death was the first homicide in human history—a case of sibling rivalry gone wild. As God enters the stage of the crime scene, He begins the interrogation process. His grilling of Cain would have pleased the likes of Sherlock Holmes or even Hercule Poirot.

"Where is your brother Abel?" God asked. His first question was quick and concise—no dawdling softballs here. God's intention was to send a fastball into the glove of Cain's guilty conscience. Even though God never runs out of time, He doesn't waste it either.

On a side note, my father served as a police officer for nearly thirty years before retiring. He said something to me once about investigating murders that surprised me. "The murderer always lies," he said. "If you find the lie, you have found the murderer."

Cain's answer to God's question fit my dad's axiom perfectly. "I don't know," he said. This was a bald-faced lie. What was he thinking? Cain miscalculated two very important factors here. One, God is everywhere and He knows everything. Two, there was an eyewitness to the murder. The voice of Abel's blood saturating the ground cried out to God for justice. God hears sounds the human ear cannot fathom.

Although it has been thousands of years since Abel's murder, I can still hear the echo of biting sarcasm in Cain's voice as he asked God, "Am I my brother's keeper?" (Gen. 4:9). Of all the things to ask the Creator, this one seems very odd. The answer was obvious or God wouldn't have asked where Abel was in the first place. Also, consider that this was a dead-end question. If God answers, "Yes," then there's no place left to run away and hide. This reminds me of something my wife frequently says to our two sons: "Sin makes you stupid."

Now back to the debate I had with this pastor's daughter. She argued that God never answered Cain's question. Furthermore, she said the answer is nowhere to be found in all of Scripture—from Genesis to Revelation. My response was that God either didn't need to answer the question because the answer was self-evident, or He simply declined an answer because the Creator refuses to have absurd arguments with His creation. My next statement to the pastor's daughter sadly reflected my age and maturity level at the time. I told her she needed to study harder before she offered any opinions about the Bible. "To do otherwise would be dangerous," I said. As best I can remember, I don't think she ever spoke to me again.

My approach has softened over the years. Today I would say it this way: God never directly answered Cain's question, "Am I my brother's keeper?" After Cain asked it, however, every chapter of every book in the Bible answers the question: "Yes! You are your brother's keeper. You always have been, and you always will be."

Who Is My Neighbor?

This question surfaced again during Jesus' ministry, although in a slightly different form. It came from a lawyer, a scribe who had advanced training in the interpretation of religious law. He asked Jesus how he might inherit eternal life (see Luke 10:25). Unfortunately, the lawyer wasn't searching for the answer in any personal sense. The question was posed as a test. It was a cunning trap. If Jesus answered incorrectly, the lawyer could argue before the curious crowds that Jesus lacked credibility and authority. The scene reminds me of a press conference where reporters try to stump the guy behind the microphone with sticky questions.

As Luke narrates the story of Jesus, this is the first time the question of how to obtain eternal life is posed. Consider that Jesus left the safety and comfort of heaven "to seek and to save what was lost" (19:10). This was the perfect question for all ages to come. It was even the *right* question. But unfortunately, it was asked with the wrong motives. Of what value is a sincere answer to an insincere question? What should Jesus do? If He answers the question, it may very well fall on deaf ears. If He doesn't, His silence will be used against Him.

You must appreciate what came next. Jesus clearly saw the lawyer as a puppet to the spiritual forces operating behind the curtains. In a brilliant maneuver, He turned the table on the lawyer and asked him to answer the question for himself. What an opportunity it must have been for the lawyer to seize the stage, demonstrate his vast knowledge of the Old Testament law, and capture the admiration of all who listened to his voice. Without hesitating, the lawyer blazed a trail directly to The Great Commandment: "Love the Lord your God with all your heart and with all your soul and with all your strength and with all your mind,' and 'Love your neighbor as yourself'" (10:27).

Bravo! Game over! He answered correctly. He should have stopped right there, high-fived Jesus, and joined the band of disciples. But pride wouldn't allow it.

Next the lawyer did what lawyers often do: He looked for a loophole. He asked Jesus to define the word "neighbor" or, more specifically, to identify his neighbor for him. Under the prevailing legal opinion of that day, a neighbor was narrowly defined as a fellow Jewish brother. Foreigners didn't make the list unless they became "God-fearing" followers of Judaism. Tax collectors, social outcasts, and "sinners"—Jewish or otherwise—never had a chance to live in the neighborhood. The important thing to remember is this: If you didn't make this highly exclusive roll call, you were considered worthless, not just in the eyes of man but in the eyes of God as well.

As a master rabbi, Jesus loved to seize teachable moments, and this was certainly one of them. Jesus launched one of the most famous stories ever told, describing the tragic affair of a man traveling from Jerusalem to Jericho. Along the way he was ambushed and beaten senseless by thugs. Next he was robbed and stripped naked. His blood-soaked, half-dead body was dumped along the roadside to feed the buzzards. Too weak to save himself, death appeared inevitable.

In the next scene we find two professional clergymen walking down the same road. Two temple workers, a priest and a Levite, pass by hurriedly but offer no assistance to the dying man. Unfortunately, they don't even stop to take a closer look. As they cross over to the opposite side of the road, they somehow justify their actions. Who knows what they're thinking? Perhaps they're afraid of touching human blood and becoming ceremonially unclean. Maybe they fear for their own safety along this bandit-infested terrain. Surely they're not so cold-hearted that they've lost the capacity to feel this man's suffering. Whatever the reason or the excuse, they simply walk to the other side and fade into the distance. (Sometimes I have to ask myself which side of the road *I'm* walking on!)

Suddenly Jesus turns on the spotlight. Now enters the unlikely hero. He steps across the stage. He stands over a dying man. The crowd hisses. Mothers hide the faces of their children. A Samaritan of all people—a member of the most despised ethnic group of that day, considered to be a half-breed dog by most Jews—stops!

Why? Will he finish the job? As he gazes upon the unfortunate traveler, our eyes are frozen in suspense. Will the Samaritan behave as his Jewish enemies expect? Is this his moment to unwrap the sweet gift of revenge? What we don't realize yet, as we hear the story with first-century ears, is that the Storyteller has taken command of our emotions. This cliffhanger is just seconds away from being resolved by one great act of mercy.

The Samaritan bends his knees lower as he hovers over the unfortunate traveler. He discovers the broken body still breathes. There is a pulse. Yes, he's alive! Unlike the Levite and the priest, the Samaritan's heart is crushed by the weight of pity. Without delay, he bandages the man's wounds and takes him to a lodge to recuperate. He even pays for it out of his own pocket. Then Jesus ends the story. But don't leave your seat yet. This parable, like many of the verbal images Jesus crafted, has an unexpected twist.

Look again at the question He asked the lawyer: "Which of these three do you think was a neighbor to the man who fell into the hands of robbers?" (v. 36). The "expert" lawyer knew clearly who had behaved as a neighbor. It was the man who had mercy, the Samaritan. Jesus told him—and us, I might add—"Go and do likewise" (v. 37).

The point of the story is this: Real love does not need to ask the question, "Who is my neighbor?" Our answer may fall into the pit of personal prejudice or the sinkhole of subjective emotions. If I'm not careful, I'll choose only those neighbors who are easily and painlessly loved. For love to be anything of great and noble value, it must be pressed to its limits. Real love says, "When you're in need, I'm your neighbor." There is only one question real love asks of another person: "Do you need love?" If you know the answer to this question, then you'll understand the first phrase of the most famous verse in the Bible. It reads, "For God so loved the world that He gave…" (John 3:16). The whole world needs love, and I am its neighbor.

So when God said, "Love your neighbor as yourself," He wasn't joking. Until you seek to meet the needs of your neighbor, you can never love him or her as much as you love yourself. Why? It's a fact: You love yourself enough to meet your own needs. If you didn't, you'd be dead. It's a strange irony that if you are unwilling to be a neighbor, you will eventually struggle to love even yourself. And people who don't love themselves find it even more difficult to love God. Once love is trapped inside you, it will wither away and die. So please, unlock those prison doors! Your love must be set free. "If the Son sets you free, you will be free indeed" (John 8:36).

The love of God, neighbor, and oneself are inseparably intertwined. That's why it's called "The Greatest Commandment." Jesus maintained that this has everything to do with inheriting eternal life. Love is the evidence that the gift of grace is flowing through you. Whatever justification the Levite and the priest may have used to neglect the dying man, I see selfishness at the heart of it. Selfishness and love cannot coexist in any great measure or for any length of time. One will ultimately replace the other.

Ask yourself this question: Do I place limits on the amount of love I hold in my heart because I narrowly define my responsibility as neighbor? If so, God doesn't want us to live that way. He loves us too much to let us love so little. For this reason He gave us Jesus, the perfect picture of authentic love. To follow Him is to explore all the dimensions and the benefits of love itself. He unleashes within us the very capacity to love. "We love because He first loved us" (1 John 4:19).

Jesus had compassion for people who needed rescue and deliverance. He was a neighbor to those living in crisis. He could have stayed on the foreign soil of heaven and let us rot in our mistakes and misery. But He didn't. Thank God! Love found a way to split the heavens wide open and plant the Son of God in the womb of a peasant girl from Galilee. For thirty-three years during His physical life, Jesus was no stranger to our needs. In the end, He sacrificed Himself to meet the very deepest ones. Today He invites us to His neighborhood and showers us with grace—a grace that is greater than all our sins.

Someone might ask the question, "Is this offered to everyone?"

Yes!

"Can it happen to anyone, no matter how dark their lifestyle may be?" Absolutely!

"What about the person who lives in such a way that everyone has abandoned any hope of change?"

God is at work!

"Can the love of Jesus change the most despicable person on the planet?" Undeniably!

"What if that person lives within an inch of hell itself?"

It doesn't matter!

"Prove it."

Not a problem. Turn the page....

6

THE THROWAWAY MAN

*No man knows till he has suffered from the
night how sweet and dear to his heart and
eye the morning can be.*
–Bram Stoker

A long time ago, in a graveyard far, far away…the story begins (see Mark 5).

My imagination takes flight when I meditate on the man who called himself "Legion." Strange. Could this be his personal name? Did it form in his mother's heart on the day she first held him in her arms? No, this name is descriptive, born out of some kind of strange alliance with the darkness. Whatever personal identity he once possessed has now faded away and vanished in time.

In that region known as the country of the Gaderenes, Legion lives a squalid and treacherous life. His mind is agitated. He moves about frantically and aimlessly as he wanders across the rolling hills. One spot in particular is his favorite—the burial ground just southeast of the Sea of Galilee.

No one has the ability to rein in his antisocial behavior. Once his clothes were merely weather-beaten, shredded, and immodest. Now he wears none. And he is a cutter. His skin is covered with scars and sores. The rancid odor of infection and the lack of personal hygiene alone are enough to keep him isolated from the rest of humanity.

His agony appears self-inflicted and runs as deep as a bottomless pit. He cries out night and day. His shrieks send chills down the spines of all who pass by. On nights when the wind is still and the mist hangs over the lake, his cries penetrate the thin walls of the village homes nearby. His howls sound like someone being tortured in the distance.

His neighbors don't know whether to feel pity or fear. Is he a man or a beast? It's hard to tell. His eyes, the windows to his soul, are disconnected at times from our world of senses. He sees and hears things, voices and images that drive him mad. He has become the feral child of an unfamiliar, unseen world.

But there's more. If you were to walk into Legion's domain accidentally, you might feel something sinister in the atmosphere. Call it "the horror of his presence." He watches people from a distance, not out of curiosity but out of some kind of sordid interest. He has become a human plague on society. And like the ninth plague that fell on Pharaoh's Egypt so long ago, it was a darkness that could be felt.

Earlier, people had tried to calm him down or "tame him," as the Bible says. Counseling didn't work. Then, in a more drastic maneuver, he was apprehended and bound—fetters for his feet and chains for his hands. Astonishingly he smashed the shackles and continued to threaten Gadara's law-abiding citizens. Other people who suffered from a similar condition were physically "brought" to Jesus for help. But Legion was in a category all to himself. No one forced him to do anything or go anywhere.

Society has no place for one such as this, yesterday or today. We don't expect they'll change...ever. But Legion did change. He got worse. He wasn't suffering from depression. He wasn't paranoid schizophrenic. He didn't need a happy pill or a padded cell. He needed deliverance from darkness.

The Invasion

Sybil was the bombshell novel written by Flora Schreiber in 1973. It chronicled the real-life journey of a young lady who was diagnosed with sixteen distinct personalities. A few years later the book was made into a shocking television movie with Sally Field playing the main character. As a young teenager, I remember sitting on the edge of the family sofa, spellbound as I watched it. There was something terribly frightening about the possibility of having sixteen people living inside one person's head.

By comparison, Legion would have made Sybil appear quite ordinary and well-adjusted. His very name, Legion, was taken from a specialized military term used in the ancient world. A Roman legion consisted of somewhere between 3,000 and 6,000 battle-hardened warriors. They existed for the sole purpose of serving Caesar and bringing glory to Rome. They suffocated their opposition and crushed their enemies by brute force. Their strategies of warfare were brilliant. Their tactical precision on the battlefield is still admired and studied today in military academies across the world. If a Roman legion stood against you on the field of battle, you didn't have much sand left in the hourglass.

Somewhere beyond the flesh-and-blood realities of Legion's tragic existence, a devastating war was being waged. His heart was ground-zero for a massive invasion of evil forces. He was occupied territory. His personality had been hijacked and locked away in some invisible prison. The hellish hoards that possessed his tortured soul joyfully embraced the name Legion, a triumphant declaration of the frightful things hatching inside their host.

Let's not be confused. This tormented man did not suffer from a "multiple-personality disorder" or from the newer classification, "dissociative-identity disorder." No, Legion diagnosed himself as having a "multiple-demon disorder." It's difficult to grasp how one man could have become the focal point of thousands of demons. The Bible doesn't give any indication what Legion did to bring this upon himself. Whatever the cause, hell allocated a tremendous amount of resources to conquer this man's soul.

The Bible mentions he had a family. Does this mean he had a wife and children? If he did, what a tragedy this must have been! Imagine how many tears they shed. How many sleepless nights were spent wondering if he would come home? How many meals did they miss after he lost the ability to support them financially? Did they become beggars on the street?

I've known many families who have embarked on a painful journey alongside someone they love. To witness this firsthand, to gaze helplessly upon a loved one as he or she is sucked into the vortex of moral failure, is the worst type of agony imaginable. How far did Legion's family allow him to pull them down before they finally detached and let him to slip away?

The Tactics

How could this have happened to any man? At some pivotal moment, Legion's heart was hacked by Satan. He probably didn't do anything so drastic as to "sell his soul to the devil," like Faust. No, the enemy's tactics are more subtle, less predictable, and far more insidious.

Satan is a schemer. He plots and orchestrates circumstances to lure people into his game. The first demon that invaded Legion's life was probably not a hideous monster—no fangs to cause him pain and no claws of consequences to frighten him away. Hell's first wave of attack most likely came from the pawns—the simple seducers, who first tease and then expose every vulnerability for future opportunities.

During the early stages of the war, Legion may have felt the illusion of short-term happiness or the thrill of pleasure. Undoubtedly, this is how many are drawn deeper into the enemy's territory. Legion would have done well to understand the law of diminishing return. As Robert Burns said in his 18th-Century poem "Tam O'Shanter":

But pleasures are like poppies spread;

You seize the flower, its bloom is shed.

Satan didn't allow Legion's first joyride to last forever. In order to recapture the original buzz of ecstasy, he had to open the door ever wider. His casual flirtation with the dark side would soon escalate out of control.

Perhaps Legion convinced himself he was in full command of his sinful desires, that he could stop and reverse course anytime he pleased. He was dead wrong. Self-deception is the worst form of deceit on record in all of human history. You might compare it to drifting slowly down a gentle river. The first hour won't set any distance records. But over weeks or even months, the river will carry a person farther than he or she wants to go.

Consider the number *one*. We often say the journey of a thousand miles begins with a single step. Tactically, the devil is looking for *one* strategic opportunity to begin walking alongside a clueless traveler. Every cycle of sin begins with *one* failure to overcome a temptation. Every alcoholic started with *one* drink. For people who are in bondage to pornography, the journey began with *one* illicit snapshot that saturated and enslaved the mind. Every drug abuser initiated the downward spiral with *one* dose—that first hit of pleasure.

There's a well-known song by Three Dog Night that names the loneliest number as *one*. In Legion's case, one quickly became two. Two became three. Each demon recruited a friend, and each day grew more sinister. The physical suffering and mental anguish intensified until he lost sight of the man he used to be. The new normal was escalating misery—until one day he lost the battle entirely. And from hell's perspective, the invasion was *fait accompli*, check and mate.

If hell ever had a porthole on earth through which it could break free and rampage, it must have been the ground beneath Legion's feet. Legion became a puppet. He did what the demons commanded. He spoke as they spoke. It's a shock to our theological senses to think this man was "fearfully and wonderfully" created in the image of God, just like you and me.

Satan hates God and anyone created in His image. Our adversary is forever weaving webs to ensnare unsuspecting travelers who wander into his territory. He "masquerades as an angel of light" (2 Cor. 11:14). He appears harmless at first, but he will partner with anyone who underestimates his resolve and is willing to make a series of uncalculated and unexamined choices. He will facilitate the development of these choices into destructive patterns of behavior. His sleight of hand creates the illusion of liberty, to introduce someone to the beautiful side of evil. If he tries this with you, run away…as fast as you can! The end game is always death or even worse—a living death.

It would be tempting to move on with the story at this point, but something needs to be said here. Don't be too quick to cast judgment and condemn Legion. Temptation is a common denominator among all humans. We should all look at the miserable condition of Legion and say, "There but for the grace of God go I."

C. S. Lewis, one of the most brilliant Christian minds of the twentieth century, understood this reality as well. In his autobiography, *Surprised by Joy*, he described the events leading up to his conversion to Christianity. "For the first time I examined myself with a seriously practical purpose," Lewis wrote. "And there I found what appalled me: a zoo of lusts, a bedlam of ambitions, a nursery of fears, a harem of fondled hatreds. My name is legion."

Something Wicked This Way Comes

Perhaps Dante was thinking about Legion too when he wrote the epic poem "The Divine Comedy." In this fourteenth-century classic, he described an imaginary journey to hell and back. In the book, as Dante begins the descent toward the abyss, he says, "I entered on the deep and savage way" (Inferno, Canto II:142). His use of the word "deep" is both powerful and evocative. Tragically I've watched people slip and slide into the deep. Sometimes they never hit bottom. They just kept falling, faster and farther, crashing through one false bottom after another. The phrase "savage way" suggests that the quality of life one might expect during the descent is both treacherous and barbaric.

Somewhere, and on some fateful day, Legion put his canoe into the lazy river of Styx. It felt good at first, just enough to make him feel at home. He should have been alarmed as the gentle drift gave way to the roar of the rapids, but he stubbornly maintained a direct course. In the distance he must have heard something that sounded like thunder. I wonder, as he neared the waterfall, if he observed a sign hanging over the precipice: "All hope abandon, ye who enter in!" (Inferno, Canto III:9). Or maybe that's when he saw Jesus.

Jesus and His twelve disciples arrived by boat the day they set foot in Legion's domain. It had already been an eventful and extraordinary day. Just moments before making landfall, the twelve disciples battled an unexpected squall as they crossed the Sea of Galilee. It rose suddenly and nearly sent their boat plunging into the deep. Had it not been for Jesus commanding the wind and the waves to be still, they surely would have perished.

Many of Jesus' followers were fishermen before they linked up with Him. They knew what it was like to be out at sea and caught in a fierce storm, but this last battle with nature brought the terror of death to their hearts. They were drenched with seawater, perhaps even seasick. Their hair was disheveled. Wet clothes hung awkwardly from their bodies. As they disembarked, they felt the security of dry ground beneath their feet. They were thankful to be alive. One brush with death was over; the next was just beginning.

Legion watched them from a distance and noticed something unusual about this crew. The voices inside his head began to stir violently. A cacophony of sounds swirled through his mind. The inner chaos intensified.

Then came Legion's moment of truth. One Man who stepped off that boat had unlimited power and authority, not merely over the natural world but over the supernatural as well. Wickedness gripped Legion's heart. "He's coming for me!"

The Encounter

Legion sprang from his trap in the graveyard and sprinted toward Jesus Christ. A few inches from the Messiah, he fell to his knees and begged Jesus not to torture him. Strange, isn't it, to ask the Son of God not to torture you? That is, until we realize how greatly evil is tormented by the presence of goodness. Consider how backwards Legion's thinking had become! His mind casually accepted the belief that real freedom was torture, and bondage to evil was freedom. That's about as upside down as the brain can get.

Who would have desired a face-to-face confrontation with this man? No doubt the villagers avoided the graveyard for the most part. Unsuspecting travelers like the disciples occasionally crossed paths with this sad shadow of a human being. And since human nature was the same then as it is today, I'm sure the word spread quickly: "Avoid all contact with the demoniac!"

But Jesus took a different approach. This was no chance encounter. The Master always comes through divine appointment, and the Man of Destiny had arrived. Jesus spoke directly to the evil spirits possessing Legion's soul. How long had it been since someone asked him the question Jesus now asked: "What is your name?" (See Mark 5:9.)

In the second half of verse 9, the demons spoke in unison: "My name is Legion, for we are many." These chilling sounds from a fallen choir of angels must have shivered the spines of the disciples. The dirge continued as Legion repeatedly begged Jesus not to send "them" out of the area. But wait a second! If my home or your home were in a graveyard, we would beg Jesus to send us anywhere else. The Sahara or even Siberia would be a far better place to hang our hats. "For heaven's sake," I would pray, "please don't leave me to live out the rest of my days in a cemetery."

The demons, however, begged Jesus to send them into a nearby herd of pigs because they knew they were about to be evicted anyway. Jesus once taught what happens to an evil spirit when it's banished from a human soul. He said, "It goes through arid places seeking rest and does not find it" (Matt. 12:43). Apparently it's pure torture for a demon to be in a barren land with no potential candidates to possess. Amazingly, Jesus granted the request.

Why? It must be for what Legion saw next. As the demons rushed into the pigs, they fell down a steep embankment and drowned themselves in the Sea of Galilee. About two thousand pigs perished. (No deviled-ham puns, please!) As Legion regained the faculties of his mind and witnessed the destructive power of the evil spirits, he finally understood. Perhaps his thinking tracked this way: "That's what the demons were trying to do to me. Day by day, Satan was destroying my life. Never again!"

What happened next is my favorite part of the story. The Bible says Legion was "fully clothed and perfectly sane" (Mark 5:15 NLT). This phrase has become one of my favorite metaphors for change. When I see someone who is radically transformed by Jesus' power, I say to myself, "There's another person who's fully clothed and perfectly sane." The opposite of this phrase reminds me what the devil does to so many people. He strips them naked and plants the seeds of confusion. In fact, there is a story in Acts 19:16 about a demon-possessed man who physically attacked the seven sons of Sceva. He left them naked and bleeding.

The thing that makes the story of Legion so unique is not that he was demon-possessed. As Jesus walked the dusty roads of Galilee and Judea, He healed many others of the same condition. Neither was it the vast number of demons that lived inside Legion that made him so singular. What was special about this man is that Jesus found him and changed him. Everyone touched by the Master's hand becomes extraordinary. The most priceless thing about you is that Jesus delivered, saved, and changed you. Some may plunge into darkness in greater depth than others, but the ground at the foot of the Cross is always level.

In the final analysis, it really doesn't matter what you were, where you've been, or what you did before you came to know Jesus. The only substantive issue is that you've met Him, and He's taken possession of your life. In the grand scheme of eternity, it's what really matters most. Does Jesus possess you? It's the only cure for the darkness.

> *But you are a chosen people, a royal priesthood,*
> *a holy nation, a people belonging to God, that*
> *you may declare the praises of him who called*
> *you out of darkness into his wonderful light*
> (1 Pet. 2:9).

A Church for the Legions

For he has rescued us from the dominion of darkness and brought us into the kingdom of the Son he loves (Col. 1:13).

Let's bring the ministry of deliverance back into the mission of the contemporary Church. This emphasis was so apparent during the life of Jesus. How could we ever miss it? He really did deliver people from darkness. And they changed—radically and undeniably—stark-raving mad one moment, fully clothed and in their right minds the next.

I dream of the day when Christian churches in America are packed with multitudes of people. I am convinced, however, that we will never reach the legions until we go after the Legions. Their number is increasing. The darkness is growing in our country. Most Christians I talk to feel it in their bones.

Rather than feeling defeated, we should be challenged and exhilarated. God is not surprised. He has a plan to defeat the darkness, and we have been chosen to play a critical role. We're children of the King. "And who knows," as Mordecai said to Esther, "but that you have come to royal position for such a time as this?" (Est. 4:14).

Some people may not love this type of emphasis in their church initially. They may prefer their church remain an exclusive friendship club or a type of network for people of similar culture, class, and creed. Any attempt to change this paradigm is like rolling up a newspaper, climbing a ladder, and swatting a hornets' nest—risky and painful! (I have the x-rays to prove it.)

Some parents don't want their children to mix with Legion's children. It leaves many people in the average church a little uncomfortable. Imagine little Hannah Legion confessing to her third-grade Sunday school class, "Please pray for my dad. He just came home from living in the cemetery. He wears clothes now, which is a big change from the time he was streaking between the tombstones."

What do we do with that? "Okay, mental note here: No fellowships or small-group meetings in Legion's home. Awkward conversation. Somebody go warn the pastor."

But consider this: The testimony of Legion spread like a California wildfire. Jesus told him, "Go home to your family and tell them how much the Lord has done for you, and how he has had mercy on you" (Mark 5:19). Legion did this throughout the entire region of Decapolis, a Greek word meaning "ten cities." The Bible says everyone marveled at what Jesus had done for the man.

Later, when Jesus went back to that region, four-thousand people were gathered to see and hear what He had to say. Legion's deliverance set the stage for one of the greatest miracles Jesus performed—the feeding of some four-thousand people with seven loaves and a few small fish (see Mark 8:1-10). Never underestimate the power of one changed life.

Safe House or Danger Zone?

Some Christians go to church to feel safe or comfortable—or both. As a leader, I confess the majority of our energy is focused on providing spectacular worship experiences and motivational preaching. No one says we shouldn't do these two things with excellence. But are we missing something great and exciting?

Many people have never experienced what it is like to follow Jesus into the danger zone. But this I know to be true. I've seen it with my own eyes. The danger zone is the place where the gospel shines the brightest. It's where we experience the saving power of Jesus Christ and the glory of the gospel in all of its relevance.

The first-century Christians knew what this was like. They met outdoors in the "hardhat area." We even have accounts from the first few centuries of Church history that describe how Christians met and worshiped in cemeteries. Ironically they were unwelcome in most other places. People like Legion were always nearby and within reach.

Oh, how we've changed over the years as we have grown in affluence and financial resources! Are we making progress today? The statistics say no. The social scientists keep reminding us that America is becoming a postmodern, post-Christian society. We no longer fear being eaten alive by lions or worry about being slain by gladiators. There is a new Coliseum in our land. We are being slaughtered by cold indifference.

The New Reality

How could this be? Many older churches occupy the most prominent hill in their city. Newer churches are buying up land near the demographic sweet spots where their communities are expanding. But are we positioning ourselves to engage the messy lives of the Legions who live in our world? If we don't, we'll be at risk of losing our birthright. The breathtaking stories that tell of Jesus' power to change lives are of far greater value than all our silver and gold.

Peter and John experienced this firsthand. One day they were walking toward the temple in Jerusalem. There they met a lame man who asked them for a handout. Peter, realizing he didn't have any money, said, "Silver and gold have I none; but such as I have, give I thee: In the name of Jesus Christ of Nazareth rise up and walk" (Acts 3:6 KJV). Instead of getting a handout, the man got a hand up. If Peter had reached into his pocket and pulled out a nickel, the man never would have gotten new legs. But Peter was broke. Thank God! He depended completely on the power of Jesus to deliver this man from the dust.

I heard an old story long ago. During the thirteenth century, Thomas Aquinas went to Rome and visited Pope Innocent IV. Thomas was amazed by the wealth of the Roman Church. Many large bags of gold were being carried into the Vatican's treasury.

Then the pope said, "You see, Thomas, we cannot say as St. Peter did of old, 'Silver and gold have I none.'"

"No," Thomas said, "but neither can you say to the lame man, 'rise up and walk.'"

With the recent financial crisis our world has experienced, the new reality will mean less money flowing into the bottom line of the average church budget. Although it makes me uncomfortable to figure out how to do ministry within this changing landscape, I'm confident God has the same plan for us that He had for Peter. We may not have much money, but we have Jesus. And He's always more than enough.

The New Battleground

As a Christian leader, sometimes my heart is deeply grieved. We're no longer waging war against the devil in the spiritual graveyards where all the modern-day Legions live. The frontline of battle has moved much closer to home. It is being fought in the pulpit, the choir loft, and in the pews. There is so much devilish behavior in our attitudes toward one another that the average church has become a spiritual and emotional wreck.

I'm not attacking the Bride of Christ. What I'm telling you is that the Bride of Christ is under attack. I wish we would admit this to ourselves, repent, and confess our sins to one another. We must break free! We must stop wounding each other with friendly fire. Either we take the offensive against Satan, or he will annihilate us in our own camp. We can't hunker down in the foxholes and survive.

The more inwardly focused we become, the less effective we'll be. It's not a matter of opinion; it's a matter of time.

For any great institution to thrive, whether secular or sacred, it needs a mission to advance. Each member must be willing to sweat out its cause and give a pound of flesh on the battlefield. Great churches are filled with average people who do supernatural things. Against all odds and with limited resources, they advance the mission of Jesus Christ.

Jesus spoke often of His mission. He said, "As long as it is day, we must do the work of him who sent me. Night is coming, when no one can work" (John 9:4). Jesus compared His work to that of a physician. He said, "It is not the healthy who need a doctor, but the sick. I have not come to call the righteous, but sinners to repentance" (Luke 5:31-32). There was never anything hazy or ambiguous about His mission. Jesus said, "For the Son of Man came to seek and save what was lost" (19:10).

Jesus loves lost people, even people like Legion. I learned an essential truth about love when I married my wife. When you really love someone, you learn to love what they love. In a successful marriage, a husband and a wife become one—hearts and souls are fused together. One of the biggest thrills of marriage is to share your love. As the old song title says, "Love Is a Many-Splendored Thing."

So how do we love people like Legion? Simple! The more we love Jesus, the more we will love the people He loves. And the more we love lost people, the more we will look and act like Jesus.

This is where the real battleground is today. It's between love and hate, or even worse, between love and indifference. This is not a new fight. Jesus Himself was caught in the crossfire of this war.

The Pharisees, those self-appointed, self-righteous religious leaders of Jesus' day, despised people like Legion. Sadly, most of the religionists were as lost as the people they condemned. Jesus wept over their empty and meaningless forms of worship. And irony of ironies, He even loved them too. They just refused to be loved. Ultimately they broke His sacred heart.

In Matthew 23, Jesus called the professional religious leaders of His day "hypocrites," "blind guides," "sons of hell," "snakes," "tombs filled with dead men's bones," and "the descendants of those who murdered the prophets." This reminds me of what Mark Twain once said: "Some of his words were not Sunday-school words." Sometimes religious people get lost within their own religion. They lose their focus, then their love. They substitute their own agenda for a genuine relationship with God. Jesus never allowed a loveless or indifferent religion to claim Him as its prize.

Christians who focus on reaching people in darkness seldom fight one another. They don't have time. They're too busy fighting against the real enemy. There is more to be concerned about than how much money is being spent or who is making all the decisions. The quickest way to remove the devil from any church is for the members of the church to join together and invade the night. So get your spotlights ready! As Jesus spoke to Paul, I believe He is also speaking to us.

> *I am sending you to them to open their eyes*
> *and turn them from darkness to light, and*
> *from the power of Satan to God, so that they*
> *may receive forgiveness of sins and a place*
> *among those who are sanctified by faith in me*
> (Acts 26:17-18).

The true Spirit-filled church will claim its authority over Satan. It will march onto the battlefield under the authority and with the power of Jesus Christ. Men and women will be delivered from darkness on the frontlines. Then we'll celebrate our victories together by telling the stories of what God is doing on this day to advance His kingdom.

There will be no need to rehash what happened in the glory days of yesterday. We will not be paralyzed by nostalgia. Our memories will not be greater than our dreams. We will regale each other with fresh stories of Jesus taking His disciples into the danger zone where people with hurts, habits, and hang-ups really live.

I confess, I love climbing to a new spiritual high. I get energized when Jesus saves a marriage from divorce, especially when I'm able to play a small role. In my imagination I can see the pigs fleeing that home and jumping off a cliff. The day I saw an alcoholic pour his liquor down the sink, then fall to his knees and invite Jesus into his heart, was a day to remember. I recall a teenager who decided to walk with Jesus and stop taking drugs. The joy in that home radiated throughout the church where I worship. One day a man swallowed his pride, confessed the sin of pornography, and cleansed his eyes from the enemy's lies. It took guts to admit he had a problem. But courage won the day!

A Courageous Dive into the River of Risk

It's a risky enterprise to send a church across the sea to reach the living-dead, whether near or far. The disciples almost died to get to Legion—or at least, that's what they thought. Jesus knew this would happen, and He didn't avoid taking them down that path. Think about that for a moment. Jesus didn't let His disciples live in safety. He could have avoided the storm on the Sea of Galilee and the trip through the cemetery, but the Great Physician decided to make a house-call that day. Aren't you glad He did?

Take a courageous dive into the river of risk. Go looking for some people who are living in darkness. I can hear the objections right now.

In fact, I've heard them all too many times. "But what if the darkness influences me and causes me to stumble?" If that's the case, you don't know the power of the Light. Light conquers darkness. The Bible says, "The darkness is passing and the true light is already shining" (1 John 2:8). You, my Christian friend, have power over darkness because you have what God gives you. And what He gives is always sufficient.

Jesus told His disciples they were the light of the world. Understand what He meant by that. He didn't mean we are to use up all the light for our own benefit. Neither did He want His followers to run and hide from the darkness. No! Crank up your candlepower. Turn up the wattage. Understand that no army of the enemy, no matter how large or formidable, can do a single thing to snuff out your light. If your light is powerless, it's because you have refused to let it shine. Stop hiding it. Begin shining it in the dark places where God's love works best.

May this be our new motto: "Give us the kind of people no other church wants, and we'll turn them into the kind of people every other church would die for." I believe this is the type of Christianity our world desperately needs. It is the type of church our Lord wants to bless. I believe it is the kind of people we will aspire to be.

Are you ready? If so, realize we may have to go though some storms to find these people. They might even terrify us at times. All I can ask of you is this: Only believe "the one who is in you is greater than the one who is in the world" (1 John 4:4). So rise up! You "are more than conquerors" (Rom. 8:37). "No weapon forged against you will prevail" (Isa. 54:17). Understand "the weapons we fight with are not the weapons of the world. On the contrary, they have divine power to demolish strongholds" (2 Cor. 10:4).

And when the day of battle comes, "Awake, awake! Put on your strength" (Isa. 52:1 NKJV). "Put on the full armor of God so that you can take your stand against the devil's schemes" (Eph. 6:11). If your emotions betray your confidence on the battlefield, then "take captive every thought to make it obedient to Christ" (2 Corinthians 10:5). And when others stand on the sidelines and call you crazy, say in return, "Let God be true, and every man a liar" (Rom. 3:4).

Church of the Lord Jesus Christ, stand and deliver!

PART 3: MULTIPLYING DISCIPLES

The mediocre teacher tells. The good teacher explains.
The superior teacher demonstrates. The great teacher inspires.

–William A. Ward

PREFACE

One of the curious comparisons I find between discipleship in our day and the early Church is this: we *add* disciples…they *multiplied* disciples. Have you ever wondered why? I have.

This question sent me on a journey. I needed to discover if we're doing discipleship differently today than how Jesus and His early disciples did it. Have we left something important behind? Or could it be we've failed to keep up with society's changes and not adapted well to the needs of our modern culture? These were the thoughts and questions I carried as I started my journey.

First I started the process by rethinking the nature of discipleship. I read through Scripture, challenged my assumptions, questioned the models, and then wrote about what I discovered. Next I looked at how to make disciples based upon what I found after taking a fresh look at Jesus Christ. Finally I dreamed of unleashing disciples according to these new convictions.

Had we been multiplying disciples all along, this journey would not have been necessary. My conclusions are less iconoclastic than they are imaginative and challenging. If they happen to seriously "mess up" your thinking as they have mine, then great. If they cause a greater degree of Christ-likeness in our lives, well, that's even better.

I'm reminded of C. S. Lewis' description of Aslan, the lion representing Jesus Christ in *The Chronicles of Narnia*: "Of course He's good. But He's not safe. He's not a tame lion!" So if you are looking for a safe place to settle your thoughts on this issue, unfortunately I may disappoint you in the end. Seldom are the followers of Jesus Christ safe when they follow Him as the Lion from the tribe of Judah. If you're willing to take this journey into the wild, where the ideas are neither tame nor domesticated, then grab your sword and let's go.

To the hunt!

I

SINE QUA NON

Jesus tapped me on the shoulder and said,
"Bob, why are you resisting me?"
I said, "I'm not resisting you!"
He said, "You gonna follow me?"
I said, "I've never thought about that before!"
He said, "When you're not following me, you're resisting me."
–Bob Dylan[3]

It was a normal day. I woke up early in the morning, drew a deep breath, coughed, and then something happened. My lungs went into spasms. For what seemed like an eternity at the time, I couldn't breathe.

Lungs

Cherry and I had been married for a little over a year. We were renting a tiny one-bedroom apartment in Ft. Worth. Our lives together had just started, and we were mystified over why my health was deteriorating so rapidly. Over the course of a few short weeks, I'd become so frail I struggled to walk up the stairs to our apartment. And I was growing weaker by the day.

---

[3] Thomas Cloud and Trey Ragsdale, Circle of Fellowship, (Xulon Press, 2009) 27.

Just a few years earlier, I'd been a member of the Texas Tech swim team. Like most of my teammates, I could easily swim a fifty-meter race without taking a breath. I'd always had lung capacity to spare. But something was stealing my wind and causing my lungs to shut down.

The school doctor at the seminary didn't have a clue what to do for me, although the penicillin he prescribed was doing wonders for my complexion—small comfort as I fought to move oxygen through my windpipes. *At least I'll look good for the viewing at the funeral home,* I thought to myself.

As I sat there on the edge of my bed, I could feel my lungs fluttering inside my chest cavity. To my utter amazement, they were in a state of rebellion against my will to breathe. I had never experienced anything like that before or since. As hard as I tried, I couldn't even gasp for air. Nothing worked.

I was terrified. As I slowly lost vision and consciousness, I could hear Cherry screaming as though she were standing at a great distance from me. "James, what's happening to you? Tell me what to do!"

I tried to say, "Call 911," but without lungs, vocal cords don't work either.

So this is it, I thought for the first time in my life. *At twenty-three, it's goodbye.* I didn't know this verse at the time, but I've spent a lot of time thinking about it since: "In his hand is the life of every creature and the breath of all mankind" (Job 12:10).

Then, as suddenly as the spasms began, they stopped. I gasped for air and thanked God I was still alive. I never found out what caused my near-death experience, but I learned to appreciate the importance of breathing.

Survival

The Latin phrase *sine qua non* means "without which not." In both philosophy and life, it describes the things we believe to be absolutely essential. It's what we cannot bear to lose and still go on living. Such things as oxygen and water are the sine qua non of our existence. Without them we die.

Another example of this is "love," for without it life becomes vain and empty. We lose our clarifying purpose. The apostle Paul understood this principle very well. He said that without love everything is just noise: "If I speak in the tongues of men and angels, but have not love, I am only a resounding gong or a clanging cymbal" (1 Cor. 13:1). Without love, relationships die, painfully and in high volume.

Consider another example. Water (H_2O) is abundant on the earth. Carbon dioxide (CO_2) is as well. In fact, every time your lungs exhale, both of these compounds escape your body. But when H_2O and CO_2 are combined with simple sunlight inside the engine of photosynthesis, oxygen (O_2) and carbohydrates are produced. Bread, sugar, fruits, vegetables, turnip greens, and pickles are all filled with carbohydrates, thanks to the miracle of photosynthesis.

A friend of mine, an optometrist by profession, recently gave me something to meditate on. He said, "Every time you eat carbohydrates, you taste sunlight. And when you inhale, you breathe in the sun."

Brilliant!

If God suspended the process of photosynthesis for just one year, all life on the planet would perish. There would be no air to breathe and no food to eat. Discipleship is to Christianity what photosynthesis is to life—intrinsic and elemental.

Discipleship is the sine qua non of the Bride of Christ. When we do it poorly, we become religious asthmatics and spiritually anorexic. If we ever stopped doing it completely, we'd suffocate or starve to death. No doubt Christianity would disappear within a generation. Discipleship is our great mandate—His Great Commission.

After the Resurrection and just before He ascended into heaven, Jesus gave the remaining eleven disciples their final marching orders. There was nothing vague or even slightly fuzzy about His expectations. Jesus said:

> *"Therefore go and make disciples of all nations,*
> *baptizing them in the name of the Father and*
> *of the Son and of the Holy Spirit, and teaching*
> *them to obey everything I have commanded you.*
> *And surely I am with you always, to the very end*
> *of the age"* (Matt. 28:19-20).

Of all the verbs Jesus used in the Great Commission—"go," "make," "baptizing," "teaching," "obey," and "commanded"—only one carries the grammatical force of the imperative mood. It's hard to see it in English, but in Greek the imperative is "make disciples!" In other words, it's not an option, a suggestion, or even a good idea. It's a command. We don't need to discuss the merits or the benefits of discipleship. We simply need to figure out how to do it to the best of our ability. It's not a matter for debate. It's a matter of survival—sine qua non.

From the Graveyard of Doubt

Jesus was a global thinker. Yet He didn't arise from any of the cultural hubs of the ancient world. He was from Nazareth, a tiny town not mentioned once in the Old Testament. It's not even recognized in the literature of the time period, Jewish or otherwise. The people raised there—in what some have termed "the armpit" of ancient Israel—would not have been taught how to wrap their arms around the globe, let alone think globally. Neither were the men Jesus called to be His disciples.

Has your sense of wonder ever spiked when you consider the worldwide movement they started? Mine does! Their plan was not all that complicated. A child could have understood their strategy. They lacked the financial resources of the older, more established institutions of their day. They didn't possess the political muscle of the elite, the relational connections of the socially prominent, or the military firepower of the kingdoms surrounding them.

What's even more amazing is that the disciples stumbled out of the starting blocks. They didn't possess the breed of courage that would inspire the confidence of others. Neither did they have the brand of faith that would lend credibility to their witness. Shortly after His Resurrection and just moments before He launched the Great Commission, Jesus met with the disciples on a mountain in Galilee. "When they saw him," the Bible says, "they worshiped him; but some doubted" (Matt. 28:17).

Doubted? Are you kidding me? Were they nuts? What was left to doubt? The resurrected Lord stood right in front of their noses. I'm stunned that Matthew would be so transparent as to record this about the other disciples. Or perhaps... Was he referring to his own disbelief? On second thought, I wonder which group I would have stood in—worshipers or doubters. What group are you in right now?

Sticky question!

If you were a betting man or a wagering woman, what odds would you have placed on the survival of Christianity at this point? Everything seems so delicate and fragile. God's big plan to save the world seems to be hanging in the balance. The slightest breeze might have disrupted their equilibrium.

And if you were Jesus, would you have chosen this moment to throw the fastball of the Great Commission at them? I wouldn't. I've seen big ideas crush little minds. I've heard the awkward silence of passive resistance. And yet I see three things in what Jesus said that won the day and saved Christianity from the graveyard of doubt.

First, His plan was simple. The big and irreducible idea of the Great Commission is this: Multiply disciples! Jesus wants us to model for others what He has already done in us, *one* life at a time. All this takes is to find *one* person who is interested, and then begin the journey. It doesn't take an advanced degree, only a transparent, flexible, and willing heart. So who is your *one*? Can you fill in this blank with a name? _____

Second, His authority was unlimited. Jesus said, "All authority in heaven and on earth has been given to me" (Matt. 28:18). "All" doesn't mean "some," "most," or even "a clear majority." All means *all*. Jesus had it. Then He shared it. From that moment on, it belonged to His disciples. Today nothing has changed. Do you believe you have the God-given, Christ-sanctioned, Holy Spirit-empowered authority to make disciples? Circle **yes** or **no**.

Third, His presence was permanent. In the last sentence of Matthew's Gospel, Jesus said, "And surely I am with you always, to the very end of the age" (v. 20). Jesus assured the disciples He would personally advance His kingdom through them. In other words, they didn't have to do it alone. We never have to do Christ's work without Christ. In fact, I would highly recommend you not even try.

Have you discovered yet that the effort to make disciples through your own strength is the quickest path to failure? I have! And it was a painful lesson. No matter how hard I tried, I kept failing. You cannot do this in your own strength, in your own flesh, even if yours is "Type A" or "Grade A" flesh. The apostle Paul learned this lesson—like many of us—the hard way: "For I know that in me (that is, in my flesh) nothing good dwells," and "those who are in the flesh cannot please God" (Rom. 7:18, 8:8 NKJV).

Never give God the best of what He doesn't want, nor the world more of what it doesn't need.

An Exciting Adventure

Personally I've discovered our world isn't very interested in me. I know this is an odd thought, but it's probably not all that curious about you either. The world doesn't give much positive attention to Christianity simply because it believes we have so little to offer.

However, there is one thing that causes people to turn their heads and take notice. One thing captures their attention and creates interest. When the world sees evidence that Jesus is working in us and changing us, it becomes curious. Jesus' presence has never failed to attract attention. This was true in the New Testament, and it's still true today. The world's curiosity about the real, compassionate, life-changing, and all-powerful Son of God is our open door.

I have this crazy dream we're about to step through in a big way to the other side. I believe the Body of Christ is tired of stumbling across the threshold with embarrassment. I'm convinced Jesus wants our generation to advance the Great Commission like never before. My prayer is that we will live to see this day with our own eyes. Before we draw our last breath, as God is our witness, let's do this together.

As for me, I want "all nations" to see Jesus, "the author and perfecter of our faith, who for the joy set before him endured the cross, scorning its shame, and sat down at the right hand of the throne of God" (Heb. 12:2). A new day for discipleship is on the horizon. I sense it in my spirit and in my toes. We know we'll never multiply disciples through our own strength. We understand the clones of man will never advance the kingdom of God. And we're finally tired of the lifeless traditions of stale religion. It's Jesus, plain and simple, most marvelous and glorious, who makes disciples through us. Christ in us will give birth to Christ in others.

Let's dig deep and find the courage to fix what's broken about discipleship in our day. As you are presented with the challenge of rethinking this issue, seize it. When you're asked to raise the level of personal risk, go after it. And when the Lord calls you to make the big change to your own life, love it.

This will be an exciting adventure. Will you join me? With every breath, please say "Yes!" And walk with me through the next few chapters as we dig even deeper into the nature of biblical discipleship.

I'll see you there.

RETHINKING DISCIPLESHIP, PAST

*Nature never appeals to intelligence until habit and instinct are useless.
There is no intelligence where there is no change and no need of change.*
–H. G. Wells, *The Time Machine*

If you could go back in time, where would you go? Would you use your knowledge of future events for profit or for gain? If you could witness your own birth, would you seize an opportunity to be there? Or would your interests lie elsewhere? Perhaps you might use the opportunity to rectify a mistake or reclaim some precious time with someone who is no longer with you.

Imagine that you have in your possession the incredible stainless steel DMC-12 DeLorean featured in Robert Zemeckis' *Back to the Future*. It's equipped with that mysterious flux capacitor that activates time travel at 88 mph. There is but one limitation, however. You may visit and safely return from just one moment. What to do? Where to go?

If it were my choice, I might think about stopping at Southampton, England, on April 10, 1912. I'd look for Captain Edward John Smith. If I could find him on the deck of the Titanic, I'd warn him that he was about to embark on a fatal voyage, and that 1,517 people would soon die in the frigid waters of the Atlantic—himself included. But who knows what the unintended consequences might be?

Thinking back further, I might plan to visit Fairfield, Connecticut, on August 14, 1901. I'd search the skies to see if I could find Gustave Whitehead, a Bavarian immigrant, flying the airplane he called "Number 21" across the golden coastline. If he could be spotted, I might solve the controversy among aviation buffs as to whether Gustave preceded the Wright Brothers in manned-powered flight. Ah, but who would believe me once I returned?

I've always dreamed of what it would be like to stand before the Castle Church in Wittenberg, Germany, on October 31, 1517. Did anyone else hear the sound of the hammer striking the nail as a troubled Augustinian monk fixed his grievances to the door? Did anybody stop what they were doing on that day? Was there someone who noticed the precise moment when Martin Luther began the Protestant Reformation?

The choices are endless. It would be interesting to meet Helen of Troy and see if she really had a "face that launched a thousand ships." And Nero—did he really fiddle while Rome burned? What about Alexander the Great—can we believe he wept when there were no more worlds left to conquer? Did Caesar see it coming—"Et tu, Brute"? And what was so interesting about Cleopatra anyway? As Spock would say of this entire discussion, "Fascinating!" On and on we could go.

My choice? Well, it would have to be Jesus. (Is that my final answer? Most definitely!)

A Child among Rabbis

My primary interest for sending myself back through time would be to understand how Jesus made disciples. By the way, I'd like to take you with me. But for this to work, we'll need to dispense of everything we think we know about discipleship. We must start with a clean slate—*tabula rasa*—an essential step in order to rethink this issue.

So pack lightly. Leave behind the contemporary notions you have on the subject. Jump into the DeLorean with me, and let's fire up the flux capacitor. Our destination is first-century Israel.

Let's meet Jesus on His own turf. We'll learn considerably more by exploring Him in His own environment and culture. Our first stop is Jerusalem, specifically Herod's temple as the Passover feast comes to a conclusion. Our first discovery is this: Jesus was a really smart kid.

In this scene, Jesus was only twelve. The men surrounding Him were much older, but age didn't seem to be the issue here. He looked young, but He stood toe-to-toe with the brightest minds of His day. The hot topic of discussion was the law. Jesus asked questions—not the type normal boys ask but the kind that gives evidence of a brilliant and lively mind. The conclusion was clear: He was a child prodigy.

The teachers, or "rabbis," as they were called, gathered every year in the temple courts during the Passover feast. They debated the most pressing issues of the day. Jesus fit right in among them. One of the rabbinical techniques of discovering truth was to ask the appropriate questions, to challenge everything, but respectfully and within the boundaries of orthodoxy. Jesus did this, and they were "amazed at his understanding" (Luke 2:47).

Next they asked Him questions. Jesus answered each one. Once again they were impressed, but this time "his answers stunned everyone who heard him" (v. 47 GW). The rabbis must have wondered, *Who's been teaching this kid, and how does He comprehend things well beyond His years?* Ironically this wouldn't be the last time they had these thoughts. In the future they'd do more than think it; they'd ask the question out loud.

A Rabbi among Critics

I'd hang around until years later when Jesus came back to the same location as an adult. What puzzled the scribes and religious leaders about Jesus is reminiscent of His earlier visit. The question they asked was highly thought-provoking: "How did this man get such learning without having studied?" (John 7:15). The Greek provides a further clue about what they were suggesting by their query. It's difficult to put into English smoothly, but you'll get the point. They said, "How has this One known the letters without having learned through instruction?" The point they were making was clear. Jesus didn't follow a rabbi; neither had He been seen with one. Therefore anything He taught was held under the shadow of suspicion.

It was considered outrageous for someone to bypass the traditional avenues of rabbinical training and interpret the Old Testament law for the masses. In that society it was worse than performing surgery without a license. It didn't matter if you *could*; it was simply unacceptable that you *would*.

The reason Jesus gave for doing this was even more shocking. He said, "My teaching is not my own. It comes from him who sent me" (v. 16). This statement must have driven them insane. In essence what Jesus said was this: "God is my rabbi!" Add to this claim that many were already wondering if He was the promised Messiah, and you have a powder-keg waiting for a spark. The situation almost exploded: "At this they tried to seize him, but no one laid a hand on him, because his time had not yet come" (v. 20).

The Traditional Rabbis

The Hebrew word "rabbi" was a title of respect and honor given to exceptional teachers. It means "my great one" or "my master." Rabbis were the recognized authorities in teaching the Old Testament law. In the New Testament they are sometimes referred to as "scribes" and "teachers of the law" because they were experts in all matters of legal opinion. Their influence in the daily lives of average people was immense. In their heart of hearts, most people wanted to understand and obey the law of God. And for one reason: the Mosaic Law was the cornerstone of God's covenant relationship with His people.

If you had a question about whether something pleased or displeased God, a rabbi was the person to see. He could tell you how far you were permitted to travel on the Sabbath before you broke one of the Sabbath laws. He knew how much weight you could carry before you were found guilty of working on the Sabbath. Rabbis debated such issues as to whether it was justifiable to heal someone on the Sabbath, which laws were absolutely necessary to guarantee eternal life, and when it was permitted to divorce your wife. Simply stated, people looked to the rabbis to help them understand God's will.

Rabbis also functioned as the gatekeepers and guardians of the sacred status quo. When I read the New Testament, I get the impression they operated as a type of "thought police," or an activity patrol. They were constantly on the prowl to find some poor unsuspecting soul who broke one of the Old Testament laws, or at least, their interpretation of the law.

And they struck like lightning whenever someone challenged their conventional views, even if that person happened to be another rabbi—a rabbi by the name of Jesus. This explains why we read things in the Bible like "…the teachers of the law were looking for some sly way to arrest Jesus and kill him" (Mark 14:1). And "…the teachers of the law mocked him among themselves. 'He saved others,' they said, 'but he can't save himself.'" (Mark 15:31). These verses remind me of a quote from George Orwell's *1984*: "Thoughtcrime was not a thing that could be concealed forever. You might dodge successfully for a while, even for years, but sooner or later they were bound to get you."

For the average person searching to find God, this type of religious expression was a never-ending source of spiritual frustration. Men and women found it increasingly difficult to connect with the God of Abraham, Isaac, and Jacob. Many of their rabbis practiced heartless rituals and modeled meaningless worship. Jesus quoted the prophet Isaiah to them: "They worship me in vain; their teachings are but rules taught by men" (Matt. 15:9). Religion was no longer about a relationship with the Lawgiver, but blind obedience to the traditions of men and the crafty interpretation of Old Testament laws. Never was the question put more clearly than when Jesus asked, "And why do you break the command of God for the sake of your tradition?" (v. 3).

On top of all this, there were several competing schools of thought among the rabbis, each debating what obedience to God should look like. The variety of legal viewpoints on the table was as confusing as the inside of Legion's mind. There were frequent disagreements about the most important issues. Most men and women grew increasingly confused, if not altogether lost, as the exchanges became more heated between the experts. Jesus saw this clearly enough and took the rabbis to the woodshed when He said, "Woe to you experts in the law, because you have taken away the key to knowledge. You yourselves have not entered, and you have hindered those who were entering" (Luke 11:52).

Ouch!

So what were unschooled, common peasants supposed to do? How could they hope to find God in all this mess? Discovering God's will should never have been a matter of debate but simply a matter of fact and devotion. But sometimes religion becomes more lost than the people it attempts to convert. For all of their religious zeal, the rabbis ventured far beyond the realm of truth and into the swampy mire. The masses were bogged down in confusion. Sometimes I wonder if the first century was much like our twenty-first century.

The bottom line was that many people had already stopped trying to find God by the time Jesus arrived. It's a sad irony because long ago, through the prophet Isaiah, God said to Israel, "Nations will come to your light" (Isa. 60:3). But at this moment in history, Israel was failing to shine upon her own confused and hurting people.

In fact, the religious establishment even had a name for these people. They were unfavorably termed the *am ha-aretz* in Aramaic, which translated means, "the people of the land." They were viewed as intellectual oafs with crude habits and unsophisticated behavior. The am ha-aretz were scorned as sinners, people who no more had an appetite for God than a pig might have for pearls.

Then Jesus came along...and not a moment too soon. Thank God! He was a different kind of rabbi. He taught with clarity and conviction. The Bible says, "The people were amazed at his teaching, because he taught them as one who had authority, not as the teachers of the law" (Mark 1:22). The am ha-aretz—the sinners—"welcomed him gladly" (Luke 19:6). And when He spoke, "The common people heard him gladly" (12:37 KJV).

Jesus shook up the system. He didn't pass through their schools, follow their leaders, accept their presuppositions, or play their games. He didn't even ask them to become His disciples. He went straight to the ones everyone else left behind—the people of the land. From among them He gathered a group of twelve and started a revolution.

The Rabbi from Nazareth

Jesus was a first-century Jewish rabbi of another sort—uncommon and creative, a true iconoclast from the uncelebrated city of Nazareth. "Nazareth! Can anything good come from there?" (John 1:46). Yes, they were bewildered. The pieces of the puzzle didn't seem to fit the picture on the box.

Their confusion was best summed up by another statement: "But we know where this man is from; when the Christ comes, no one will know where he is from" (7:27). To this Jesus replied, "I am from him [God] and he sent me" (v. 29). In other words, His teachings predated their birth. He was and is the eternal Word sent from God—heaven's glorious Rabbi.

It's interesting to note that Jesus never claimed the title of rabbi for Himself. He never said, "Call me 'Rabbi.'" In fact, the people who envied this title drew His criticism. Jesus said, "They love to be greeted in the marketplaces and to have men call them 'Rabbi.' But you are not to be called 'Rabbi'" (Matt. 23:7-8). Nevertheless, His disciples still referred to Him as Rabbi or Teacher, and many others did as well.

A more intensified form of rabbi is the Aramaic word *Rabboni,* which means "my great master" or "my master teacher." The Bible recorded two examples in which someone used this title to address Jesus. The first was when Jesus asked a blind man what he wanted. Bartimaeus said, "Rabboni, that I may receive my sight" (Mark 10:52 NKJV). The second instance occurred when Mary Magdalene discovered the empty tomb shortly after the Resurrection. When she suddenly realized she was talking to Jesus instead of a gardener, she cried out, "Rabboni!" (John 20:16).

The significance of the word Rabboni is this: *Vine's Expository Dictionary of the New Testament* says this title was used almost exclusively for the president of the Sanhedrin. The Sanhedrin was the supreme judicial council of Judaism and the highest authority in the land. It was composed of the top seventy-one most acclaimed and influential rabbis. Among these seventy-one men, ten had the most power and control. They were called the "chief priests." One of these ten functioned as the president or the High Priest of the Sanhedrin. The writer of Hebrews would later say, "Therefore, since we have a great high priest who has gone through the heavens, Jesus the Son of God, let us hold firmly to the faith we profess" (Heb. 4:14).

When Bartimaeus and Mary called Jesus "Rabboni," they attributed to Him the highest degree of respect and honor imaginable. They were saying He was the greatest religious authority in the land. They were devoted to Him heart and soul. It blows my mind that the two people who figured this out were a blind beggar and a woman who had been delivered from seven demons—not the usual authorities in such matters. But now you have a peek into how Jesus' followers viewed His teaching and authority.

Gathering Disciples

It was unusual for a first-century rabbi to go searching for his own disciples. He didn't need to go looking for them; the best and the brightest found him. But Jesus broke with this tradition. He went searching for His own. And we know of at least one who was stunned by His choice. Peter fell down at Jesus' knees and said, "Go away from me, Lord; I am a sinful man!" (Luke 5:8).

Peter knew he was not the type of man any other rabbi would have selected. He didn't have the slightest chance—unless it happened on Saint Never's Day. Fortunately for Peter—and us—Jesus was not the typical rabbi. He reminded His disciples, "You did not choose me, but I chose you and appointed you to go and bear fruit—fruit that will last. Then the Father will give you whatever you ask in my name" (John 15:16).

Admission into the circle of a respected rabbi was difficult to obtain. A disciple had to prove his own worth. It was first-century Ivy League at its best. Average people need not apply. If the rabbi deemed the candidate to be exceptional, the door swung open wide. And once he walked through, the newbie disciple was bound to his teacher for the rest of his life. Peter must have had this on his mind when he said to Jesus, "We have left all we had to follow you!" (Luke 18:28).

Here is where the word "yoke" comes into play. In the literal sense, a yoke was a harness worn by an animal. Originally it symbolized slavery and servitude. But during Jesus' time it came to represent such ideas as "Torah," "wisdom," and "God's instruction." When a Rabbi used the term yoke, it often referred to his teaching.

First-century disciples were married to the rabbi's interpretation of the Law of Moses. They embraced his ideas and his philosophy of life. On occasion, wearing their yoke around the neck led to a backbreaking and miserable sort of existence. The super-rabbis of the day were the Pharisees. Jesus said to them, "You travel over land and sea to win a single convert, and when he becomes one, you make him twice as much a son of hell as you are" (Matt. 23:15).

Jesus had a very different reality in mind. He said to His disciples, "Come to me, all you who are weary and burdened, and I will give you rest. Take my yoke upon you and learn from me, for I am gentle and humble in heart, and you will find rest for your souls. For my yoke is easy and my burden is light" (11:28-30). For the people who were burned out on religion, Jesus said, "Come." To every man and woman who suffered under the misery of guilt and shame, Jesus said, "Watch and learn from Me." For the masses who were confused by the rules and regulations of manmade creeds, Jesus said, "Let Me teach you how to find rest for your souls."

It's true—everyone wears a yoke or carries some kind of burden. The difference with Jesus is that His yoke won't break your back or kill you. His teachings will give you back your life and sanity. Perhaps the best news of all is that you get to choose whose yoke you will wear. So pick it out very carefully. If it feels too heavy and doesn't fit, you chose the wrong one.

The Great Adventure

Jesus invited His disciples to put on His yoke, take up their cross, and follow Him into the wilds of grace. Discipleship, Jesus-style, was a great adventure. He didn't say, "Sit with Me," or "Spend a few hours listening to Me." He said, "Follow Me!"

The disciples left everything behind to follow Jesus. Some left their nets and their boats. One left his tax collector's booth on the side of the road. Some counted the cost but were unwilling to leave everything behind. One "went away sad, because he had great wealth" (19:22). Tragically, he walked away from the opportunity of a lifetime. He wouldn't risk what he had in order to gain what he didn't. "If you have not chosen the Kingdom of God first," William Law said, "it will in the end make no difference what you have chosen instead."

What bothers me most is that this high-stakes, all-or-nothing call to discipleship sounds so foreign to our ears today. Jesus didn't call part-time disciples. He said, "No one who puts his hand to the plow and looks back is fit for service in the kingdom of God" (Luke 9:62).

Have we forgotten how to drop all other priorities and seek the kingdom of God first? Are we so secure and comfortable in our world that we don't think about changing it anymore? Are we not experiencing life together with our fellow believers in the Rabbi's presence? Could it be that our American mantra of "rugged individualism" has isolated us and sapped our combined strength? We need to rethink what we're doing so poorly and recapture a blinding vision of Jesus Christ. Let's reengage our minds and our feet to follow our Rabbi.

Following the Rabbi Today

Ray Vander Laan has written a captivating book on discipleship titled *In the Dust of the Rabbi: Becoming a Disciple*. The idea behind the book comes from an old Jewish proverb taken out of the Mishnah. It says, "Follow the rabbi, drink in his words, and be covered with the dust of his feet." I've never discovered a more intense student/teacher relationship than the one that existed between a rabbi and his disciples. When he traveled, they went with him. They ate together and often slept under the same roof. A disciple followed his master so closely he would often be covered with the dust thrown off by the rabbi's feet.

Personally I find something thrilling and exciting about this image. It leaves me wondering if we could somehow recapture this model and implement it in our churches today. Imagine having an opportunity to follow Jesus for one day just like the original disciples did. What would it be like to be covered in the dust thrown off by our Rabbi's feet?

Someone might be thinking right now, *Jesus is in heaven. How am I supposed to follow Him on the dusty roads of Galilee and listen to Him like those first disciples did?* Great question! Here's my answer: Jesus said He would ascend to His Father in heaven, but He would never abandon us to live out our lives on this planet without Him. He said we would never be spiritual "orphans" (see John 14:18). He sent the exact representation of Himself to live inside us. The Holy Spirit is the internal presence of our invisible Lord.

In the Greek New Testament of John 14:26, Jesus referred to the Holy Spirit as the *parákletos,* or as we say in English, Paraclete. This word is rich in meaning. Personally I love the various nuances brought out by each Bible translation. The Paraclete is sometimes called "Counselor" or "Comforter." Likewise, the Holy Spirit is a "Helper," an "Encourager," and a "Friend." And sometimes He is our "Advocate" and our "Defender." The literal meaning of parákletos is "the One who is called to walk beside us."

Isn't that exactly what Jesus did with His own disciples? Absolutely! He walked alongside them. He called them His "friends" (see 15:15). He provided them comfort (see 11:31). He did every one of the things "in the flesh" that He later promised the Holy Spirit would do in the future, but at a much deeper level—"in our hearts." Centuries earlier, God spoke of the day when this would happen. He said, "I will give you a new heart and put a new spirit in you; I will remove from you your heart of stone and give you a heart of flesh" (Ezek. 36:26).

Our Rabbi is more accessible today than He was in the first century. Jesus is no longer "on the outside looking in," as He was with His first disciples. He's inside us, looking out for us. And He will never check out of your life. He will never send you to some spiritual orphanage. Neither in this life or the next will He abandon you to a meaningless fate.

The earlier question posed was, How am I supposed to follow Jesus like the early disciples did? Don't miss this fact! Here's how to be covered in the dust of your Rabbi. You and I are blanketed by Paraclete dust every day. He first came to your side when you called upon the name of your Rabbi for salvation. You did the calling; Jesus did the sending. Now you both do the walking. The Paraclete is kicking up dust everywhere you travel together.

Were you aware of this reality when you rolled out of bed this morning? What a captivating image! It will do your heart some good to pause and meditate on these two verses for a moment.

> *"But the Advocate, the Holy Spirit, whom the Father will send in my name, will teach you all things and will remind you of everything I have said to you"* (John 14:26).
>
> *As for you, the anointing you received from him remains in you, and you do not need anyone to teach you. But as his anointing teaches you about all things and as that anointing is real, not counterfeit—just as it has taught you, remain in him* (1 John 2:27).

As a Christian, my friend, you don't have to go back in time to be covered in your Rabbi's dust. You don't even have to hop on a plane and fly to Galilee so you can fire up your imagination. The Paraclete is inside you right now as you are reading this book. He's inside you when you walk down the hallway and check on your children at night. He's with you when you go to school, or even when you do the dishes and mow the lawn. He'll be there when you drive to work tomorrow and when you go to lunch with your colleagues. If you're listening, He's teaching and you're growing.

All that's necessary is for you to be aware of who you are in Christ and live each moment in the realm of God's reality. Never miss the wonder and the majesty of "Christ in you, the hope of glory" (Col. 1:27). So the next time someone is looking for a committed Christ-follower, a Holy Spirit-filled believer, and a fearless disciple of the resurrected Rabbi, may you arrive to greet them in a swirling cloud of Paraclete dust!

3

Rethinking Discipleship, Present

Test pilots have a litmus test for evaluating problems. When something goes wrong, they ask, 'Is this thing still flying?' If the answer is yes, then there's no immediate danger, no need to overreact.

–Alan L. Bean

Can I borrow your imagination again for one moment? Place yourself in this scenario. What if this were your story?

Ground School

You've wanted to learn how to fly an airplane for as long as you can remember. During your childhood, others were content to play with their buckets in the sandbox, but not you. Your eyes were fixed on the skies above. You marveled how the birds of the air ascended on the wings of freedom. In your dreams at night, your subconscious enabled your body to defy gravity. You floated effortlessly above all the tiny people below. Parents, friends, and even school bullies envied your ability to slip the surly bonds of earth. But alas, it was only a dream.

Then one fateful day you receive a postcard in the mail. There's a new flight school at the airport offering discounts for new students. It seems all the circumstances have now aligned for you to achieve a lifelong dream.

After a brief tour of the facilities, you sign up for the private pilot course. You are told ground school will last a mere six weeks, after which you will be required to pass a comprehensive test in order to graduate.

Your brain functions like a sponge. During the course of study, you learn the basic skills of flight planning and navigation. Your instructor teaches you how to master the six basic flight instruments used by pilots everywhere to fly the highways in the sky. You learn how to operate and communicate on the radios. From the safety of your desk, you discover the physics behind why airplanes fly and how to manipulate the flight controls to carry you to destinations unknown.

On the last day of class, your teacher delivers the final speech. "In this classroom I have taught you almost everything I know about flying a basic single-engine airplane," he says, beaming. "I have described for you what it feels like to fly among the birds of the air and dance around the clouds. There is no greater thrill."

As he talks, you imagine yourself experiencing the same exhilarating freedom for the very first time.

He continues. "You have heard me explain the various conditions of flight, like weather, wind, and air turbulence. You know how these may affect your movement through the atmosphere. I've illustrated from my own personal experience how flying will make you feel, sometimes free and other times nauseous. At length we've discussed the importance of safety and sound decision-making skills. I've prepared you to know what to do in case of an emergency and how to choose the best option for survival."

He pauses momentarily for emphasis. Your mind keys in on the word "survival." It's an important concept and something you want to achieve when you begin flying.

Then your instructor softens his voice as he leans toward you and the other students. "But what's most important is that you have passed your final exam. You are now finished with ground school training. So here are the keys to the airplane. It's the one sitting on the tarmac just outside the classroom."

He places the keys on your desk and smiles with confidence. "Now fulfill your dream. Go fly!"

There's just one problem. You've never actually flown a plane before. What's even worse is that you're on your own. No one is going with you on your inaugural flight. Sounds risky, doesn't it? You'd do well to be horrified.

In reality, the FAA would never allow anyone to solo an airplane without first receiving adequate instruction in a real cockpit under the conditions of actual flight. I know this to be true because I happen to be a flight instructor myself. We know the best classroom for teaching someone to fly is in the cockpit of a real airplane. It's the only way to measure whether someone is ready to fly solo and land their own aircraft safely.

The stakes are very high—higher than in most learning environments. If a flight instructor fails to transfer the appropriate knowledge and skills to a student, he or she could have a very bad day. The only other profession that logs a higher fatality rate than pilots is the fishing industry. The air and the sea are hostile and unnatural environments for human beings. The statistics prove it.

But when I compare the intensity of instruction that takes place in a flight school with the anemic discipleship strategy of the average church, it makes me wonder if the FAA is more serious about teaching students how to fly than we are about teaching someone how to follow Jesus Christ. I get the fact that a poorly taught student pilot could crash and burn, but are the spiritual risks of poor discipleship any less perilous?

Physical death is one thing; spiritual death is another. I would argue the worst type of fatality is eternal death. That's why I believe Jesus' command to make disciples is the highest priority ... ever! He said, "*Therefore go and make disciples of all nations, baptizing them in the name of the Father and of the Son and of the Holy Spirit, and teaching them to obey everything I* have commanded you. And surely I am with you always, to the very end of the age" (Matt. 28:19-20).

At no other time in the course of human history has a more important task been assigned by one person to another. So we have to ask ourselves these questions: Are we engaging the most important task with the greatest amount of effort? Are we really serious and passionate about discipleship? Are we even open to evaluating how well we're doing in this area?

Grim News

The September-October 2009 issue of *Ministry Today* contained an article titled "The Great Commission Suggestion" by Steve Murrell. It originally caught my eye because the bright red cover of the magazine shows the word Commission x'ed-out with bold black lines. Underneath, the handwritten word Suggestion is added as an ironic twist. The opening statement is, "What's happening to real discipleship in America ... and how we can get back on track?"

Murrell gathered several statistics from Pew Forum on Religion and Public Life. The research is grim. I hope it hits you as hard as it did me. It demonstrates clearly how we are failing in our discipleship efforts.

Fact: Seven out of ten self-identified, born-again Christians don't believe in moral absolutes. Only ten percent base their moral decision-making on biblical principles. And get this! Only thirty percent of this same group correlates spiritual maturity with "having a relationship with Jesus."

Fact: Fifty-nine percent of Christians believe Satan is merely a symbol of evil, not an actual being. Fifty-eight percent believe the Holy Spirit represents God's power and presence, but that He is not a distinct person within the Trinity. Astonishingly, thirty-nine percent of Christians surveyed believe Jesus sinned while on earth.

Fact: Sixty-one percent of the people who were once active in their church youth group are "spiritually disengaged" during their twenties. More than half of all Protestants who drop out of church say the main reason is because they "stopped believing its teachings." Seventy-one percent say they gradually drifted away. Nearly forty percent indicate their spiritual needs were not being met while attending church.

The saddest fact of all: Forty percent of all Christians do not believe they have a personal responsibility to share their faith with anyone.

What are we to make of this? I don't know that we've ever faced a greater threat to American Christianity than we do today. We're persecuting ourselves from within. The silent killer of our faith is a lack of knowledge, which leads to a lack of conviction, which leads to a lack of passion. Somewhere along the way we decided to dumb down the process of discipleship. But at what cost?

Reality

I've heard it all before:

- People are too busy.
- There's not enough time.
- Accommodate their demanding lifestyle.
- Be culturally relevant.

But lately I've grown frustrated and weary of trying to fit the gospel into the mold of our contemporary culture. We shouldn't let go of the belief that the gospel is supposed to change and revolutionize our culture. I can't help but wonder what would happen if we each led the type of magnetic, contagious life that led the world to say, "We want to be like them. They've got it. We need it. Show us the way!"

Should we believe it's too much to ask someone to lay down his or her life for the cause of Christ? Is it really true the average person is too busy and out of time? Are we to roll over and accept this as reality? Before we're tempted to do this, let's consider the facts.

The New York Times published an article on July 31, 2009, titled, "For the Unemployed, the Day Stacks up Differently." But what caught my eye was a graph that showed the results of a 2008 study focusing on how people spend their time. On average, during every evening of the week at precisely 8:50 p.m., thirty-nine percent of all Americans ages sixteen and above are watching television and movies. No other activity even comes close to this. At the same time only one percent are engaged in religious activities. In fact, religion never occupies more than two percent of the total activity in America when averaged over a weekly period for any hour of the day!

So the question is not *if* we have the time to do a better job at making disciples. It's not a matter of time; it's a matter of priority and commitment.

Where does this leave us today? Perhaps Murrell summed it up best: "If modern discipleship is confusing or complicated, it is because we have strayed from biblical principles and the simple biblical process that Jesus lived and taught His disciples. Sadly, the fruit of this departure is glaringly evident today."

I believe we can change the current reality. I also believe we must. The Great Commission was not a suggestion. The mandate to "make disciples" was never rescinded. We need to evaluate and rethink how we're currently doing discipleship. Let's continue to analyze the One who did it best.

The Greatest Teacher

Jesus was the greatest teacher of all time. Could anyone find a better teacher with greater effect, or produce a more outstanding role model than that of the Carpenter from Galilee? Consider that no one from any field of study or any discipline has mastered the human heart as did Jesus Christ. In all human history, there has never been a more effective teacher/student relationship than the one Jesus forged with His disciples.

Even an atheist can admire the results produced by His words over the centuries. The effect of Jesus' teachings on art, literature, philosophy, politics, philanthropy, sociology, and ethics is unequalled. Believe Him or not. Worship Him or not. But acknowledge that no other human being has had greater influence—not Darwin, not Marx, not Einstein, or even John Lennon. Anyone who questions this need only consider that the image of Jesus has appeared on the cover of more contemporary news magazines than any other person from antiquity.

And what about His influence on religion? Could there be any doubt that if He had never been born, civilization would look vastly different today? Imagine a world with no churches. Take Jesus out of human history, and many orphanages, hospitals, benevolence organizations, and universities disappear into thin air. His teachings have shaped society in ways we often fail to consider. This is pretty amazing for a man who began His life in a rented stable and ended up in a borrowed tomb. Mark Hopkins, a nineteenth-century Christian educator, said it best: "No revolution that has ever taken place in society can be compared to that which has been produced by the words of Jesus Christ."

The Greatest Methodology

But it was more than what Jesus said that shaped our world. We seldom consider another crucial element when we think about the influence of Jesus' words. For most of my ministry, I focused on *what* Jesus taught. My thoughts centered on understanding the information He shared with His followers. Of equal importance to the what, however, is the *how*. How did

Jesus make disciples? I'm convinced the how has been neglected to a large extent. Both are important; neither should be minimized.

Jesus' teaching methodology demonstrated the perfect combination between the *what* and the *how*. He explained and then He applied. He spoke it, and then He lived it. His words and deeds merged into one.

Think back to the opening illustration about flight school for a moment. Jesus didn't make disciples in a sterile classroom environment. He invited them into the cockpit, where they learned what He said under the actual conditions of real-life experiences. He didn't sign them off to fly solo after a few hours in a simulator. He lived with them for three years. Each disciple saw with his own eyes, in real time, how Jesus applied what He taught.

In essence, what Jesus was saying as He called each disciple was, "Come fly with Me. Jump into the cockpit, and let's take off." When Jesus called Nathanael to be one of His disciples, He said, "I tell you the truth, you shall see heaven open, and the angels of God ascending and descending on the Son of Man" (John 1:51). He didn't say, "You will learn about how the heavens opened in the days of old," or "I will teach you the names of all the angels of heaven."

One of the Greatest Ironies

It's one of the greatest ironies of all time. Every church that claims Jesus as her Cornerstone and Lord has more technological tools to advance the mission of Jesus than He had Himself. We have smart-phones that keep getting smarter, social networking tools that can find the person we played with in the sandbox when we were two, Al Gore's Internet, Wi-Fi that used to be Sci-Fi, Bible translations that speak our language, inspiring architecture, and cars. (Imagine what Jesus could have done with a car or even an airplane!)

And consider there is no record that Jesus ever wrote any of the things He said and did. But we know He could read, for He read from the prophet

Isaiah in His hometown synagogue. And we know He could write. On one occasion, He stooped down and wrote in the dust before the feet of an angry mob who sought to stone an adulteress. Jesus left His words and His story in His followers' shaky, uncertain hands. That was a gutsy and unimaginably risky thing to do.

If the disciples had not written the Gospels and preached the gospel, all that might remain of His legacy would be a few quaint references by a few Roman historians. Add to this a handful of official letters and general correspondence—all written by people who made disparaging remarks about His followers. If this were the case, all we would know about Jesus was that He was an executed criminal, and His followers were disturbing the peace.

Had His words and deeds not left such an imprint on His followers' minds, today we'd know almost nothing about Him. The Jesus of fact and history would have disappeared almost entirely. It happened to others, but it didn't happen to Him.

Do you want to know why?

The Greatest Resources

What Jesus relied on was so basic I think we may easily overlook it in our advanced society. Jesus gathered a group of ordinary people and changed their lives. The before-and-after snapshots of the disciples are nothing short of amazing. Life-change is the irrefutable evidence that something has worked.

Jesus took a crusty old fisherman by the name of Peter and transformed him into a fearless, passionate preacher. Peter was the first disciple to go public with the Master's teachings. And he did it in a big way. It happened just fifty days after the Resurrection and during the Jewish Feast of Weeks, which we now call Pentecost. On that day, Peter stood before a vast crowd in Jerusalem and unloaded an evangelistic message that "cut to the heart"

(Acts 2:37). What was the result? Three thousand people were persuaded to believe in Jesus Christ—just like Peter himself had come to believe.

Some might consider this approach backward. If you know you'll need a public orator, you start by finding the best one available. Tell the person what you want spoken, the results you're looking for, and then hope for success. But Jesus didn't do that. He found twelve people He could pour His life into.

Progress must have seemed slow at first, especially in Peter's case. Peter frequently tried to correct what Jesus said, and challenged Him over some of the things He did. But in the end, Jesus got what He went looking for—not a hired gun but a changed life to put on display before a curious world.

Consider what happened in the lives of James and John. They were two hotheaded, self-promoting young men in the early days of following Jesus. Once they wanted to call fire down from heaven on a city that had refused to welcome Jesus. That's nice, isn't it? "If they don't believe, wipe 'em out!" It gives a whole new meaning to the word evangelism. Can you imagine how awkward that approach would be to implement in the average church today? If it were effective over time, there wouldn't be any lost people left to reach; they'd all be dead. I'm glad Jesus said to them, "The Son of Man did not come to destroy men's lives, but to save them" (Luke 9:56 NKJV).

What later happened to John, this fire-breathing disciple, was epic. He became the Apostle of Love. Of all Christ's disciples, John held up the value of love like no one else. He wrote about it, taught about it, and uncompromisingly lived it. Love is such a nebulous term at times that we need flesh-and-blood examples, or real-life stories to illustrate it for us. John's transformation provided just that to the watching, listening world.

The Greatest Challenge

For the Church to restore its witness and credibility in our contemporary age, we need to deliver the only thing that will capture our society's eyes and ears. Changed lives are the irrefutable evidence that what we say and believe is true, simply because it works. When a man or a woman changes for the better, or when their lives are drastically improved, people ask, "Why?" If they look deeply enough into their own lives and find a degree of frustration or despair, they might also ask, "How?" Then they're ready to listen to what we have to say.

Discipleship changes people. "But wait a second," someone might say. "Focus on Jesus. He's the one who changes people." That's correct. Focusing on Jesus and following Him is the driving, thundering heartbeat of discipleship.

These two words, "Follow Me," changed the lives of eleven ordinary men. Unfortunately, Judas broke the dozen when he quit the team to become a free agent. As to the others, four were unlucky fishermen. One was a despised tax collector—a Roman collaborator considered to be a traitor by his Jewish brothers. Another was a Zealot—a political rebel with a big chip on his shoulder. None of them were politically powerful or socially prominent in the larger scheme of things. They were underdogs, like the Man from Nazareth whom they followed. And yet, something happened to make this team of ordinary men extraordinary.

The Greatest Lessons

The greatest lessons are taught and then caught. They weave themselves into our life experiences. Superior teachers incorporate all the senses and emotions, every resource at their disposal, and all the tools of learning to help their students develop both knowledge and skills. They're highly intentional, interactive, and interpersonal. And no one, I tell you, did this better than Jesus Christ.

I believe we remember the great things Jesus taught, but we fail to remember why He taught them in the first place. Consider the three parables Jesus shared about the lost sheep, the lost coin, and the lost son, recorded in Luke chapter 15. Each of these three stories focuses on outrageous love—a painful yearning for that which was lost. In essence, Jesus tells these stories to illustrate God's passion for finding people who have wandered a great distance from His love.

The parables themselves become more meaningful when we realize what prompted Jesus to share them. Here it is: "Now the tax collectors and 'sinners' were all gathering around to hear him. But the Pharisees and the teachers of the law muttered, 'This man welcomes sinners and eats with them'" (Luke 15:1-2). These "mutterings" of the religious snobs and aristocrats could not go unchallenged. Jesus wouldn't stand for it, especially considering it was a personal attack against Matthew, a former tax collector, and many of the so-called sinners who were following Him. Jesus pushed the throttle to the firewall and challenged the offensive nature of their prejudiced statements.

But He did it in a highly strategic and artistic manner. He shared some stories. Storytelling lowers the defenses of any audience. Everyone loves them, especially if they have twists and pack an emotional wallop. So grab an energy drink. Pop some corn. Sit back and be entertained.

Oh, how those Pharisees and the highbrow lawyers must have been lured into a false sense of security as Jesus began talking about things of little value to their world: sheep, small change, and insolent children. But He drew them into the story. And like moths, they flew closer to the flame.

I'll skip the details of these familiar stories in Luke Chapter 15 and get to the point Jesus drove into their heads: God gets excited when the lost are found. When a sinner repents or when the spiritually dead decide to live again, all the angels of heaven celebrate. The last story Jesus told of the bad kid who left home in a huff, who burned through his father's cash, who partied for months, who lost everything he had, who humiliated himself, ended with a twist. When he came home groveling, the father was so moved with compassion that he threw a party.

How like God!

The good brother who never left home? Oh, he was bitter! The father in the parable, who represents the heavenly Father, said to him, "But we had to celebrate and be glad, because this brother of yours was dead and is alive again; he was lost and is found" (v. 32).

Wait a minute, the Pharisees and religionists imagined. *Is He saying we're like the bitter brother? Is He implying we don't understand God's heart? Is He telling us our attitude stinks?*

Gotcha!

The master Rabbi continued telling the kind of stories that challenged the Pharisees' backward thinking until they "were sneering at Jesus" (16:14). They were lured into His blinding light of truth. It singed their wings and caused them to fall from the lofty heights of pride and prejudice.

Here's the point: This is the type of interaction we often miss when discipleship is confined to the classroom. But take it into the cockpit, into the streets, or into the arena where the chariot's wheels meet the pavement, and it suddenly becomes relevant. When a teacher walks daily with his students and interacts with their world, they learn.

We have more labels for this process than we actually have legs to implement it. We use words like "mentoring," "accountability," "life application," "share groups," "coaching," and "counseling." All of these are good words that label what we do poorly. Something else is missing, and I believe I know what it is.

Speaking into Another's Life

In the first section of the book I said this: "People usually don't make changes until they receive enough that they are able to change, learn enough that they want to change, or hurt enough that they have to change." Most people wait to make significant modifications in their lives until after a meltdown occurs and they have no other choice.

We need to rethink this whole process. It's too painful. Learning from your mistakes is not the only way to grow. Some people do this over the course of their entire lives. We call it "learning the hard way." It seems to be our default setting. And it's also a big problem. We finally arrive at the end of our lives having learned the things it would have been nice to know years earlier. By the time you're smart, it's time to die. Don't just learn from making your own mistakes. Let others make the mistakes and learn from them!

When a teacher molds a disciple the way Jesus did, he will speak truth into the disciple's life. Everyone needs to give someone the permission to do this, however painful the experience might be. But make sure the person who speaks truth into your heart is spiritually mature, gentle, and free from the trappings of self-interest. If you haven't given permission to someone you trust to do this, the devil is always willing to provide this service for you—free of charge, consequences included.

Educators call this "the critiquing process." Here's how it works: If I were your teacher, in order to help you move forward I'd need access to some important information. I'd need to jump into your life, even the private areas, and ask you where you're struggling to make progress or are just simply stuck. You'd need to be honest. You couldn't leave anything off the table or hidden behind a closed door and still expect me to be able to help you. In other words, I'd need the truth, and you'd need to trust. The Bible says, "Wounds from a friend can be trusted, but an enemy multiplies kisses" (Prov. 27:6). This proverb seems upside down to the way we normally process our emotions. But it's true. Not everyone who kisses you is your friend, and not everyone who wounds you is your enemy.

Jesus lived with His disciples. It's hard to hide anything from someone you're with on a daily basis. I've often marveled at what I've learned about people from their spouses during a marriage counseling session. Often the public persona is vastly different from the private person. This type of Jekyll-and-Hyde lifestyle always leads to some kind of implosion in the end.

I've known spouses who grew to detest the carefully crafted image their husband or wife portrayed in public. It wasn't that it was bad—quite the contrary. It was just fake. Pretty masks make horrible marriages. I've heard women say things like, "It would be nice to see the same engaging personality at home that we see in our church or among our closest friends. You don't know the real man." And more than one man has said to me, "She may appear sweet to everybody else, but she tears down my self-esteem and bites my head off daily."

People don't make much progress in the home, at work, or in any social environment until they're ready to face the truth about themselves. We're all flawed, just in different ways. We all have blind spots, just in different areas. And we're all stubborn, just about different things. The key is to admit this to yourself. Decide today to make a change. Consider that life change always follows a heart change, but no heart will change until it's open. Who has access to speak into your heart and life? Think about it.

Walking into Another's Life

Perhaps the question we need to consider as we rethink discipleship is this: Why do we keep trying to do it differently than the way Jesus modeled? Jesus did more than help His disciples learn about the truth. He personally taught them how to understand it, and then He showed them how to apply it.

Jesus didn't lay down an anchor. His classroom was mobile. It moved from soul to soul, day to day, and from one situation to the next. He didn't arrive on the scene with workbooks, videos, graphs, and complicated strategies. For Jesus, making disciples was as natural as breathing. It was simply the way He chose to live His life. It was His Father's plan, and it flat-out worked.

How refreshing!

In the kingdom of God, each of us started out needing growth. Afterwards, we're under a mandate to disciple the next generation. You and I must help others grow—up close, personally, and face to face—just like Jesus did it. Your involvement in the lives of others is more important than your reluctance, your fears of failure, or even your schedule. This is about our survival. We must reverse the cascading trends in America!

In the final analysis, you're either a mature disciple who makes disciples, or you are a maturing disciple in need of discipleship. If you're mature, who are you maturing? If you are maturing, who is your mature mentor helping you to grow? Let me ask again. Can you write a name in this blank?

_____

The reason Christianity succeeded is because Jesus multiplied Himself through the lives of others. It's the most brilliant strategy ever invented. If you chose just one person to pour the Christ-life into for the next three years—just like Jesus did with His disciples—at the end of that period there would be two Christ-followers. Then teach them how to do the same thing, and begin the whole process all over again. At the end of the next three years, there would be four Christ-followers. In nine years there would be eight, twelve years—sixteen, fifteen years—thirty-two, eighteen years— sixty four ... After this point, the numbers start to go crazy.

How much time do you have left to do this? Subtract your age from seventy-eight—the average life expectancy in America—and divide it by three—the number of years Jesus spent in public ministry. This equals the number of three-year periods you have remaining to make disciples the way Jesus did.

Tick Tock!

BECOMING A DISCIPLE

Jesus said, "I no longer call you servants, because a servant does not know his master's business. Instead, I have called you friends, for everything that I learned from my Father I have made known to you" (John 15:15).

Jesus called His disciples "friends."

If you were to remove friendship out of the equation of discipleship, it would lose its heart. There is no Lone Ranger model for discipleship to be found in the Bible—no solitary super-heroes standing alone to advance the kingdom of God. One thing I discovered as a kid while reading comic books is that super heroes don't reproduce themselves. They just end up in fights with each other, break things, and hurt a lot of people in the process. Have you ever heard of such a thing happening between two believers?

There is a better way. Here's how it worked in the New Testament world. Jesus said, "I and the Father are one" (John 10:30). I'd say that's a pretty tight relationship—the tightest on record! The Father sent Jesus. He started with twelve men. Their number eventually grew to seventy. According to Clement of Alexandria, an early Church father, Barnabas was a member of the seventy. He mentored Paul. Then Paul took Timothy under his wings. Timothy discipled people in both Philippi and in Corinth. During the first century, the gospel spread with the force of a mass contagion.

From there, the story continues to this very day. In fact, you can draw an unbroken line from Jesus to yourself, from person to person, spanning nearly two-thousand years of Christian history. Holy Spirit-orchestrated relationships were the vehicle through which Christianity spread throughout the centuries.

Each of us needs two things to happen in our lives. First, God wants you to have a true friend who can mentor you, regardless of how mature you may already be. No matter how much you know, there's always more to learn. The Jewish Talmud puts it this way: "He who adds not to his learning diminishes it." Second, God wants you to be a friend and find someone you can mentor. Don't be a clog in the kingdom plumbing. Let God's work flow through you. Believers shouldn't behave like beavers. Each of us needs to tear down the spiritual dams and let the river flow to the people living down below.

What Matters Most

There are more books today on how to apply biblical truth than at any point in Christian history. Add to this the study Bibles, devotional guides, DVDs, satellite seminars, webinars, Internet churches, pamphlets, podcasts, radio broadcasts, television ministries, and world-famous Christian gurus. With all these resources at hand, one might come to the conclusion that Christ's modern-day disciples are about to conquer the world. But think again. Søren Kierkegaard, the Danish theologian and philosopher, once said, "There is no lack of information in a Christian land; something else is lacking." I tend to agree.

The information superhighway running through the Kingdom of God has its benefits, but it isn't enough to meet the demands of the Great Commission. Book authors and television personalities, as wonderful as they may be, don't drive to school or to work with you in the morning.

It's very unlikely that one will ever visit your home or even send you a personalized text message. You can't call on them to counsel you or answer your questions personally. Even the senior pastor of your local church is limited in the amount of time he can devote to you individually. The missing link is someone who is close enough to share your story, to participate in your journey, and to provide guidance for you along the way.

This may be a new thought for you to consider. But if you can't think of someone you can call at two a.m. when you're struggling with a painful issue, then you're an isolated believer. Someday, if you haven't experienced it already, you'll need more than a vicarious relationship with a charismatic personality. A winning smile and flamboyant personality are not enough to pull you through the tough times. You need someone up close and in the flesh.

Isn't this what God did for us? In Old Testament days He dwelled in the high and holy realm of heaven. He heard our cries from below and listened to them from above. He sent His angels and deliverers to unravel our knots and remove our obstacles. Then, one glorious day, the heavens cracked open and God arrived in person, in the flesh, by the fabulous miracle of the incarnation. The eternal Word of God became a baby to behold, a child to raise, and a Messiah to follow.

God's plan moved from Incarnation to Resurrection, from Resurrection to Ascension, and from Ascension to the Spirit's indwelling. The fellowship of all believers exists today because the Christ in each of us can connect to the Christ in the rest of us. In His kingdom we're never orphans, always family, never alone, unless we stubbornly choose to be.

God became flesh, not just because we needed Him to but because He wanted to. The incarnation was the fulfillment of an ageless plan in God's sovereign economy. And it only gets better. The principle of the Incarnation is still vital and relevant today. Why? Because discipleship takes a human touch. The best disciple-makers are the ones you can see with your own eyeballs and touch with your own hands. They'll be your friend and your traveling companion. As it was said of Jesus in Luke 24:32: "Were not our hearts burning within us while he talked with us on the road and opened the Scriptures to us?"

Skin matters!

Choosing a Mentoring Friend

Let's get one thing straight. "Mentoring" is just the latest word to describe what the Church has been trying to do all along. Mentoring is synonymous with discipleship. In Jesus' ministry, the experience was completely relational and intentional, but never programmatic. He turned strangers into friends and invited them to live out God-sized dreams as they experienced life together. "Rabbi, where are you staying?" two men asked Jesus one day. "Come," he replied, "and you will see" (John 1:38, 39). So how does one find a real friend anyway—the kind who will walk beside you and disciple you as a personal mentor? Consider the following two principles.

First, some believer in your life may be trying to mentor you right now, but you keep running away. You're playing hard to get. However confident you may be in leading yourself, or skilled in making your own decisions, don't fall prey to pride. "Pride goes before destruction, a haughty spirit before a fall" (Prov. 16:18). Overconfidence is a killer. When coupled with a reluctance to receive godly counsel, I've seen it lead people to the brink of failure. But it doesn't have to be that way. The Bible says, "The sweet smell of perfume and oils is pleasant, and so is good advice from a friend" (27:9 NCV).

Be cautious, however. Not everyone who wants to be your mentor and speak into your life is qualified to do so. Ask yourself these questions: Does this person know the Word of God? What about his or her own life? If it's a mess, keep running. Is this person controlling by nature? Run faster. Is he simply collecting trophies to increase or display his influence? Now it's time to sprint.

These traits are usually obvious and will serve as early-warning signals when you need to establish relationship boundaries. It's not your Christian duty to be sucked into unhealthy friendships. Many people wanted to get close to Jesus so they could instruct and correct Him. How ironic! They had it all backwards. "Who can know the LORD's thoughts? Who knows enough to instruct him?" (2 Cor. 2:16).

The second way to choose a mentoring friend is this: put the word out that you're seeking help in order to mature as a disciple. This may seem odd from your perspective, but it's really inspiring to others. Some people actually keep their ears to the ground in the quest to use their spiritual gifts to help others grow. Personally, I find it motivating when I come across someone who's passionate about discipleship and in hot pursuit of Christ.

So don't be ashamed. And don't imagine that everyone thinks you're the dumb one in the room because you're searching for spiritual direction and counsel. You're not alone. Deep down inside, many Christians live under a shroud of guilt and condemnation. They sometimes obsess over the fear that they're constantly falling short. As they look in the mirror, they see a spiritual pygmy staring back.

I'm convinced this is the work of our enemy. Hell puts out its own propaganda. Hit the delete key, and erase such notions from your memory. There's nothing shameful about starting a new journey to maturity. If you want to stand on the mountain summit, you begin climbing in the foothills. Disciples are made step-by-step—not born fully grown, but built over time.

R. James Shupp

Reluctance

If you're still reluctant to seek a friend who can mentor you, I believe I know why. Most people have experienced rejection in the past and fear it will happen to them again—especially if they expose their weaknesses and vulnerabilities to another person. We often carefully and selfishly guard our own secrets from the awareness of others. If you're still hurting from past rejection, then you're probably still hiding. And it's not really working for you, is it?

I've been forced to walk the plank before. I'd agree that being thrown overboard isn't much fun. However, I never understood in the slightest what Jesus went through until I experienced rejection for myself. John's Gospel tells us that Jesus "was in the world, and though the world was made through him, the world did not recognize him. He came to that which was his own, but his own did not receive him" (John 1:10-11). Rejection is one of those unfortunate events that can actually forge Christlikeness in your soul. Let God use it to build you up. Don't let our enemy use it to break you down.

The important thing to know is that God understands personal rejection. He knows how worthless it makes you feel inside. If you trust Him, He'll transform the experience into a thing of beauty. He did it for Jesus; He'll do it for you too. Our God places upon us a "crown of beauty instead of ashes, the oil of gladness instead of mourning, and a garment of praise instead of a spirit of despair" (Isa. 61:3).

King David, the man after God's own heart, experienced rejection. In spite of it he testified, "I have never seen the righteous forsaken" (Psa. 37:25). David understood that God is faithful to us even when others are not. "For the LORD will not reject his people; he will never forsake his inheritance" (94:14).

I like the fact that "discipleship," "friendship," and "fellowship" each has the suffix "ship" attached to it. The image it creates in my mind is that we're all in the same boat, with the same Savior, traveling in the same direction. We experience clear skies and sunny days together. But when the storm is surging and the waves are wicked, faint not, dear hearts. Arise! All hands, man your station. Our Captain will see us through. Listen. Watch. "Even the wind and the waves obey him!" (Mark 4:41).

THE SHEPHERD'S DANCE

The seaman tells stories of winds, the ploughman of bulls;
the soldier details his wounds, the shepherd his sheep.
–Laurence Peter

Thousands of books have been written on the subject of discipleship. Many break the process down into a measurable discipline, complete with tables and timelines, bullet points and action points. This is one approach, and it works for some people, but not everyone—perhaps not even the majority.

Our Dilemma

Here's what I've observed after two decades of being a pastor. It seems when discipleship is developed into a rigorous strategy, it triggers the flight instinct in most people. They run away and hide—quietly but noticeably. I can't say I blame them much. An invitation to watch paint dry or even live as a mountain-cave hermit might be more enjoyable. People who take the most straightforward process and then weave it into a complex web remind me of what Abraham Lincoln said so eloquently: "He can compress the most words into the smallest idea of any man I ever met."

So where does this leave us? How can we do a better job without turning the mandate "to make disciples" into a neatly packaged but highly complex program? We have more books and training literature on discipleship than ever in history. I'd argue that Christendom doesn't need more of the same. As I noted in the last chapter, something else is missing.

What is needed to recharge discipleship for this generation is not another list of things to do, but rather a model to emulate. We follow skin better than we follow strategies. This catapults me back to the person of Jesus Christ. Since He is the subject of this *One Blinding Vision* to change our world, let's dive headfirst into His teaching on the subject. I'm convinced there's no better way to demystify our dilemma.

More than a Strategy

We've already taken a peek into how Jesus—the Rabbi—chose and made His disciples. But there's even more to discover. As I plunge deeper into the mind of Christ, I find a powerful metaphor that had great importance and meaning to Him personally.

John 10:11 records Jesus calling Himself the "Good Shepherd." He called His disciples "sheep." Could there be a clearer comparison than this? Is there another time-honored profession that has greater nostalgic appeal? Often I find myself in awe of Jesus' creative simplicity. It's pure genius. Brilliance incarnate!

The image of a shepherd keeping watch over his sheep is universal. It's a timeless vocation, dating back to the earliest records of human civilization—some 6,000 years ago. Even a little child might understand that the relationship between a shepherd and his sheep is one of a kind.

But look a little closer. This is the best metaphor ever crafted to illustrate the nature of discipleship, simply because it's the one Jesus chose for us to emulate. He gave us more than a strategy or a "how to" guide for making disciples. Jesus inspired us with a series of pictures from the rolling hills of Galilee that were close to His heart and home. To what shall we compare it?

The Masterpiece

Please, step into His studio; the admission has already been paid. Let me guide you on a tour. I ask just one thing. As you walk through this chapter, let your imagination run wild. Understand that the best artists invite you to take leave of your own surroundings and move inside their canvass. So let the journey begin.

As heaven's *virtuoso artiste*, Jesus painted an enduring masterpiece to capture His convictions about discipleship. His canvas is a work of uncommon beauty, exquisite and rare, painted not with brushstrokes but with simple words and big ideas. As I've spent years gazing upon His *tour de force*, I do not see a process of discipleship but an experience, filled with breathing room and freedom. If I were to choose a name for it, I'd call it "The Shepherd's Dance."

The background you see before you is familiar yet creative. Jesus paints with the wonder of an artist expressing a vivid childhood memory. Listen to Him in His own words:

> *"The man who enters by the gate is the shepherd of his sheep. The watchman opens the gate for him, and the sheep listen to his voice. He calls his own sheep by name and leads them out"* (John 10:2-3).

In order to appreciate what you see on this canvas of words, you must dive into the culture of first-century Israel. Observe an ancient shepherd doing his job on an average day. Climb inside his skin. Pay particular attention to the nature of his sheep. Then you'll understand the Artist's heart.

The Scenery

Every city had a "sheepfold" or a "sheep pen." It was a protected area often enclosed behind the city walls. If you happened to be in this area early one morning, you'd observe a shepherd gaining entrance through the sheep gate. Once inside, in his own unique way and by the distinctive inflection of his voice, he calls out to his sheep.

These shepherds rely upon helpers who are called "gatekeepers" or "watchmen." They work in tandem to protect the sheep while the shepherd rests at night. They guard the gate against the thieves and predators who might try to steal or devour the sheep. They're paid a simple wage for a routine and oftentimes mindless job. And because the watchman doesn't actually own the sheep, other interests may motivate him as well. If an actual threat were to occur, he might weigh it against his own sense of self-preservation. Unfortunately, it is not unusual for a watchman to be subject to bribery, or even to flee in the face of danger.

> *"The hired hand is not the shepherd who owns the sheep. So when he sees the wolf coming, he abandons the sheep and runs away. Then the wolf attacks the flock and scatters it. The man runs away because he is a hired hand and cares nothing for the sheep"* (vv. 12-13).

It's important to note that several flocks of sheep, each belonging to a different shepherd, are often sheltered in the same pen. The sheep, however, know the characteristic sounds of each shepherd's call—sometimes a singsong melody, other times a familiar cry. Once they are certain their shepherd has arrived, the sheep rush to his side and depart with him through the gate. "And his sheep follow him because they know his voice" (v. 4).

This scene happens each and every day. Holy Land shepherds are compassionate and sensitive to the sheep's needs. In fact, they herd their sheep differently than is done in other parts of our world. They lead their sheep by walking in front of them. They don't drive them from behind, nor do they utilize sheep dogs to keep them in a tightly knit group. Recent studies among animal scientists conclude that sheep actually respond better and are physically healthier when they are in close contact with compassionate human beings. "When he has brought out all his own, he goes on ahead of them" (v. 4).

Typically, sheep spend an average of eight hours per day grazing. During this time, the shepherd watches over his sheep with great diligence. He scans the horizon and keeps his eyes open for potential threats. Lions, bears, wolves, poisonous grass, and vipers were natural enemies of the sheep in first-century Israel. But as long as the sheep feel safe in the presence of their shepherd, they remain calm. They're able to eat and survive.

Sheep will not follow an unfamiliar shepherd through the gate. Our Artist said emphatically, "They will never follow a stranger; in fact, they will run away from him because they do not recognize a stranger's voice" (v. 5). Sheep trust their shepherd. They will dance with no other. Only he can call the sheep from the safety of the fold to graze in the open countryside.

The reason for this exclusive relationship may be understood by what we call "imprinting" or "bonding." Because the shepherd lives with his sheep, he's present when they're born. The shepherd's image is imprinted in each little lamb's brain from the earliest of moments. This creates a powerful psychological and emotional attachment, making following their shepherd an automatic response. "I know them, and they follow me" (John 10:27).

Shepherds sometimes work together to ensure the safety of their sheep. If a common threat does arise, they band together to meet it with their collective strength. Our Artist would have seen this happen with His own eyes. And no doubt, He was familiar with the prophet Isaiah, who described one such event:

> *"As a lion growls, a great lion over his prey—*
> *and though a whole band of shepherds is called*
> *together against him, he is not frightened by*
> *their shouts or disturbed by their clamor—so*
> *the* LORD *Almighty will come down to do battle*
> *on Mount Zion and on its heights"* (Isa. 31:4).

Shepherds consider their work to be sacred and symbolic of God's own role in protecting their nation. They believe themselves to play a vital function in the economic and religious culture of their society. They raise the sacrificial lambs for the great national feasts and celebrations. Without shepherds there would be no Passover and fewer burnt offerings to present to the LORD.

Today the study of animal behavior is called ethology. Professor Warren Gill of the Animal Science Department at the University of Tennessee is an expert ethologist, specializing in sheep. In a research paper titled "Applied Sheep Behavior," he described their sense of hearing.

> *The sheep can amplify and pinpoint sound*
> *with its ears. Sound arrives at each ear at*
> *slightly different times with a small difference in*
> *amplitude which the auditory system can process*
> *into a directional signal. This can be further*
> *refined by moving the ears, head or the entire*
> *body. This skill is probably almost as important*
> *as sight and smell for keeping the sheep, as a prey*
> *species, alive.*

Although their hearing is excellent, a sheep's eyesight suffers from certain limitations. They have limited color, depth, and height perception. Like most grazers, their eyes are located on the side of their heads. This enhances their peripheral vision and allows them to detect threats such as the advance of a predator. Their pupils are somewhat rectangular in shape. This creates a wide-angle lens effect, but it reduces their ability to distinguish between people and/or objects at a distance. This is why sheep depend primarily upon the sense of hearing to identify the shepherd, and why they depend upon his eyes to lead them. "My sheep listen to my voice" (John 10:27).

Their near vision, however, is quite good. It allows sheep to distinguish between different varieties of plant life and even accomplish simple facial recognition. Add to this a refined sense of smell, and sheep become the masters of foraging for food in barren, arid environments. Sheep flock together in order to combine their visual resources into a type of collective sense. This provides them with an early-warning system against potential threats. It's their one strategic advantage.

Of all animals, sheep are perfectly suited to exist alongside man. Their relationship is symbiotic. In exchange for food, shelter, and safety, the sheep provide the shepherd with milk, wool, and lambs. Each of the sheep's senses are configured in such a way as to allow them the best chance for survival in areas where the terrain is rough and the climate is challenging—the type of land that is abundant in Israel. And this is why there are approximately five-hundred references to sheep and lambs in the Bible.

Sheep prefer predictability. It makes them feel safe. Sheep respond very poorly to change. It's a well-known fact that sheep are extremely anxious by nature. I have seen laboratory reports from scientists who obsess about the accuracy of their information, simply because sheep are too tense and nervous to be studied in such environments.

According to a 1993 study titled "The Effect of Isolation and Separation on the Metabolism of Sheep," published in *Livestock Production Science*, when sheep are isolated from one another, their baseline heart rate increases by as much as fifteen percent. But this information is not new. An old Irish proverb says, "There was never a scabby sheep in a flock that didn't like to have a comrade." Hebrews 10:25 relates this same need to us: "And let us not neglect our meeting together, as some people do, but encourage one another" (Heb. 10:25 NLT).

One theory is that sheep are skittish because they have no means to defend themselves—no chemical toxins, no fangs or claws, no intimidating postures, or even so much as a scary bleat. And they can't fight either. Have you ever read an obituary of someone who died from a sheep attack? Sometimes they do bite each other, however. But for the most part, sheep are easy prey, and they probably know they taste good too.

Of all the creatures on God's planet, the domesticated sheep is perhaps the most dependent on humans for survival. They need shepherds like the spring needs its rain.

Here's the point of "Dancing with the Shepherd": if you're going to be a disciple-maker, then you must be a shepherd. The men and women, boys and girls under your care are sheep. It's really not all that complicated when you think about it.

> *Now may the God of peace who brought up our Lord Jesus from the dead, that great Shepherd of the sheep, through the blood of the everlasting covenant, make you complete in every good work to do His will, working in you what is well pleasing in His sight, through Jesus Christ, to whom be glory forever and ever. Amen* (13:20-21 NKJV).

Thank you for attending today. If you would like to understand this masterpiece in greater detail, please join me in the next room—the next chapter.

Making a Disciple

I am the good shepherd; I know my sheep
and my sheep know me—just as the Father
knows me and I know the Father—and I lay
down my life for the sheep.
(John 10:14-15)

Welcome back! Let's continue our tour.

Jesus painted this picture for us in response to the religious mudslingers who attacked His life and work. The Pharisees were like envious little art critics, frequently scorning His every brushstroke. He could see the great deficit in human society. People were like sheep without a shepherd. Religion had not served to shepherd the wandering souls of men and women. Religion had become the butcher of the sheep.

Jesus used this familiar vocation and experience to describe the unique relationship He had with His disciples. The Good Shepherd, as He called Himself, did several things to gather and grow His disciples—the sheep of His fold. I've gleaned six principles from the Master's masterpiece in John Chapter 10, which are: calling, naming, leading, feeding, protecting, and sacrificing.

1. The Shepherd Called Them

"He calls his own sheep" (John 10:3).

Jesus called each of His disciples. He extended the invitation. Normally, people are honored when someone takes a personal interest in them. By the way, since you're reading this book, the chances are that people in your circle of influence know less about following Jesus than you do. Have you ever thought about asking them to study the Bible with you? You could meet them for breakfast one day a week or invite them over to your home. Have you ever thought about being a shepherd?

I recently had a conversation with a friend over lunch. I consider this guy to be a sold-out Christ-follower of the first order. One day I asked him, "What made you so passionate about your commitment to Christ and personal discipleship?"

I have never forgotten his response. "I was a young man attending a small church. An older gentleman in the congregation who was very knowledgeable in the Scriptures asked me if he could mentor me."

I smiled as I listened and said, "Yes!"

My friend continued. "For three years he poured his wisdom into me. He helped me to understand the meaning of the Bible and how to have a deeper, more meaningful relationship with Jesus Christ. He gave me a list of books to read. We discussed my life, ambitions, the future, and then … he cut me loose."

"What do you mean by that?" I asked.

"Well," he replied, "he told me I'd graduated. I knew enough to keep growing on my own. He made it very clear to me that my next responsibility was to go find someone else and do for them what he'd done for me. I didn't like it at first, but then I realized it was exactly what Jesus Himself had done."

Brilliant!

What would happen if every mature believer did this?

2. The Shepherd Named Them

John 10:3 records Jesus saying that the Good Shepherd "calls his own sheep by name." As Shakespeare asked, "What's in a name?"

There's an old saying: "A sick sheep is a dead sheep." In other words, by the time a sheep begins to display the symptoms of an illness, it's too late to save it. In most cases, the sickness has already progressed too far.

When the shepherd arrived in the morning, if one of his sheep lagged behind in the sheep pen, he called its name. Depending on how it responded to his voice, he could determine the sheep's physical condition. If the sheep showed subtle signs of illness, the shepherd brought food and water to the sheep. He didn't force the sheep to follow the flock. Instead, he did his best to nurse it back to health with special care.

As a shepherd takes care of his sheep, so a disciple-maker should care for his or her disciples. This is less complicated than it may be inconvenient for us. But consider that selfish shepherds never last very long themselves. A sheep-less shepherd is as unhealthy as a shepherd-less sheep. Death is on the horizon for both.

On occasion it isn't unusual for a sheep or a little lamb to get distracted while grazing and wander from the flock. This sheep is called an "outlier." A second sheep, called the "bellwether," might soon follow. It's an interesting fact that the flock will not follow the outlier, but it will follow the bellwether. If the bellwether stays behind, the outlier will ultimately separate from the flock and end up in the jaws of the wolves.

Is Jesus' day, when the shepherd noticed one of his sheep was about to stray far beyond the rest of the herd, it was time for action. Out of great love and concern for the welfare of the sheep, the shepherd lifted his voice and cried out to the outlier. When he called "his own sheep by name," it ran back to rejoin the safety and comfort of the group.

I love Psalm 23, don't you? Written by King David, it's known as "The Great Shepherd's Psalm." David called God "my shepherd." There's an interesting phrase in verse 3 that says "He restores my soul." A literal translation from Hebrew reads, "He brings me back from wandering." Sheep are not like dogs. Once they get lost, they can't find their way back home. They need the shepherd to find them and bring them back to safety.

The truth is we all suffer from sheep-itis: "All we like sheep have gone astray; We have turned, every one, to his own way" (Isa. 53:6 NKJV). Robert Robinson must have been contemplating this in 1758 when he wrote one of my favorite hymns, "Come, Thou Fount of Every Blessing."

> O to grace how great a debtor
> Daily I'm constrained to be!
> Let Thy goodness, like a fetter,
> Bind my wandering heart to Thee.
> Prone to wander, Lord, I feel it,
> Prone to leave the God I love;
> Here's my heart, O take and seal it,
> Seal it for Thy courts above.[4]

If God has given you a disciple to mentor, don't let him or her wander too far away. Call the little outlier on the phone. Chase him down if you have to, and pray for him by name. For heaven's sake, do something to get her attention, and get her back on track. We've lost too many of the Lord's sheep in the wilderness.

The Good-Shepherd model of discipleship compels us to value each soul who wanders away from the Shepherd's love. We can't say, "Oh, well, I started out with a hundred sheep and only lost one today. I still have ninety-nine!" That's not God's math. It wasn't Jesus' either, and it shouldn't be ours.

Every sheep matters. That's why the shepherd gives each one a name.

[4] Public Domain.

3. The Shepherd Led Them

Jesus said, "When he has brought out all his own, he goes on ahead of them, and his sheep follow him because they know his voice" (John 10:4). Discipleship requires leadership. Leadership is based on relationship. The sheep know the shepherd's voice, and they follow him.

Much could be said about leadership at this point. I've spent the better part of my life studying it in the context of serving a local church. But as I look upon this masterpiece painted by our Lord, I see three bedrock principles on leadership that will strengthen any leader's foundation.

First, leading takes courage. The shepherd stands between the sheep and danger at all times. His courage inspires their confidence in his abilities. If the shepherd loses his courage, the sheep will lose their confidence. The void left by the absence of courage always tends to be replaced by fear. Disciples, like sheep, don't respond well to fear, scare tactics, guilt, or even shame. Such things only cause anxiety and have a way of triggering their flight instinct.

Second, leading takes conviction. Sheep learn quickly how to walk over the back of an ambivalent shepherd. There's an old proverb that says, "An army of sheep led by a lion will defeat an army of lions led by a sheep." Disciples are inspired by their leader's convictions. Convictions arise from the combination of truth and faith. The best disciple-makers know what they believe and why they believe it. They're grounded in the Scriptures and strengthened by their own personal faith in Jesus Christ.

To keep your faith strong, you need to stick very close to the Good Shepherd. King David was aware of his own need to do this. He said, "The LORD is my shepherd, I shall not be in want" (Psa. 23:1). You will never lack for faith as long as God is your ever-present Shepherd. When your faith grows weak, it's because you've been wandering some yourself.

"For you were like sheep going astray, but now you have returned to the Shepherd and Overseer of your souls" (1 Pet. 2:25).

Third, leading takes vision. The lead shepherd was often called an "overseer." He stood on the hilltop and looked out over the horizon. On a clear day he might see greener pastures in another location. In the future he'd lead the sheep in that direction. Because the sheep were nearsighted, they relied upon the shepherd's eyes to keep them healthy and well nourished. Maintain a clear Christ-centered vision, and you'll never lead a disciple in the wrong direction.

Alexander Chase was correct when he said, "People, like sheep, tend to follow a leader—occasionally in the right direction." How sad. Excellence in leadership should never be rare. We need more leaders to step up and disciple the next generation. Do you possess courage, convictions, and vision? If so, what are you waiting for? Lead!

Jesus' heart was broken when he looked upon the crowds and saw the people were like "sheep without a shepherd" (Matt. 9:36). The more your heart becomes like His, the more you'll feel this pain too.

4. The Shepherd Fed Them

Researchers have discovered that sheep do a poor job of feeding themselves. Given the choice, they will not choose to eat the most nutritious food. Professor Warren Gill noted in *Applied Sheep Behavior*:

> *There have been experiments to determine if sheep have "nutritional wisdom." This is based on the premise that sheep will attempt to eat feeds that provide them with the nutrients they require. In most cases, sheep are unlikely to balance their own ration when provided a variety of feeds.*

Jesus said, "I am the gate; whoever enters through me will be saved. He will come in and go out, and find pasture" (John 10:9). Not only is Jesus the Good Shepherd, but He's also the Gate through which everyone must pass to find the "bread of life." Again He said, "I am the living bread that came down from heaven. If anyone eats of this bread, he will live forever. This bread is my flesh, which I will give for the life of the world" (6:51).

One of the greatest things disciple-makers can do for disciples is to teach them how to feast upon God's Word. It is often said that a man and his word are inseparable. Jesus is more than inseparable from His word. He *is* the Word. Jesus wants His disciples to devour the Word and, in turn, be consumed by it.

Jesus was so passionate about this truth that He even proclaimed it to the devil one day: "It is written: 'Man does not live on bread alone, but on every word that comes from the mouth of God'" (Matt. 4:4). Show me a disciple who isn't being mentored in the Word, and I'll show you a spiritual anorexic.

Of all the books to appear on the bestseller's list, the Bible is the only living book ever written. God has spoken! "For the word of God is living and active. Sharper than any double-edged sword, it penetrates even to dividing soul and spirit, joints and marrow; it judges the thoughts and the attitudes of the heart" (Heb. 4:12). When I compare any other book against the Bible, it looks like sterile words printed on woody pulp. Every word from Genesis to Revelation contains God's breath. "All Scripture is God-breathed and is useful for teaching, rebuking, correcting and training in righteousness, so that the man of God may be thoroughly equipped for every good work" (2 Tim. 3:16-17). Show me a Bible that's falling apart, and I'll show you a life that's not.

Nourish yourself...and then feed others.

5. The Shepherd Protected Them

"No one can snatch them out of my hand" (John 10:28).

Sheep have natural enemies from which they need constant protection, and so do disciples. Our greatest threats are three in number: the flesh, the world, and the devil. Let's look at them individually.

Our first enemy is the flesh or "the sinful nature" as it is often translated in Scripture. It compels a person to flee from the call of discipleship. The calling represents everything the sinful nature opposes—change, the loss of control, and the restraint of sinful appetites. A Christ-follower who is not growing as a disciple is in some way allowing the sinful nature to take command. If a disciple is to grow in Christ, he or she has no choice but to take up his or her own cross and live the crucified life.

Paul said, "I have been crucified with Christ; it is no longer I who live, but Christ lives in me; and the life which I now live in the flesh I live by faith in the Son of God, who loved me and gave Himself for me" (Gal. 2:20). The good news is that Jesus wants to live His life in and through us. When it comes to escaping the stranglehold of the sinful nature, He offers us more than a solution. He offers Himself. Call it the great exchange. He received our sins; we receive His righteousness. He nailed our old life to His Cross; we receive His freedom.

Our second enemy is the world. It will seize each and every opportunity to ambush a disciple of Jesus Christ. Why? Because the world hates committed Christ-followers. The Bible states this fact clearly: "Do not be surprised, my brothers, if the world hates you" (1 John 3:13). The chances are we won't roll out of bed one morning and discover the world has changed its opinion about Christianity. As my great-grandmother from Tennessee used to say, "A pig would sooner jump on a poke and into the barbeque than for that to happen."

Disciples will never find their peace in the world, and they shouldn't.

Our peace comes from Jesus alone. He said, "My peace I give you. I do not give to you as the world gives. Do not let your hearts be troubled and do not be afraid" (John 14:27). The Bible says we are like pilgrims and strangers who are just passing through this life. Real life is found by following the Good Shepherd. He said, "I have told you these things, so that in me you may have peace. In this world you will have trouble. But take heart! I have overcome the world" (16:33).

Our third enemy is the devil. He loves to pounce on disciples. Remember Judas? "Then Satan entered Judas, called Iscariot, one of the Twelve" (Luke 22:3). The Bible says the devil "prowls around like a roaring lion looking for someone to devour" (1 Pet. 5:8). The word "devour" means "to swallow whole." This threat is real. Satan is hungry. Right now he's searching for some clueless victim to add to his trophy room. A good shepherd will warn the sheep. He will prepare them for the day when the lions of hell arrive. The Good Shepherd said to one of His own, "Simon, Simon, Satan has asked to sift you as wheat. But I have prayed for you, Simon, that your faith may not fail. And when you have turned back, strengthen your brothers" (Luke 22:31-32).

I love the story of David and Goliath. When young David was trying to persuade King Saul to let him tear Goliath apart, he said, "Your servant has been keeping his father's sheep. When a lion or a bear came and carried off a sheep from the flock, I went after it, struck it and rescued the sheep from its mouth. When it turned on me, I seized it by its hair, struck it and killed it" (1 Sam. 17:34-35). No enemy—not even the devil himself—can survive an encounter with someone who possesses such a childlike faith.

Never place your faith in an object, a job, money, or something else that will eventually let you down. Place your faith in the Lord Jesus Christ, the great Shepherd and protector of us all. "I give them eternal life, and they shall never perish; no one can snatch them out of my hand" (John 10:28).

Disciples are held in the grip of grace. The Good Shepherd will never let you go, and you'll never slip through His fingers. Though He's the Ancient of Days, He doesn't get arthritis, and His hands won't grow weary from holding on to you. Satan cannot arm-wrestle you away from God once Jesus has laid hold of your life. Jesus said, "While I was with them, I protected them and kept them safe by that name you gave me. None has been lost except the one doomed to destruction so that Scripture would be fulfilled" (17:12).

We call this "blessed assurance" and "eternal security." Unlike some insurance policies, God's protection is unlimited. There are no caps. Your ultimate security is eternal life—His life lived through you. How cool is that? Why would anyone want another Shepherd?

> For I am convinced that neither death nor life, neither angels nor demons, either the present nor the future, nor any powers, neither height nor depth, nor anything else in all creation, will be able to separate us from the love of God that is in Christ Jesus our Lord (Rom. 8:28-39).

6. The Shepherd Sacrificed for Them

Even more specifically, He sacrificed Himself for His disciples. Jesus said, "I am the good shepherd. The good shepherd lays down his life for the sheep" (John 10:11). Why would He do such a thing? The answer is clear. He did it because they were His friends and He loved them. "Greater love has no one than this," Jesus said, "than to lay down one's life for his friends" (John 15:13 NKJV).

Soldiers understand these words. I have a friend who served our country in Iraq. One October day in 2006, while traveling in a Humvee through the war-torn streets of Ramadi, he and his fellow Marines were attacked. An IED (Improvised Explosive Device) buried beneath the road exploded as their vehicle passed over it. The force of the blast ripped through the Humvee and propelled my friend several yards from the vehicle. He suffered third-degree burns over most of his body. Miraculously, he survived. Three of his fellow Marines did not.

His battle continued at Brook Army Medical Center in San Antonio, Texas, where he was treated for his injuries—a ruptured spleen, ruptured vertebrae, skin grafts, facial reconstruction, and months of rehab. It was during this time that he came to my church one Sunday morning. The entire room was buzzing with excitement as people sought to express their appreciation for his selfless commitment to serve our country. With a sense of wonder, they gazed upon the charred face of courage. They drew near just to touch the hand of a hero.

He quickly became a friend to our church family—more than a member, a flesh-and-blood representation of the price of sacrifice. One day I asked him to deliver the Sunday morning message. At one point, he described the thoughts running though his mind just moments after the bomb exploded. I can still hear every word he said: "The only thought I had was to save my Marines, but I couldn't." Had he not been burned beyond recognition and restrained by the soldiers surrounding him, I have no doubt he would have rushed back into that burning Humvee.

My friend's journey from Ramadi to San Antonio forced me to ask some probing questions: Is there any other cause greater than the cause of Christ? Do we understand the level of sacrifice necessary to multiply disciples? And just how committed are we to each other anyway? If we don't even lay down our time for a friend, could we ever lay down something as great as our life?

Personally, I'm taking an inventory as I write these words. I've had to ask myself these hard, Holy Spirit-inspired questions: What am I doing right now to boost the level of sacrifice in my own life? Could I not raise the bar even higher?

I invite— No, I *dare* you to ask yourself the same questions.

✸

I pray you can see and understand His masterpiece clearly now. Call, name, lead, feed, protect, and sacrifice are the big ideas of Jesus Christ when it comes to shepherding and discipling the next generation. These are the steps in the dance between the shepherd and his sheep. I believe this is the greatest work of art ever to inspire or hang in the imagination. As it relates to discipleship, I believe it will reverse the cascading trends in America.

As hard as we might try, we would only fail if we attempted to turn this into a nice little church program. This may shock some minds, but discipleship was never a strategy in the first place. Discipleship was and is a commitment to a lifestyle. Jesus intends for it to be as natural as the rhythm of breathing. We don't set aside time in our day for breathing. We just do it. Jesus has the same thing in mind about making disciples.

I have spent years looking at His masterpiece. I hope you will too. But do more than that. Paint this picture on the canvas of someone else's heart. As a shepherd, do what the Good Shepherd instructed Peter: "Take care of my sheep" (John 21:16).

7

Myths and Seasons

Jesus promised his disciples 3 things:
They would be completely fearless, absurdly happy,
and in constant trouble.
Progress should mean we are constantly changing
the world to fit the vision; instead we seem to always
be changing the vision. The riddles of God are more
satisfying than the solutions of Man.
–G. K. Chesterton

My wife and I married right after college graduation. A few months before the wedding day, I purchased every book I could find on the subject of marriage. I read every word on every page, underlined, highlighted, and made copious notes in the margins. I gave myself pop quizzes. I was an "A" student—top of the dean's list.

I imagined my wife would be the luckiest girl on the planet after she said "I do." After all, she had *me*. No one had ever studied so hard or memorized so much material. No one had ever mastered the secrets of the female psyche—no, not like I had.

I humbly ... no, I *proudly* gave unsolicited lectures to all my single friends. I expounded upon my untested, but nonetheless airtight, strategy for obtaining marital happiness. I envisioned myself pioneering the next great renaissance in human society, promoted through my revolutionary understanding of the mysteries of matrimony. To be fair to my new bride, however, I would wait at least a year before propelling her and our marriage into the spotlight.

After the first week of marriage, I burned all my books. Apparently I had a few misconceptions. Humble pie is a dish best served cold.

One of the reasons we under-perform in the area of discipleship is because we have too many messed-up ideas about it. We need to expose some of the contemporary myths surrounding the Lord's command in the Great Commission. It might help if you put on your MythBusters' thinking cap. Let's get rolling.

Seven Myths about Discipleship

The first myth about discipleship is the belief that a person can be a respectable Christian without being a committed disciple of Jesus Christ. Discipleship is viewed as a kind of turbo-charged commitment maintained only by the spiritual elite. These mythmakers, however, feel at ease under the flimsy umbrella of casual Christianity. They believe the high-stakes call to follow Jesus down a risky road of heart-thumping adventure was merely a first-century thing. Less octane is required for the twenty-first century, right?

In his poem titled "Three Dollars' Worth of God," Wilbur Reese illustrated this view with a sprinkle of sarcasm.

> *I would like to buy three dollars' worth of*
> *God, please. Not enough to explode my soul*
> *or disturb my sleep, but just enough to buy a*
> *cup of warm milk or a snooze in the sunshine.*

I don't want enough to love a black man or pick beets with a migrant. I want ecstasy, not transformation. I want the warmth of the womb, not a new birth. I want a pound of the Eternal in a paper sack. I would like to buy three dollars' worth of God, please.[5]

Most people are surprised to discover that the word *Christian(s)* is found only three times in the entire Bible. For instance: "The disciples were called Christians first at Antioch" (Acts 11:26). The context of each usage implies that Christian was a name outsiders tagged on Christ's followers. And it was no compliment either. It was a kind of nickname meaning "little Christ," similar to the childhood games we once played of mock and scoff. Even so, Peter encouraged the disciples to embrace the title with gusto: "If you suffer as a Christian, do not be ashamed, but praise God that you bear that name" (1 Pet. 4:16).

The word *disciple(s)* is used nearly three-hundred times in Scripture. It is the term used to describe those who stand with Christ. As we discovered earlier, a disciple was a committed follower of a rabbi. The disciple gave up his own ambitions in order to learn how to think and act like his master. Jesus said, "If you hold to my teaching, you are really my disciples" (John 8:31). The first myth—busted!

The second myth claims discipleship is separate from evangelism. I've actually had people ask me, "Why are you so passionate and focused on evangelism? Shouldn't we be more enthusiastic about discipleship instead?" My response is, "Disciples don't mysteriously appear out of thin air." When Jesus said, "Go … make disciples," He intended for us to start by evangelizing our world. The early Church understood this connection: "They preached the good news in that city and won a large number of

---

[5] Quoted in Charles R. Swindoll, *Improving Your Serve*, (Thomas Nelson, 1997), 16.

disciples" (Acts 14:21). The apostle Paul instructed Timothy, his personal disciple and "true son in the faith," to "do the work of an evangelist" (1 Tim. 1:2; 2 Tim. 4:5). Evangelism is the first step in the discipleship process—both then and now. Evangelism is to discipleship as oxygen is to lungs. Of what use is one without the other? Both are necessary for life.

The third myth asserts that discipleship is a quick fix to all your problems. People don't go to sleep one night with their lives in a mess and wake up the next morning with everything neatly sorted out. Don't get frustrated because you didn't become the next Billy Graham or Mother Teresa overnight. Life-change can often be a slow process. A long time ago I heard this equation, which I love: Change equals grace over time.

I would agree there are growth spurts in every Christian's life. But Jesus intends for us to grow over the entire course of our lives. A weed may grow overnight, but it won't last as long as an oak tree. You'll appreciate this reality more when the wind kicks up and the thunderclouds come rolling in.

Life's trials and troubles require spiritual root systems that develop over time. Every learning experience is a building block to the next challenge. Life changes constantly, and so will the tests you face. Be gracious to yourself and allow God's hand to shape you for the days ahead. The Bible says "a man cannot discover anything about his future" (Eccles. 7:14). Only God knows what your future will bring. Trust Him. "There is surely a future hope for you, and your hope will not be cut off" (Prov. 23:18).

The fourth myth is usually expressed like this: "I don't need the church to help me grow as a disciple; I fly solo!" People who say this have usually been burned by some experience in a church, or they are simply against "organized religion." But I agree with D. L. Moody, who said, "Church attendance is as vital to a disciple as a transfusion of rich, healthy blood [is] to a sick man."

The reality is that Jesus established His Church while His disciples were listening to Him one day. He said to them at Caesarea Philippi, "On this rock I will build my church, and the gates of Hades will not overcome it" (Matt. 16:18). That's pretty significant! The issue is not whether a disciple *needs* a church, but that disciples *are* the Church. Paul put it this way: "Now you are the body of Christ, and each one of you is a part of it" (1 Cor. 2:27). A church is not the sum total of its buildings and budgets, but of its baptized believers. When the church comes together in worship, stands together in prayer, and works together in ministry, hell trembles.

I recommend that if you don't like your church, either help solve the problems it faces or find one that meets your spiritual needs. If that doesn't work, then start one that brings glory to Christ. For all of her blemishes and problems, the Church is still the visible body of our invisible Lord. So love her—warts and all. God does, and it's also the way He loves you. A long time ago I heard someone ask this question: "What kind of church would my church be if every member were just like me?"

The fifth myth about discipleship alleges that church attendance is the only thing required for a person to grow. No, it's only one of the spiritual disciplines necessary to achieve maturity. If you ate just one meal a day on only one day of the week, you'd starve to death by the end of the year. And even if you did survive, you'd be a mess.

People often get mad at God when they attend church and are still confused, or when their lives remain in disarray. Don't blame Him; look within. Are you talking to Him daily through prayer? Are you consistently reading His Word and deepening your understanding of what it means? Do you worship God and ponder His holiness and majesty throughout the week? Have you ever fasted? Are you applying truth to areas where you need to improve your life and relationships? If not, start today!

Jesus didn't call part-time disciples. Discipleship is a poor hobby, but it's a great lifestyle. Jesus said, "No man who puts his hand to the plow and looks back is fit for service in the kingdom of God" (Luke 9:62). A plowman who looks over his shoulder will dig crooked furrows. This makes planting seeds and harvesting crops all the more difficult. When it comes to discipleship, keep your hands on the plow, your feet to the fire, and your eyes on the prize. And when the harvest comes, you'll be rewarded for your labor.

The sixth myth says growth happens automatically. "It's a funny thing," Arnold Palmer said. "The more I practice, the luckier I get." Growth requires effort. Nothing flourishes without undergoing some kind of struggle. The Bible says, "… continue to work out your salvation with fear and trembling" (Phil. 2:12). Have you ever noticed that *improvement* begins with "I"? The most spiritually mature people I know understand there's always room for improvement, and it's usually the biggest room in the house.

Consider the grass in your front yard for a moment. It appears to grow effortlessly, but each tiny blade needs the biochemical engine of photosynthesis to keep it alive. Babies don't grow by themselves either. They require bottles, a king's ransom in diaper provisions, and lots of love. Likewise, the young love of a newlywed couple will deplete itself faster than a couch potato sprinting uphill unless it is exercised daily. Many of us learned that lesson the hard way. It doesn't take long for the new car smell to fade away.

If you want something to grow, work at it and keep it healthy. The same principle holds true for discipleship. That's why the words *disciple* and *discipline* are so closely related.

The final myth is sometimes expressed this way: "How well I'm doing as a disciple is a private matter—between me and God." It's easy to hide in a pew or in a classroom and never open yourself up to accountability. You're not in a safe place if you're flying under the radar. Pilots understand this. That's why they stay in constant communication with the personnel on the ground who monitor their transponder signals. They also maintain contact with other pilots who share their airspace. Fly under the radar long enough, and you'll hit an immovable object. If you really want to grow, you need people you can trust—the kind who share your burdens and give godly counsel when you need it. As John Donne said, "No man is an island."

Harold Geneen, former CEO of ITT, said it best: "We must not be hampered by yesterday's myths in concentrating on today's needs." Don't allow any of these seven myths to stunt your growth as a disciple. Imagine how heartbroken you would be if your newborn baby stopped growing and never learned to walk or speak. The writer of Hebrews must have had this in mind when he wrote:

> *By now you should be teachers, but you need someone to teach you again the first lessons of God's message. You still need the teaching that is like milk. You are not ready for solid food. Anyone who lives on milk is still a baby and knows nothing about right teaching. But solid food is for those who are grown up. They are mature enough to know the difference between good and evil* (Heb. 5:12-14 NCV).

Jesus wants you to grow. How far you follow Him down the pathway of maturity is your choice. So count the cost and make the courageous decision. Follow in His steps. The really good news is that God has a plan to develop you throughout each stage of your journey and through each season of life.

R. James Shupp

The Seasons of Discipleship

I remember one day considering the words of the apostle Paul when he wrote to Timothy, "Do your best to get here before winter" (2 Tim. 4:21). Paul was sitting in a Roman jail cell awaiting execution under the rule of Emperor Nero when he wrote these words. He was on the last leg of his earthly journey. Time was of the essence, and he wanted to see Timothy one last time.

But Timothy needed to arrive before winter and bring Paul's cloak with him. Without it, Paul would suffer from misery and over-exposure to the cold. To Paul, winter was more than a season; it signaled the end. He said, "For I am already being poured out like a drink offering, and the time has come for my departure" (2 Tim. 4:6).

Solomon said, "There is a time for everything, and a season for every activity under heaven" (Eccles. 3:1). I often use the four seasons to describe the four phases of discipleship. The first is spring. This is the season of new life, first love, and brisk growth. Solomon was meditating on spring when he sang, "Flowers appear on the earth; the season of singing has come, the cooing of doves is heard in our land" (Song of Sol. 2:12).

Shortly after a person becomes a new Christian, he's like a sapling. He drinks in the Son-shine and feeds off the rich nutrients in God's Word. It is often a time of rapid growth and enthusiasm. I love to watch people in their spring season of discipleship. Paul experienced such a season after he met Jesus. He spent the first three years after his conversion experience in Arabia simply learning and soaking up everything he could about Jesus Christ.

Then comes summer. It's the season of maturity. Things heat up and become very busy during this time. It's the season when you learn how to incorporate into your life the things you've learned from Jesus. It's not without its stress however. On occasion you may find yourself juggling the desire to serve the Lord with family expectations and work-related responsibilities.

For Paul, the summer days were a time of turbo-charged ministry activity. He went on three different missionary journeys. He established new churches everywhere he went. He carried the gospel into the gentile regions of Asia and then into Europe, perhaps even as far as Spain. He wrote letters to the churches he established and laid the foundation for the worldwide advancement of Christianity. Summer was his season of productivity.

And how we love the next season! Autumn brings with it the beauty and the spice of life. The hint of something special is in the air. It's a time of harvest. Now life's journey brings a person to the place of perspective and wisdom. Disciples in this phase of life know they'll not be around forever. Life is short. So we must fill the earth with the beauty of the glory of God, and leave our legacy behind for the next generation. Often I have seen a seasoned disciple in the autumn days of their Christianity become more sacrificial, more patient, and more loving of those around them. This period is the crescendo of the Christian life.

Winter is the season of "goodbye." A disciple should expect some difficulty in reconciling conflicting emotions during these final days. Even brave hearts will dream of the bygone days of spring and summer. Paul expressed this when he said, "Yet what shall I choose? I do not know! I am torn between the two: I desire to depart and be with Christ, which is better by far; but it is more necessary for you that I remain in the body" (Phil. 1:22-24). Just as there was grace to be found at the beginning of spring, it will also find you in the dead of winter.

The thing we need to understand is this: The seasons come and go for everyone, just as they did for Jesus. As a disciple of Christ, make the best use of each one. "However many years a man may live, let him enjoy them all" (Eccles. 11:8). Never waste a day. Seize it. One of the great theological minds of our day (Yoda) put it this way: "Always in motion is the future." In other words, you can't go back. Time lost is time wasted. "Remember your Creator in the days of your youth" (12:1).

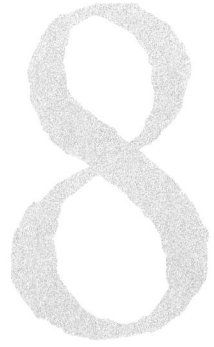

8

UNLEASHING DISCIPLES

"I want to know God's thoughts...the rest are details."
–Albert Einstein

Isaac Newton didn't invent gravity. He described it mathematically. Albert Einstein didn't invent relativity. He merely theorized its possibilities. God created the physical universe. In doing so, He designed the fundamental principles by which it operates. Then He gave us the miraculous ability to perceive our surroundings. All of this is summarized by the first ten words of the Bible: "In the beginning God created the heavens and the earth" (Gen. 1:1).

RD+MD+UD=XD²

Isn't it ironic how the entire field of science has worked feverishly to conceptualize what happened in the first verse of Scripture? We say God. They say Bang. I say my God is bigger than their bang! (That was free.)

God invented the math. It's His universe. The brightest human minds struggled for millennia to wrap their understanding around that which existed all along. It's a discussion for another book, but how can anyone describe, whether by mathematics or any other means, the symmetry in the universe without coming face-to-face with God? There is a rhythm to reality, a flow in the force of nature, and a harmony in the heavens. Pull back the curtain, and you will see God.

This notion inspired a crazy thought one day. If we could resurrect Einstein's brain and apply it to the study of Scripture, I wonder what fruit would develop. If we said to the German physicist, "Here is this reality called discipleship. It's in a state of chaos today. But we believe you have the ability to see order and harmony where others see disorder and confusion. As you gave us $E=MC^2$ and revolutionized our understanding of physics, help us understand what we are not seeing today in the Great Commission."

In my imagination I see Einstein walking over to a low-tech chalkboard, picking up an antique piece of white chalk, and writing down this simple equation: $RD+MD+UD=XD^2$. Then he says in a thick German accent, "Rethinking discipleship (RD) plus making disciples (MD) and unleashing disciples (UD) will equal multiplying disciples (XD^2)."

Quick Rewind

The truth is it doesn't take someone with the mind of a genius to see this reality. Every generation must do its best to rethink discipleship. Please don't misunderstand. To rethink does not mean to reinvent! We don't reinvent the wheel each time a new type of road is developed. We adapt the wheel to meet the changing road conditions. In the same way, the Great Commission is timeless. The command of Jesus "to make disciples" does not need to be reinterpreted; it needs to be reinstated. But we can't neglect the fact that our culture is changing. Jesus wants us to roll up our sleeves and get serious. He wants us to figure out how to adapt His mission within the context of our changing culture.

This isn't new. In fact, you do it yourself all the time. Every time you read the Bible, whether consciously or subconsciously, you ask yourself two questions: What did it mean back then? And in light of what it meant back then, what is the timeless truth I need to apply to my life today? The Bible was written centuries ago, but we still believe it is relevant and that it will never lose its relevance. The same is true of discipleship.

In the previous chapters, we took a hard look at discipleship. We initiated the rethinking process. We asked some difficult questions and came up with some surprising discoveries. Then we considered how to be a disciple and make disciples in this generation. All of this has been undertaken by studying the example of Jesus Christ. He is our *One Blinding Vision*, the Alpha and the Omega, where we started and where we will end. Now a final task remains with respect to discipleship. We must turn our attention to unleashing disciples.

How should this be done today? Glad you asked. Let's look at another masterpiece in Jesus' art studio. Once again, He presents us with a brilliant metaphor—a mental image to help us achieve clarity. Gaze upon it long enough, and you will understand what He wants you to do. I call this work of art "The Harvest."

The Harvest

As Jesus looked across the broken landscape of lost humanity, His eyes saw fields ripe for harvest. To seventy-two of His disciples He said, "The harvest is plentiful, but the workers are few" (Luke 10:2). It's difficult for us to understand the significance of the harvest. Most Americans have never experienced an agrarian lifestyle. And among those who have, the differences between today and the culture of ancient Israel are stark—at least as great as the feather pen is to a personal computer.

A few years back, a friend invited me to ride in his combine. This occurred during the wheat harvest. I was stunned. The cab was more comfortable than a living room sofa. It was pressurized, air conditioned, and had a sweet stereo system. The threshing cylinder was a mechanical wonder. It cut such a beautiful swath through the field that if Adam had been there, he might have exclaimed, "The curse has been lifted!" The control panel had more switches and gauges than an airplane of equal size. I was impressed. I think Jesus would have been too.

In ancient times, the harvest was a time of urgency. It imposed the most significant deadline of the year on society. Compare it to all the pressure you feel on April 15th and December 24th crammed into a single day, and then multiply that by ten. Harvest the crops, and you might live another year. But let them rot in the fields, and you could begin kissing your friends and family goodbye.

Sometimes I wish the Bible had accent marks to help us understand the inflection of Jesus' voice. When He said, "the workers are few," I wonder how it sounded pouring from His heart. One thing I'm convinced of: He said it with an emotional force that echoed inside His disciples' minds.

The effect was clear. In one unprecedented move, a remote Jewish Rabbi mobilized and unleashed seventy-two men. They stormed the fields of humanity and gathered a rich harvest. Up to this moment in human history, nothing like this had ever happened before. There is no parallel, either in scope or effect.

The Produce

Before we look specifically at the instructions He gave, consider the results—the produce. Jesus said Satan fell "like lightning from heaven" (Luke 10:18). The forces of darkness were defeated when the disciples were unleashed. I don't know how you define spiritual success, but I think that's pretty cool.

Jesus said something very curious when they returned: "For I tell you that many prophets and kings wanted to see what you see but did not see it, and to hear what you hear but did not hear it" (v. 24). Jesus used this same phrase again in Matthew 13:16. It happened just moments before He explained the "Parable of the Sower" to His disciples. Such a statement would have sounded very strange coming from the lips of any other man, but not from Jesus. He came from the place where kings and prophets go after they die. On another occasion, Jesus said, "Your father Abraham rejoiced at the thought of seeing my day; he saw it and was glad" (John 8:56).

Consider Leonardo da Vinci for a moment—that fifteenth-century Italian Renaissance genius. He spent a good portion of his life dreaming about flying. He wrote a book on the flight of birds. He even produced detailed sketches of flying machines—helicopters, hang-gliders, and parachutes. But sadly, he never flew. He died nearly four-hundred years too early. As a pilot myself, I get sad just thinking about it.

Just imagine how excited Leonardo would have been to fly across the Atlantic in a 747. He'd be happier than a little boy on Christmas morning. If you can appreciate this thought, then in some small way you might understand the elation Jesus experienced over unleashing the seventy-two. History had been waiting for this moment since the beginning of time. For all that Abraham, Moses, David, and Isaiah experienced, they would have exchanged it gladly to be a member of the Messiah's inaugural harvest.

When disciples are unleashed in the world, Jesus gets wound up with excitement. I imagine seeing a smile on His face each time someone steps through a fear. Jesus was straightforward with His disciples when He said, "Go! I am sending you out like lambs among wolves" (Luke 10:3). When one of His courageous little lambs enters a den of wolves with an attitude—watch out! The hounds of hell are but mere underdogs by comparison. They can't survive a battle with the weakest lamb in the Kingdom of God. No wonder Satan tries so hard to keep us away from the harvest.

I believe that *all* heaven, from the angels of God to the saints of glory, applauds when we set our face toward the harvest. They understand why it matters so much because they have an eternal perspective. And we should too.

> *Therefore, since we are surrounded by such a great cloud of witnesses, let us throw off everything that hinders and the sin that so easily entangles, and let us run with perseverance the race marked out for us* (Heb. 12:1).

Jesus intends for His Church to unleash disciples into the harvest. Although the world has changed over the last two-thousand years, the need is just as great. If the harvest rots outside the Church's walls, it's not long before the saints inside rot as well. We'll starve spiritually if we stay glued to our pews.

Luke 10:1-24 records Jesus giving seventy-two disciples a set of timeless instructions on how to enter the harvest. I picture these taking the form of seven steps. And they're not complicated at all. Rather, compare them to the first steps of a little child, who one day learns how to tread confidently upon the ground beneath his feet. No doubt, we can do the same. Just remember to take one step at a time. If we do this, our days of slowly crawling toward the Great Commission are over.

The Principles of Unleashing

The first step is to pray. Jesus instructed the seventy-two to lift their petitions to heaven, and "ask the Lord of the harvest, therefore, to send out workers into his harvest field" (Luke 10:2). God owns the fields. The people who are ready to enter the kingdom are waiting for us to arrive. But before we go, we must pray.

I learned some great theology when I was a kid, but I didn't know it was happening while I read my comic books. I discovered Spiderman got his superpower from a radioactive insect bite. The Hulk got his from a gamma bomb. Superman carried his superpower with him from another planet.

I'm convinced our superpower comes from "the Lord of the harvest," and it's activated by prayer. Andrew Murray, a nineteenth-century prayer warrior, said, "In prayer we exchange our natural strength for the supernatural strength of God." Don't you think we should remove the kryptonite from our personal prayer closets? I do. Dwight Moody never read a Marvel Comic, but this statement suggests he would have loved them: "Christ's soldiers fight best on their knees."

Personally, if I had a choice between preaching better sermons or praying more effective prayers, I'd choose the latter. John Henry Jowett, an acclaimed preacher in his own day, said, "I'd rather teach one man to pray than ten men to preach." Jesus was the best preacher who ever lived. But consider this: His disciples never asked Him to teach them how to preach. Neither did they ask Jesus to teach them how to do miracles. They did ask Him, however, to teach them how to pray. They understood that His abilities came down from the Father above. Jesus explained it this way: "I tell you the truth, the Son can do nothing by himself; he can do only what he sees his Father doing, because whatever the Father does the Son also does" (John 5:19).

Jesus said, "My house will be a house of prayer" (Luke 19:46). Whatever it takes, we should restore the primacy and urgency of prayer in our worship gatherings, our small groups, our committees, and our business meetings. When we stop running away from prayer, we'll regain our supernatural power. I agree with J. A. Wallace when he said, "Prayer moves the hand that moves the world."

The second step is to "Go!" Jesus gave the seventy-two an early glimpse into what would later be expressed in the Great Commission—"Go and make disciples." But what did Jesus mean when He said He was sending them out like "lambs among wolves"? Did He mean "to the slaughter"? Were they the martyr brigade—frontline cannon fodder? Hardly! When they returned, there were no reports of injuries. No lamb chops. No one died.

Lambs attract wolves, and Jesus relied on this fact but in a good way. He intended for the seventy-two to flush out the packs of humanity from their hiding places. And it happened. Luke said they returned with joy. See, it was painless ... no bite marks! They said, "Lord, even the demons submit to us in your name" (10:17).

Many people believe they are too busy to "Go!" I'd put it this way: If you're busy, chances are you're already going somewhere. The most joy-filled people I know realize every step they take is under God's divine purpose and direction. "In his heart a man plans his course, but the LORD determines his steps" (Prov. 16:9).

When you walk into a classroom, your office, or even when you run errands, keep your eyes open for divine appointments. You are God's charming little lamb. The world is curious about your Shepherd.

The third step is to stay focused. Jesus said, "Do not take a purse or bag or sandals; and do not greet anyone on the road" (Luke 10:4). At first glance it may seem Jesus was advocating rudeness. Again, not true! Here's the point: Don't walk through life with such a load of baggage that you're unable to consider anything but your own traveling burdens. And don't waste all your time on idle chitchat or meaningless activities. When Jesus assigns you a mission to accomplish, go straight to it. His mission is the most important thing on your calendar. Focus on it like a laser. Attack it like a samurai.

The fourth step is to seek a man of peace. Jesus said, "When you enter a house, first say, 'Peace to this house.' If a man of peace is there, your peace will rest on him; if not, it will return to you" (10:5-6). This is a fascinating concept, one I've heard my missionary friends talk about over the years. When a missionary seeks to plant the gospel in virgin soil or within an unreached people group, they begin looking for a "man of peace." Normally this is the type of person who is friendly to strangers, open to new ideas, and highly influential. Often such a person is the key to reaching an entire village for Jesus Christ. He or she is the gateway into the harvest.

After the tsunami of December 26, 2004, one of my friends gave His life to serve Christ on a small island in the Indian Ocean. The population is predominately Muslim and very hostile to Christianity. He's not supposed to be there, technically, and above all, not for the cause of Christ. My friend completely understands that he and his family are living as lambs among wolves.

Here's the most amazing part of his story. Before he went to serve as a missionary, I had him speak to my church family one Sunday morning. He specifically asked us to begin praying for the "man of peace." We did. On the first day he and his wife set foot on the shore, with their two children by their side and with what little remained after selling their worldly possessions, the man of peace presented himself. He walked over to shake my friend's hand and welcomed him to the island. Later the man became a believer. Together they started a church.

We should learn to do at home what we have learned to do so well on the foreign mission field.

The fifth step is to deliver the message. This is how Jesus instructed us to enter the harvest: "Heal the sick who are there and tell them, 'The kingdom of God is near you'" (v. 9). Some people are sick from disease. Others are sick from their sins. It's a fact! The Great Physician works best among the sick. On another occasion Jesus said, "It is not the healthy who need a doctor, but the sick … For I have not come to call the righteous, but sinners" (Matt. 9:12-13).

The message is twofold. Jesus wants us to deliver people, and He wants them to know God's kingdom has arrived. Everyone chooses whether to grow his or her own kingdom or to become a citizen of God's. The major difference between the two is that our tiny little kingdom can't stand against the assaults, either from without or from within. Our self-built kingdoms are temporal and fading. God's kingdom will never falter. It's built with a solid foundation that will never be shaken. This is good news. People desperately need you to deliver this message.

The sixth step is to move past rejection. Jesus said, "But when you enter a town and are not welcomed, go into its streets and say, 'Even the dust of your town that sticks to our feet we wipe off against you. Yet be sure of this: The kingdom of God is near'" (Luke 10:10-11). How dramatic! I've heard of Christians kicking the dust off their feet in front of other Christians just before they came to blows over some church conflict. But clearly this is not what Jesus had in mind.

People need to understand the gravity of turning away from Jesus. They may not fully realize it, but it is a devastating choice. I've had people look me in the eye and say things like, "Let me think about it"; "Maybe tomorrow"; "Perhaps after I clean up my life"; or "When I get past this big problem I'm having." These excuses don't sound as hardcore as full-fledged atheism, but the results are often the same.

Every time someone says no to Jesus, a change occurs inside that person's heart. Blockages develop. The arteries through which God's love may flow develop resistance. Saying no becomes easier with each passing encounter. A diseased heart may take time to develop, but the harder it becomes, the harder it is to say yes on another day.

It's never a good idea to run away from an encounter with Jesus Christ. Expertise in this area of running from Christ leaves a person in a far worse condition. It's not a popular thing to do in our society, but when someone rejects the gospel, let them know clearly what they've done. But do it with love and compassion. Don't wipe the dust off your feet if there are no tears in your eyes. Jesus sends only broken-hearted people into the harvest.

One more thing: Don't let fear of rejection keep you from sharing the Good News in the first place. It may feel personal to you, and it probably is to some extent, but this is more about Jesus than about you. We should have a greater fear of not warning someone than of being told no. God holds us accountable for our witness. God spoke these words though the prophet Ezekiel:

> *But if the watchman sees the sword coming*
> *and does not blow the trumpet to warn the*
> *people and the sword comes and takes the life*
> *of one of them, that man will be taken away*
> *because of his sin, but I will hold the watchman*
> *accountable for his blood* (Ezek. 33:6).

The seventh step is to celebrate. After the seventy-two returned, they testified of what they experienced. The enthusiasm was thick. Notice the phrases that described their emotions in Luke 10:17-24: "returned with joy"; "full of joy"; "rejoice that your names are written in heaven"; "I praise you, Father"; "good pleasure"; and "blessed are the eyes that see what you see."

Jesus loved the harvest. He invites us to celebrate with Him. He was no wet blanket—no stick in the mud. No! He's the Master of ceremonies. Our joy hits new highs when our Lord unleashes us to fill the earth with His presence. You'll miss the celebration if you are on a leash tied to a stake in the ground. Whatever you must do, please break free. Unleash yourself and join the party!

Have you noticed how much the world likes to party? Invite them to ours. It's how we multiply disciples.

PART 4: BUILDING BRIDGES

Men build too many walls and not enough bridges.
–Sir Isaac Newton

PREFACE

*The test of a man or woman's breeding is
how they behave in a quarrel.*
—George Bernard Shaw

Years ago I read a parable written by that poorly paid storyteller named Anonymous. Over the years it has appeared in many different forms, but the point is always clear. Here's my rendition:

Once upon a time, two brothers who lived on adjoining farms fell into a troubling conflict. What began as a small misunderstanding grew into a major disagreement. One day the tensions exploded into a bitter exchange of words followed by weeks of uncomfortable silence. Their longstanding partnership fell apart. This was the first major rift after forty years of farming side by side without any serious problems. But now they stubbornly refused to share equipment or exchange labor and goods with each other.

Early one morning there was a knock on the door of the older brother's home. He opened it to find a man with a carpenter's toolbox. "I'm looking for a few days' work," the stranger said. "Perhaps you have some small jobs here and there that I could do for you. Please, I would love to help out in any way I can."

"Okay," the older brother said. "I do have a job for you. Do you see the farm across the creek? That's my neighbor. In fact, it's my younger brother. Last week there was a meadow between us. He drove his bulldozer over to the river levee and tore it down. Now there's a big creek between us. I believe he did this to spite me. I want to get even. Do you see that pile of lumber by the barn? I want you to build me a fence, ten feet tall. I never want to see his place or his face ever again!"

The carpenter said, "I think I understand the situation. Show me the nails and the post-hole digger. I'll do a job that pleases you."

The older brother had to go to town, so he helped the carpenter get the materials ready. Then he was off for the day. While the sun shone overhead, the carpenter worked diligently—measuring, sawing, nailing, and building. About sunset when the farmer returned, the carpenter had just finished his job.

Stunned by what he saw, the farmer's eyes opened wide. His jaw dropped. There was no fence there at all. It was a bridge—a bridge stretching from one side of the creek to the other! It was an exquisite piece of work, handrails and all. And the neighbor, his younger brother, was coming toward them with his arms outstretched.

"Brother," he shouted from across the creek, "you are quite a fellow to build this bridge after all I've said and done."

The two brothers stood for a moment at each end of the bridge. Then a miracle occurred. They each began walking toward the other until they met in the middle. There they hugged in a heartfelt embrace. From the corner of their eyes, they noticed the carpenter. He was pleased. Satisfied his work was complete, he quickly hoisted his toolbox onto his shoulder and began to walk away.

"No, wait! I haven't paid you," the older brother said. "Please stay a few days. I've a lot of other projects for you."

"I'd love to stay here," the carpenter said, "but I have many more bridges to build. And by the way, I work for free!"

How like Jesus! I wonder if we could figure out how to build more bridges ourselves. We start by looking at Jesus, our *One Blinding Vision*.

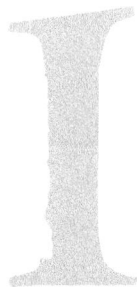

I

Last Things

The end is where we start from.
–T. S. Eliot

People have long been intrigued by how things end.

Consider Hilton Crawford. For the main course he requested twelve beef ribs, three enchiladas, chicken-fried steak with cream gravy, a crispy bacon sandwich, and a loaf of bread. On the side, he wanted an order of French fries, onion rings, and plenty of ketchup. To wash it all down, he asked for three Cokes and three root beers. Dessert was simple. He ordered cobbler. Such was his last meal. His crime was murder. Crawford was executed by lethal injection July 2, 2003, in Huntsville, Texas.

Last Request…Words…Testament

In the end, we all reap what we sow.

Consider the last recorded words of a few famous people. Just moments before he died, American frontiersman Kit Carson said, "I wish I had time for one more bowl of chili." Winston Churchill's final words are reported as, "I'm bored with it all." Salvador Dali inquired, "Where is my clock?" Leonardo da Vinci confessed, "I have offended God and mankind because my work did not reach the quality it should have." Queen Elizabeth I pleaded, "All my possessions for a moment of time."

In the end, some people say the most unusual things.

Now consider Mark Gruenwald. He loved comic books. As an impressionable young boy, he was the industry's biggest fan. As a young man, he quickly rose through the ranks of Marvel Comics as a multi-talented writer, penciller, inker, colorist, and cover artist. By his mid-thirties, Gruenwald had become a living legend. He edited some of the most popular magazines ever to fall into the hands of young boys and girls, such as *Avengers, Spider-Man, Iron Man, Captain America, Spider-Woman, Squadron Supreme, X-Men,* and *Wolverine*—just to name a few.

His memory was encyclopedic. For a time, Marvel hosted an annual contest where fans were challenged to stump Gruenwald. He was presented with the most obscure questions from the universe of superhero trivia. He never lost, so the contest was discontinued. It came as no surprise when—not once but twice—Gruenwald won the prestigious "Fan Award" issued by the industry-standard *Comics Buyer's Guide.*

Then, unexpectedly, during the height of his career, he died from a massive heart attack. He was only forty-three. His last will and testament requested he be cremated and his ashes mixed with ink. This bizarre compound was used to print his magnum opus—the first twelve issues of *Squadron Supreme* collected into one graphic novel. Four-thousand copies were sold.

In the end, fact is stranger than fiction.

Twenty-Four Hours

Finally … consider Jesus.

He lived only thirty-three years, but we know more about His last twenty-four hours than any similar period of time, and for good reason.

Long before Adam took his first breath, before the very first star pierced the darkness, behind some eternal door in the most secret place, God ordained the perfect plan. The date was fixed. God orchestrated the last night and final day in Jesus' life to take center-stage. Every passing second ticked toward this moment like a foot soldier swiftly advancing toward the place of battle.

For those of us who believe Jesus Christ is the Son of God, the Messiah sent to rescue us from the penalty of sin, we reflect on this day with reverence. We don't just read the story; we see it unfolding. His life is intertwined with our own. We feel it, deeply and sometimes painfully.

It's not hard to imagine standing next to Peter as he warmed himself by a fire that night. Our hearts are torn by the storyline—the denial and the betrayal, the mockery and the hypocrisy. We feel the force of the blows to Christ's face, the shredding of flesh, the wounded brow, the nail-pierced hands and feet. By midday, we watch the sky grow dark as all creation groans against this crime. Then we hear, "It is finished" (John 19:30). Sometimes I forget to breathe as I read the story.

The Return to Glory

But before the chaos, there was calm. At some point between the Passover supper in the Upper Room and arriving at the Garden of Gethsemane, Jesus prayed one final time with His disciples. This prayer is found in John Chapter 17, and it happens to be our Lord's longest recorded prayer. It is called "The High Priestly Prayer." Jesus has much to say. The disciples have much to hear. We have much to learn.

First, Jesus prays for Himself. But He doesn't pray like most of us would pray before facing a painful execution. Jesus prays with a sense of anticipation. He's eager to return home, to rejoin the intimate, triune fellowship with the Father and the Spirit.

Here is a great mystery to fill the imagination: Jesus yearns for the Father to give Him the glory they shared together "before the world began" (v. 5). Jesus is eternal and has never been less than "fully God," even when He became "fully man" during the incarnation. He wasn't half God and half man or any percentage in between. He was fully both—completely God and completely man.

That's the mystery!

But there were self-imposed limitations on the divine part of His nature. Jesus chose to veil His eternal, glorified state as He walked among His own creation. Paul expressed it this way: "Though he was God, he did not think of equality with God as something to cling to. Instead, he gave up his divine privileges; he took the humble position of a slave and was born as a human being" (Phil. 2:6-7 NLT).

Who can fathom all He left behind to live as we live? His descent from glory into humanity was greater by comparison than if you or I suddenly became a single speck of sand. And He did it willingly, humbly, unselfishly—all so we could experience God, up close, in the flesh, with our eyes wide open.

Throughout the centuries, this mystery has mystified the minds of common Christians and ivory-tower theologians alike. But it's a beautiful reality to ponder. It captures the heart, especially when you meditate on the full significance of what Jesus did—all for the glory of God … and all for you!

A Fall from Glory

On a mission trip in 2004, I had an opportunity to visit the Forbidden City in Beijing, China. The six-hundred-year-old palace is the largest surviving palace complex in history. It covers 181 acres, and it took more than one million laborers fifteen years to build. The architecture is stunning.

The palace contains the largest collection of ancient wooden structures in the world. Over the course of five centuries, it was home to twenty-four emperors who ruled the vast Chinese empire. Standing at the entrance, I reflected on the fact that no one entered or exited without the emperor's permission. The mere sight of it left me in a state of awe.

While there, I had a chance to study in some detail the life of Emperor Puyi, who died in 1967. On the twentieth anniversary of his death, Columbia Pictures released "The Last Emperor," a movie about his life. On the silver screen and in reality, his life was epic and tragic. He ascended to the throne at the tender age of two. Everyone treated him like a god. Everywhere he went people kowtowed in his presence.

But when Communist leader Mao Tse-tung came to power, Puyi was sent to prison for ten years. He was reeducated and then transformed into a common citizen. He lost his power and his freedom, and then lived the rest of his life in shame. The lament David sang about the death of King Saul, "How the mighty have fallen …," reminds me of Puyi. What a plunge from the heights of glory!

On that same trip, I visited a museum in Changchun that showcased Puyi's prison garments and simple gardening tools. I asked our Chinese tour guide if people felt a sense of sadness that Puyi had fallen from such lofty heights—from a god to a gardener, from a palace to a prison.

Wrinkles formed on her brow. Then a spontaneous flash of anger came across her face. "No!" she snapped. "He got what he deserved."

Rarely does someone lay aside power voluntarily. It's human nature to reach for more, not less. History records many stories of dictators who had control pried from their hands. Czar Nicholas II, Adolph Hitler, Benito Mussolini, Pol Pot, Idi Amin, and Saddam Hussein each lost everything in the end. "What good is it for a man to gain the whole world," Jesus asked, "yet forfeit his soul?" (Mark 8:36).

Jesus never fell from glory. He *came* from glory. He had immeasurable power before He came to walk the earth. No one possessed more than He did, ever! And no one gave up more. He checked out of heaven's royal palace to spend His first nine months in the womb of a peasant girl. Then He landed in a manger—a feeding trough for livestock. No one had the power to take His glory from Him—no dictator, no king, no emperor. In the most sacrificial way, Jesus willingly gave up His glorified state. He became like us, yet "without sin" (see Heb. 4:15).

It's no great wonder that during His last night, Jesus yearned for heaven—His true home. He longed to step into the courts of praise, to see the Father's face, to hear "well done," and to sit by His side. As Jesus prayed for Himself in John chapter 17, I can't help but feel the sense of expectation and joy that filled His heart. The time had come for Him to go home.

The Prayer for the Disciples

But His prayer didn't stop there. He also prayed for the disciples. In a few hours they would desperately need His intercession. They, like Jesus, were about to be caught in the crosshairs of a bloodthirsty mob. Soon they'd be dazed and confused. So, twice, Jesus asked the Father to protect His disciples.

The word *protect* has an interesting meaning in the Greek language. It was used by prison officials, who *guarded* their prisoners. Other times it conveyed the sense of *preserving* or *keeping*. This was the same word Jesus used in Revelation 3:10 when He promised the believers in the church of Philadelphia, "I will also keep [protect] you from the hour of trial that is going to come upon the whole world to test those who live on the earth."

In the hours preceding the Crucifixion, the disciples needed divine protection like the spring needs rain. But physical safety wasn't enough. They also needed to be convinced the Father had sent Jesus Christ. So Jesus prayed, "They knew with certainty that I came from you, and they believed that you sent me" (John 17:8). Their physical safety would be threatened, and their convictions would be tested. But in the end, Jesus' prayer was answered. God never fails.

The Prayer for Us

Finally, Jesus prayed for us—all believers across all ages. This is both wonderful and fascinating. Jesus saw that you and I would be part of God's kingdom one day. This is the most forward-looking, far-reaching prayer ever prayed. It spanned every century of Christian history. And consider that the power of His prayer will be felt hundreds of years from now, or at least until He comes to take His people home.

If you happened to be there in that holy moment as Jesus began praying for you, would you have a special request? I've been in thousands of prayer meetings. Normally, before someone prays, requests are taken from those in the audience. I remember an appeal from a little boy who wanted his hamster to go to heaven. Over the years, I've had people ask me to pray for family members, friends, co-workers, health issues, enemies, and even the deceased.

If I had been with Jesus hours before He went to the Cross to die for my sins and He said to me, "I'm about to pray for you," I might have given Him the biggest request imaginable. Wouldn't you? We might ask something like, "Jesus, please don't let me die from cancer." Maybe the request would be, "Lord, I never want to bury my own child," or "Please keep me from ever losing my job, going bankrupt, or experiencing a divorce."

But Jesus didn't pray any of those things for us. What He did pray was surprising. As He gazed into the future and saw all believers across the ages, He prayed, "My prayer is not for them alone. I pray also for those who will believe in me through their message, that all of them may be one, Father, just as you are in me and I am in you. May they also be in us so that the world may believe that you have sent me" (vv. 20-21).

The disciples asked Jesus to do many things for them, but they never asked Him to unify them or help them get along. But during this high and holy moment, He prayed His followers would be one. Had we been there, it's probably not the prayer we would have asked for. Yet it's the prayer we got.

Tri-unity and Our Unity

Why? What makes this so important to Christ's heart? Why did He bypass seemingly greater issues the Church would face throughout the centuries? Jesus answered these questions clearly. He wanted us to reflect the glorious, transcendent unity that exists within the Trinity. He prayed that we would be "one" just like He was "one" with the Father.

Words and imagination fall short when we attempt to describe the relationship between God the Father, God the Son, and God the Holy Spirit. This side of heaven there will always be an element of mystery that veils our understanding. We know the Three are separate, yet One. They are distinct persons with individual personalities, yet One. They have existed throughout all eternity, co-equal, without beginning or end, yet One.

Tri-unity. Mathematicians can't formulize it. Scientists can't explain it. And philosophers can't comprehend it. Nevertheless, the Trinity is a deeper reality than all known realities combined. Before anything existed, our triune God was on His throne. He is Three. He is One.

What a relationship!

His prayer, "May they also be in us," is now reality. Our unity with each other is a witness of the Trinity. Jesus said, "… so that the world may believe that you have sent me." If ever there was a reason for all believers to be unified, this is it. Our unity with one another has an impact on whether the lost world believes the Father sent the Son. And it has everything to do with whether they believe our message.

We can't afford to ignore this. There is more at stake than our petty differences, our preferences, or our past hurts. The issue is not whether we like the fellow believers who share our space. No, the real issue is far more significant. Our disunity impedes our mission. Might there be people in hell at this very moment who chose not to believe in Jesus Christ because of the lack of unity among believers? Most likely! Why would they have believed in a message that didn't work for the messengers?

We should grieve over this fact. Our spirits would be devastated if we could fully understand how division breaks God's heart and creates disbelief among the people we're trying to reach. We must take this prayer as seriously as Jesus did. Considering all the things He could have prayed for us, He prayed for our unity.

The next time you get mad at another believer, don't spend all your time trying to figure out who's at fault or who needs to apologize first. Think about Jesus on the last night of His earthly life praying that you would be one with that person. Realize the spirit of dissension and unresolved bitterness damages the kingdom. Resolve matters quickly between a brother or sister in Christ. Lay your pride aside and make things right.

I'm not asking you to compromise your convictions or admit fault where there is none. I'm asking you to give your best effort to something that mattered greatly to your Lord. We should all be glad Jesus didn't require us to apologize first or confess our sins before He went to the Cross. He took the first step toward Golgotha. He completed the work to show you first how much your unity with Him really matters.

If we understood God's grace, we'd be more graceful to others. Our sinful nature expresses itself most unmistakably when we fight so hard to get our way. Many people hate to admit when they're wrong or even consider there is more than one way to look at a particular issue. It's impossible for every believer to get his or her way in a church. It's ridiculous to expect the leadership in the church to please everybody. It will never happen if we require our needs to be met first. We will be most pleased in our Christian life when we put Jesus' desires first. We must be humble enough to admit we could be wrong about some things. We must evaluate our positions and longstanding convictions, and be willing to change when necessitated by the truth. It's how we grow.

Do you examine your convictions to determine whether they're correct? Some things are clear and obvious and need no evaluation. For instance, I don't need to examine whether faithfulness in marriage or staying away from pornography is God's will. These are seldom the things that divide churches. It's usually things like the style of music, the subject matter of the message, or how the money is allocated.

When we get to heaven, the Lord will correct our misguided thoughts and expose what really mattered most. I don't know exactly what this experience will be like, but I'm certain we should strive to get things right— here and now. Who wants to step across the threshold into heaven to hear God say, "What were you thinking?" I'd rather deal with this today so when I get to heaven I might hear, "Well done, good and faithful servant."

One of the things Christians do well is fight. This reality exposes the worst in us. It leads to broken relationships. It steals our time and passion for our mission. In such times, we display our hypocrisy to the world in its most raw and elemental form. Shame on us when we gossip about and slander our fellow believers! Is there another option?

Absolutely!

What if we built bridges across the great divides? I propose we stop basing everything on our feelings and self-interests. Let's base things on Jesus' desire. He's already told us what He wanted. He wants us to be "one."

He couldn't have been clearer.

2

BOHEMIANS FOR CHRIST

I have but one passion—it is He, it is He
alone. The world is the field and the field is
the world; and henceforth that country shall
be my home where I can be most used in
winning souls for Christ.
–Count Nicholas von Zinzendorf

The Bethlehem Steel Corporation was a powerhouse of industrialism and capitalism on the American landscape for nearly 150 years. Founded in Bethlehem, Pennsylvania, in 1857, it became the second largest steel company in America. Countless bridges, railroads, skyscrapers, and ships around the world were built using Bethlehem steel. From the first day I heard about the company until its bankruptcy in 2001, I wondered where its name originated.

Here's the backstory. The original city of Bethlehem was the home of King David and the birthplace of Jesus Christ. But to discover how it was selected as the name for a village in eastern Pennsylvania, we need to travel back through time nearly three-hundred years. Our destination is a place on the opposite side of the Atlantic. There we find a man who sees possibilities more clearly than reality. He's a fresh thinker and a pure leader by design—applauded by theologians as a spiritual revolutionary, admired by historians as a dominant force for change in the world.

Nicholas von Zinzendorf was born in Dresden, Germany, on May 26, 1700. Although his father died shortly after Nicholas' birth, the boy had all the privileges and pains of an aristocratic upbringing. His fortune would be secure, but his destiny was already settled. It was assumed he would ultimately mature, embrace his nobleman status, and fulfill the responsibilities of a typical European Count. But those who watched Nicholas, even as a child, noted his deep piety and mystical leanings.

As a young man, Nicholas visited a museum where he saw a painting by the great 17th-century Italian artist Domenico Feti. It was called *"Ecce Homo,"* or "Behold the Man." It features a portrait of Jesus Christ—His eyes drooping in a listless gaze, a crown of thorns upon His head, wearing a seamless flowing robe, pale, with arms folded, and hands resting on a wooden beam. The Latin inscription on the beam reads, "This have I done for you—Now what will you do for me?"

Nicholas was spellbound. Warm tears streamed down his face. He stood motionless before the painting for five hours. A life-changing moment was brewing deep inside. Nicholas felt as though Jesus were speaking those words directly into his heart. And on that very day, he dedicated his life to serve Jesus Christ. Little did he know what this would mean for his future.

It became clear, however, when in 1722, a group of Moravian exiles, traveling from the region of the modern-day Czech Republic, asked Nicholas if they could live on his estate. The Moravian Christians (sometimes called Bohemian Brethren, or *Unitas Fratrum*, "Unity of the Brethren") had experienced an appalling degree of religious persecution in their homeland. Nicholas listened to their stories and was moved with compassion. And because he was so deeply sympathetic to their plight, it was an easy decision. He agreed. This small band of Moravian believers established a new community they called *Herrnhut*, or "The Lord's Watch," then set out to reconstruct their lives.

Unfortunately, the refugees argued and fought over the most trivial matters for five long years. They were angry people from a variety of backgrounds who had experienced overwhelming hardship in their lives. Understandably, it leaked out in bitterness and hostility. The fragile community was in jeopardy of splintering away and disappearing entirely.

Let me push the pause button on this story for a moment. If they had failed to get their act together, the world would be a different place today. At this moment in our story, who could have looked upon this uprooted, rag-tag bunch of refugees and seen much potential? Who could have seen that movements were about to be born to advance God's kingdom? The issue for us is the same. Do we expect God to do great things in our midst? Do we have the firm conviction that He desires to? I'm reminded of what the apostle Paul said to the Corinthians:

> *Brothers, think of what you were when*
> *you were called. Not many of you were*
> *wise by human standards; not many were*
> *influential; not many were of noble birth.*
> *But God chose the foolish things of the world*
> *to shame the wise; God chose the weak*
> *things of the world to shame the strong. He*
> *chose the lowly things of this world and the*
> *despised things—and the things that are*
> *not—to nullify the things that are, so that no*
> *one may boast before him* (1 Cor. 1:26-29).

Sensing the Lord's direction once again, Nicholas decided to leave behind the public life of nobility and aristocracy. He devoted himself entirely to the task of building a unified, Christ-centered community among the uprooted Moravians. His goal was to build a bridge between his world and theirs, then step over to the other side. Nicholas was convinced that redirecting their focus to Jesus Christ was the answer. "I have but one passion," he said. "It is He, it is He alone."

Challenging the community to capture a fresh vision of Jesus wasn't easy, but it worked. Nicholas spent three hours on May 12, 1727, speaking to the Moravian refugees on the subject of spiritual unity among believers. After he finished, the effect was immediate. The Holy Spirit moved. They repented, wept, and confessed their sins to one another. The rifts between believers mended at an even greater pace when Nicholas took communion into their homes. As they broke bread with one another, old hurts and tensions were laid aside. Relationships healed. Their fellowships grew sweeter and more enjoyable as the days marched on.

Following these events, the Moravians established a code of "Brotherly Conduct"—a set of biblical principles to govern their relationships and foster unity. They started the first around-the-clock prayer vigil, which remarkably lasted more than one-hundred years. Also, they began the first emphasis on organized meetings to pray specifically for the cities in which they lived. As this spiritual renewal gathered steam, they became known as "God's Happy People."

When others began to hear that God was doing something special through the Moravians, the little community of Herrnhut began to blossom. People from a variety of backgrounds came to experience what was known as the "Moravian Pentecost." One such man was a former slave from the West Indies named Anthony Ulrich. He had recently converted to Christianity. He shared in great detail the misery and suffering experienced among the slaves living on the Caribbean islands.

Two young men, Leonard Dober and David Nitschmann, were so touched by Ulrich's stories that they decided to go to St. Thomas and live among the slaves. But there was one problem. The landowner didn't want the Christian ethic to interfere with his profitable business. He refused—quite passionately—to allow outsiders the chance to preach the gospel to his slaves. So Leonard and David came up with a plan. They sold themselves into slavery, so that as slaves they might evangelize other slaves. They gave up their freedom to share Christ's love with those who were perishing. Their friends and family members were grief-stricken by this decision. They begged and pleaded for them to reconsider, but to no avail. To them, the Word of God was clear enough. As the apostle Paul said, "Though I am free and belong to no man, I make myself a slave to everyone, to win as many as possible" (1 Cor. 9:19).

Finally, the day came for the ship to set sail. David and Leonard watched from the deck as their friends and relatives wept over their departure. No one ever expected to see them again or believed they would survive for long. As the ship embarked and her distance increased, a loud cry was heard echoing across the water. One of the two young men—no one knows which one—called out, "May the Lamb that was slain, receive the reward for His suffering!"

That phrase became the rallying cry for Moravian missions all over the world. These men were the very first Protestant missionaries, and their example launched a worldwide movement. By the end of Zinzendorf's life in 1760, his missionaries were serving from Greenland to South Africa. Out of six hundred inhabitants of Herrnhut, seventy followed Christ to another land.

Unprecedented!

Moravian missionaries also came to America. In fact, they had a significant influence on John Wesley during the time he was in Georgia. The Moravians had joy; John was burned out and miserable. It wasn't long before Wesley came face to face with his own moral failure and personal disappointment. Embarrassed, he went home to England. In his diary Wesley said the Moravian brethren "endeavored to show me a more excellent way. But I understood it not at first. I was too learned and too wise; so that it seemed foolishness unto me."

Perhaps it was Wesley's flagrant pride that led God to place a few Moravians on his voyage back to England. When a fierce storm threatened their ship, Wesley was terrified. By contrast, he observed the Moravians sitting together in one corner of the ship, peacefully singing hymns. After the wind and waves died, they encouraged him to attend a small gathering of believers who met on Aldersgate Street in London.

Once back in England, Wesley wrestled with this invitation. But with nothing else happening, he begrudgingly decided to give it a try. "In the evening I went," Wesley said, "very unwillingly." As he listened to someone read the introduction to Martin Luther's commentary on the Epistle of Romans, Wesley felt his heart "strangely warmed." For the first time in his life, he understood God's wonderful grace. He placed his faith in Christ and ceased all his striving to earn God's favor. Wesley's conversion eventually led to the founding of the Methodist church and fanned the flames of the First Great Awakening in America and England.

Imagine how different our world would be today without John and Charles Wesley—the churches that would never have been built, the hymns that would never have been written. During Christmas you wouldn't hear, "Hark! The Herald Angels Sing." Other hymns, "O For A Thousand Tongues To Sing" and "Come, Thou Long-Expected Jesus," gone! It would be difficult to assess what the absence of the Wesley brothers would have meant to the Awakening in which they played such a prominent role. Now think back to that moment when it appeared those early Moravians would ultimately fail for lack of unity. Thank God that didn't happen!

I'd like to share one final historical detail: Moravian missionaries traveled as far north as Pennsylvania. This brings me back to where our story began. Bethlehem, Pennsylvania, was founded on Christmas Eve, in 1741, by Count Nicholas von Zinzendorf—the Christ-centered servant, missionary zealot, and humble bridge-builder for Jesus Christ. It's an irony, but one worth noting. Nicholas didn't build his bridges out of steel. They were constructed out of simple things like brotherhood and unity, born out of an all-consuming passion for Jesus Christ. He too had *One Blinding Vision*.

> *Take my poor heart and let it be*
> *Forever closed to all but Thee!*
> *Seal Thou my breast and let me bear*
> *The pledge of love forever there.*
> *"Song of the Moravian Revival"*
> –Zinzendorf [6]

Final Thoughts

Spiritual unity among believers really matters. When great things are done to advance the kingdom, be assured it has everything to do with common goals, shared passion, and a compelling purpose. The opposite is true as well—painfully so. The hardest part of what a particular church does is not the work itself, but getting rid of what kills the joy in our work. It's nearly impossible to love what you do if you don't love who you're doing it with. This is why the most important task for a community of believers is to come together, to be united.

Have you noticed it's always harder to do things by yourself? If I want to champion a cause, it helps to have many champions of that cause. There's a great synonym for introverted champions who fight all their battles by themselves: martyr. A man will not be successful at anything for very long unless others want him to be. He will either burn out from exhaustion or fail because of too much opposition.

One of the biggest threats to our unity is lingering and unresolved

---

[6] Public Domain.

R. James Shupp

conflict. The least efficient method of exerting energy in life, if not bloodiest, is done fighting uphill battles against opposing forces. I'm convinced of it. The first work, before all other work can be successful, is to be one with my fellow workers in Christ. Like most people, I find this is the easiest step to neglect when I hatch my ideas and launch my plans.

If we do the difficult work of unifying our hearts and minds for the glory of God, He will be most pleased. Our failure to do so only grieves the Holy Spirit of God within us. And it's all too easy to detect when this happens. Since His Spirit is in our spirit, when He is grieved we cannot avoid feeling grieved as well. Inside every failing endeavor for the cause of Christ is a mournful ache within the body, a spiritual distress over the failure to unify. It should come as no surprise that when we drench and quench the Spirit, our bright and glorious flame becomes a fragile, smoldering wick.

We must guard ourselves from the spirit of contention. I confess it's easy for me to get disgruntled and disturbed. Sometimes it's difficult to keep my spirit free and make the choice to cast off the yoke of bondage. Rude, thoughtless, or inconsiderate people—intentional or unintentional—can really mess up the circuits in my frontal lobe.

Spiritual warfare always begins in the mind. Granting free access to godless thoughts has brought more than one saint to the brink of the abyss. "Take captive every thought," the Bible says, "to make it obedient to Christ" (2 Cor. 10:5). Say this next sentence with me, out loud: "Any thought I allow in my mind, unleashed by the enemy, unexamined by the Word, or untouchable to the Spirit, will cause unlimited amounts of damage, both to me and those closest to me."

Thoughts like seeds are thrown.
Once planted,
they are quickly grown.

Here's a better thought: One man or woman completely sold out to Christ, possessing the mind of Christ, consumed by His life, fearless in unifying and rallying other believers to live the same, will draw from Christ's unlimited power and authority to change the world. It's happened before. It can happen again.

Let's go and do this together.

May we each stand with the prophet Isaiah and say, "Here am I. Send me!" (Isa. 6:8).

3

Mammy

*Even when I am old and gray, do not forsake
me, O God, till I declare your power to the
next generation, your might to all who are to
come.* Psalm 71:18

My great-grandmother was born in 1892. She was in her mid-seventies when I began forming my first impressions of her. Most of the time she was confined to a wheelchair. Long before I was born, an unfortunate car accident had severely damaged her knees. On good days she was able to move about slowly by means of a walker. I called her "Mammy," and I loved her dearly.

When I Was Four

Mammy had two speeds: Go and sleep. To this day I've never seen someone get so much done without really going anywhere. From my four-year-old perspective, she did the important things like snapping beans and peas for dinner, managing the finances for the chicken farm, and barking orders to the hired workers. In between periods of keeping everyone on task, she worked crossword puzzles, played solitaire, and regaled me with tales that kept me entertained for hours.

I'll never forget the story of "the mysterious snake that swallowed chickens whole." As Mammy told the story, "It came from the Hatchie River Bottoms, a place of unspeakable terror for little boys." It slithered its way into her massive chicken barn one hot Jackson, Tennessee, afternoon. On that day she heard thousands of chickens making "a fuss that in all my years of raisin' birds, I'd never heard before."

All this happened before the accident when Mammy was still in the prime of life. During those days, she carried her four-foot-nine-inch body with formidable agility. She often assured me I would never have been able to outrun her "before my knees left dents in the dash." I never doubted this as a little boy—and still don't.

She continued. "I ran outside, grabbed the hoe"—which she kept razor sharp—"charged into the barn, and peered through the faint light. As my eyes adjusted to the darkness, I could feel the presence of something terrible … watching me … waiting."

She paused momentarily, scanning my tiny adolescent frame. Already my eyelids were stuck wide open, drying out from a lack of blinking.

"Then I saw it." Her words erupted with a deep southern drawl. "It was standing on its tail looking at me straight in the eye—a snake with a body nearly as big around as my leg. It had fins below its head and bright colors that formed a pattern I'd never seen before."

"Mammy," I squeaked, "was it poisonous?"

"You bet'cha," she whispered. "Whenever it struck a chicken with its fangs, the bird dropped where it was that instant and swelled up like a basketball. The feathers would stick straight out like a porcupine's quills. The poor chicken's eyes never closed. The last thing the bird saw was the snake coming to swallow it whole."

"Were you scared?" I asked.

"No, but you should be," she warned. "You never want to go into that chicken barn alone. There are things in there that could eat a little boy up or carry him off. We'd never see you again."

"Mammy, what did you do?"

"That snake and I stared at each other for what seemed like an hour. His forked tongue came in and out of his mouth, over and over, vibratin' like a leaf blowin' in the wind. I think he was tryin' to hypnotize me, or taste me from a distance—figurin' out what to do."

Mammy looked right past me, peering off somewhere in the distance, conjuring up that decades-old scene in her mind's eye. Time passed. And though I was filled with anticipation, I dared not crash the silence. Then all at once she cleared her throat—dramatic effect—and narrated the furious details of the death match, voice rising and falling like the clash of thunder.

"That snake whipped his head back, showed his proud fangs, and struck at me. I moved, and just in time. He missed me by a hair. I swung my hoe as hard as I could. I hit him ... knocked him over."

"Did you kill him?"

"No, not then," she said. "That hoe just bounced off his scaly skin; don't think it hurt him much. He just slithered off toward the tractor. The chickens were jumpin', slappin' their wings against the dusty barn floor, cacklin' so loud my ears were ringin'. Feathers were floatin' up into the air so thick I could hardly see."

"What did you do next?" I gasped.

"I chased him. If I didn't kill him, he'd eat all my chickens. I wouldn't be able to pay all my hired hands. If that happened, you'd have to move here and take care of my place for me."

I thought about that for a moment. Living with Mammy in Tennessee would have been the fulfillment of a childhood dream. She had all the things little boys love—a big house with many rooms to get lost in, closets packed with stuff accumulated over decades, land as far as the eye could see, animals, adventure, and the best southern cooking I had ever tasted in my life. As my mind considered the possibilities, I nearly forgot about the snake.

"I chased that snake." She bobbed her head. "Yes, I did. We fought over every square inch of that barn. Some of the chickens got so scared they died from a heart attack. But I kept fightin'. I swung at it nearly fifty times before I hit it somewhere that made it hurt. It rolled up into a ball and started floppin' its head against the floor. That's when I hit it one last time … took its head off with my hoe."

Then came the important lesson. "Boy," she said to me, "never touch a dead snake. First of all, it might not be dead, just sleepin'. And second, a snakehead can bite you even without a body. That dead snake twitched for hours."

Mammy told this story to me repeatedly as I grew up. Every summer we visited her in Tennessee, I asked her to share it with me all over again. Sometimes new details emerged. She proudly shared how she put the snake in the back of her pickup truck, carried it to the university, and asked the professors to identify it.

"Those scientists and scholars had never seen a snake like that before," she said. "It was one of a kind." Mammy searched reptile books throughout her life trying to identify her snake. She never could. Guess that's what made it so "mysterious."

When I Was Sixteen

I never got to live with Mammy in Tennessee. It broke my heart as a child, but I kept the disappointment to myself. However, Mammy came to live with us in Midland, Texas. She finally hit that season when she couldn't take care of herself any longer. So one day we got into our family car, drove to Mammy's house for the last time, loaded up her stuff, and moved her to a "place where trees couldn't grow"—west Texas.

Over the preceding twelve years, Mammy had slowed down tremendously. She needed help to do anything or go anywhere. That's where I came in. My job was to get Mammy to church every Sunday morning that she felt well enough to attend. Her trailer house was on a direct route to the small country church where we worshiped, but I always arrived early enough to give her ample time to move at her own pace.

The technique of getting her into my 1972 Ford Maverick was rather complex. We used a walker to get down the stairs. In the front passenger seat, I placed a blanket. When she sat down I pulled the blanket from the driver's side of my car. Sometimes she giggled as her frail body slid across the seat. She'd comment on how strong I was and how proud she was to see me grow into a fine young man. I'd load the walker and wheelchair in the trunk, and off we'd go to church. I must have been the only teenager in Midland who arrived in the front parking lot with his great-grandmother sitting in the front seat.

The preacher of the small Baptist church we attended always knew when Mammy was there. He made sure each time she arrived that we sang her favorite song, "When the Saints Are Marching In." Mammy would clap and sing with all the enthusiasm she could express. I have no doubt she was looking forward to that day herself.

One day as I took Mammy home after church, I asked her to tell me the story of the mysterious snake again. I listened and interacted with her in much the same way I did as a child. She retold it with the same enthusiasm, although somewhat diminished as her voice cracked more frequently. After she finished, I asked her the question I was too afraid to ask as a little boy.

"Mammy, how much of that story is true?"

She looked at me, grinned, then spoke: "Mostly."

"Mostly," I repeated.

"I loved telling you stories," she said. "You loved to listen. And I loved your attention. Always have."

Throughout my life, Mammy fascinated me with stories of her Alabama childhood. She taught me more than I realized at the time. Widowed at an early age, she helped me understand what it was like to lose someone you dearly loved. On a family vacation to the Gulf of Mexico, her husband got caught in a riptide, had a heart attack, and drowned. It was a shock from which I don't think she ever fully recovered. When Mammy sang songs in church about heaven, I knew she was thinking about seeing her husband again.

When I Was in College

The news came from my mother while I was attending Texas Tech University in Lubbock. Her voice trembled as she spoke. "Mammy died today. She's with Jesus now. She loved you so much."

Faint echoes of that song she sang with passion stirred in my memory. Sometimes our imagination is more powerful than reality. I could see her sitting in her wheelchair, a big radiant smile on her face, slapping her knee, keeping the beat, shouting through frail vocal cords:

> *Parted friends shall meet,*
> *On the golden street,*
> *When the saints are marching in,*
> *Spotless robes shall wear,*
> *Victor's palms shall bear,*
> *When the saints are marching in.*[7]

I didn't attend the funeral. For some strange reason, I couldn't. I had been to only one other funeral. I was much younger and didn't even know the person who was being buried. But Mammy was different. I wanted to remember her alive, snapping peas and chasing snakes with her hoe. I'm

---

[7] Public Domain.

certain I'll see her again in heaven. She'll be more alive than ever before. And I can promise you this—there won't be any snakes up there!

Reflections

Over the last thirty years, I've watched the relational distance between the young and old increase dramatically. There's something about this reality that causes a deep ache in my heart. I know I'd be a different person today had it not been for all the elderly men and women who played such significant roles in my life.

In fact, when I began serving as the pastor of my first church, I was only twenty-four. Many of my members were in their seventies and eighties. As a young man, my life was enriched by the godly examples of seasoned saints. I was constantly exposed to their wisdom, experience, and genuine love.

The elderly deserve our respect, and the Bible clearly teaches this truth. "Rise in the presence of the aged, show respect for the elderly and revere your God. I am the LORD" (Lev. 19:32). When a man or a woman has walked with the Lord for decades, they have much to offer the next generation. "They [the righteous] will still bear fruit in old age, they will stay fresh and green" (Psa. 92:14). Consider all this world's timeworn generation has lived through—love and loss, tragedy and triumph, pain and pleasure. Everything life will throw your way has already been experienced by someone else—most likely someone older than you. This is why the Bible says, "Gray hair is a crown of splendor; it is attained by a righteous life" (Prov. 16:31).

If you are already in the twilight years of life, let me say a few things to challenge you. Don't give up on the younger generation; encourage them. When you find yourself gravitating toward negative thoughts, stop! Remember what it was like so many years ago when you were trying to figure out life for yourself. Jump into the lives of some young people around you. Explore their thoughts and listen to their ideas with an open mind. Join their social networks, and find out where their passions lie.

Consider that the distance between the young and old is greater today than when you were a child or a teenager. And it will only increase if we don't do something to bridge that gap. Be intentional. Put your fears of rejection and feelings of awkwardness behind you. Look for the open door into some young person's heart. Be patient. Be gentle and loving. Respect them and find common ground. Be willing to serve them, and they may do the same for you.

Remember the most important thing you leave behind is your legacy, not your money. Mammy has been gone for nearly thirty years now, but her memories will live on and be passed down throughout the generations. People will also talk about you decades from today if you pour yourself into their lives now. You will stand in the company of that "great cloud of witnesses" revered by the next generation (Heb. 12:1).

To my younger readers I say this: Seek out someone much older than you for wisdom and advice. As A. W. Tozer once said, "Listen to the one who is listening to God." Put on a spiritual hardhat, and build a bridge into their world. Then cross over to the other side. You won't regret it, and you'll be surprised over the way your life will be enriched.

When you're struggling, confused, discouraged, or lonely, someone has already visited those very same places before you. If you're a new parent trying to figure out how to raise your baby, guess what! There are grandparents and great-grandparents out there who have "seen it all." Are you struggling with your career or a business decision? There are people who have retired and then spent years reflecting on their experiences in the workplace. Better yet, there's probably someone out there who's willing to help troubleshoot a problem for you. All they want in return is the opportunity to feel useful again—and the chance to get to know you personally.

Church

There is no better environment for mingling with people of different ages than a local church. I get a surge of adrenalin and a jolt of excitement every Sunday morning that I'm able to mix it up with different generations. I guarantee you will too. So the next time you go to church, don't move in all your familiar circles. Branch out! Get out of your comfort zone. You don't have to abandon all your friends to make new ones.

For God's sake and ours, let's reverse the negative trends. It's not rocket science. We don't need more surveys and statistics about the widening chasm that exists between the young and old. We feel the problem in our bones and grieve over it in our hearts. Just do what Christ did. Leave your comfortable space and take a risk. If Jesus could walk across heaven and enter our world—all so we might understand God—maybe you could walk across a room.

Let's all burn a few calories for the Kingdom of God!

4

CULTURES AND CLASSES

Though I am free and belong to no man, I
make myself a slave to everyone, to win as many as possible ...
To the weak I became weak, to win the weak.
I have become all things to all men so that by all possible means
I might save some. I do all this for the sake of the gospel,
that I may share in its blessings.
1 Corinthians 9:19, 22-23

My sophomore year at Texas Tech University in Lubbock, Texas, was a turning point for me. For the first time in my life, I began reading the Bible on my own. I found a band of brothers who were growing in their faith. We sharpened and encouraged one another. It wasn't long before I began volunteering for a variety of leadership positions. I signed up to be the fellowship director in the Baptist Student Union, a Sunday school teacher in a bilingual church, and even a spring-break missionary to inner city Houston.

My First Sermon

In Houston I was unexpectedly given my first opportunity to preach. Children came to the mission center to hang out after school. They were given snacks, played pool, jumped on the trampoline, and were kept off the streets where the gangs were recruiting. The only stipulation was they had to listen to the plan of salvation at the conclusion of the activities. The person who was supposed to do the preaching that day never showed up. My friends who were participating in the spring-break trip looked at me and said, "We think God wants you to do it."

I didn't have a clue about what to do, nor did I have any time to prepare. I found an old King James Bible, front cover torn off, lying on one of the tables. Not long before, I'd read the dramatic story of Paul's conversion on the Damascus road. So with fifty Hispanic preteens sitting at my feet, I read the story. After reading, I narrated what I had just read, making sure to add great emphasis to each word and phrase.

"Every breath he took," I told them "was an angry breath. He was quickly becoming known as the butcher of Christians. One man had already died. More would follow. He was looking for followers of Jesus Christ."

I paused momentarily for emphasis. Then I asked, "Is there a follower of Jesus Christ here in this room today? If so, you would have been his next victim. It looked as if nothing would stop this man. That is, until he saw a bright light shining from heaven. It was so intense that it blinded him. He heard the voice of Jesus calling to him from the light. Jesus said, 'You are persecuting me every time you injure one of my followers.'"

Then I reread Acts 9:5 to them. "And he said, Who art thou, Lord? And the Lord said, I am Jesus whom thou persecutest: it is hard for thee to kick against the pricks" (KJV). My next comments to them were a huge mistake, and I'm somewhat embarrassed to say it hasn't been my last. I asked these inner city boys if they knew what it meant to be *"kicked against the pricks."*

Snickering broke out all over the room. Bursts of laughter followed. One of my friends clutched his side then turned around to face the wall.

Next the kids began saying things like, "Yea, I know what that means. It happened to Juan last week. He got really sick." Another said, "I wouldn't kick Jesus there; he might get mad and throw a lightning bolt at you."

Up to that point they'd given off expressions of boredom. For better or worse, I had their attention. Seizing this unique opportunity I said, "Jesus doesn't like to be kicked around. He's the one person you can't bully in life. Every time you tell Him you're not going to be a Christian, you're kicking Him. Every time you make fun of someone who becomes a Christian, you're kicking Him. Every time you cuss and swear in God's name, you're kicking Jesus Christ. But when you kick Him, it only hurts you. They even kicked Jesus into an early grave. But that didn't matter. Right now He's sitting next to God in heaven. If you're still trying to kick Him, you have to do it in front of God. God won't tolerate you kicking His Son for too many more days. One day He's going to find all those people who kicked Jesus and kick them into hell, where they will spend forever with the devil."

The laughter stopped. Faces were motionless. I painted a picture of these kids kicking Jesus from every direction and angle. They looked shocked if not sad. Then I said, "If you want to stop kicking Jesus and start following Him, you can have a second chance, like Saul. How many of you want to ask Him into your heart right now?"

Several hands went into the air. I asked them to repeat after me as I led them in the sinner's prayer. Then I sent them home to tell their parents what the preacher talked about at the mission center.

Jumping the Great Divide

I was a kid in 1974. I have a lot of great memories from that time. I remember watching ABC's "Wild World of Sports" and being mesmerized by Evel Knievel. One afternoon, on the eighth of September, he attempted to jump Idaho's Snake River Canyon on a motorcycle. It actually looked more like a rocket to me, and to most Americans as well, but that was beside the point. Evel said it was a motorcycle, and we believed him.

Actually, a former NASA engineer designed the rocket-propelled motorcycle, called the Skycycle X-2. It was created specifically for Evel to accomplish this quarter-mile jump. It looked crazy, and I was convinced he'd die. But like most people of that day, I was fascinated by Evel's showmanship and appetite for risk-taking. He was known for breaking his bones and cheating death. "I did everything by the seat of my pants," Evel said. "That's why I got hurt so much."

When the Skycycle blasted off the ramp, the parachute accidentally deployed. Unfortunately, it created too much drag for Evel to make it to the other side. The rocket plummeted 500 feet to the bottom of the canyon. Although it was only minutes before we knew he survived, the suspense made it seem like hours. Evel once said, "I'm a lucky, lucky person."

Luck? How about something more powerful—like Divine intervention?

For years, the Snake River Canyon jump has served as a parable to me about the challenges of crossing great divides. It's difficult and sometimes painful to bridge the gaps that exist between different cultures and classes of people. I learned this lesson first in Houston, and nearly every day I continue to see the struggle of initiating Christian community with people who are different from me.

Love for the Nations, Beginning to End

The most important questions for us to consider are: "What does God want?" and "Where is His heart in this matter?" The Bible maintains that God loves the nations. Each individual from every background really matters to God. Jesus died for the rich and the poor, the privileged and the disadvantaged. As a kid sitting next to my parents in church, I heard this statement from the pulpit numerous times: "The ground at the foot of the cross is level." This is true for people from every nationality and tongue.

Our pigmentation is simply part of the spectrum of God's glorious image, the stamp of His creation. Whatever the color of your skin, it's beautiful in God's eyes.

God's love for the nations is established in the first book of the Bible. He called Abraham to be the father of "a great and powerful nation." Then God declared, "All nations on earth will be blessed through him" (Gen. 18:18). There was a very specific and sovereign purpose in this decree. God wanted a special people—the Jewish nation—to be His "inheritance" (see 1 Kings 8:53). As such, she was to become a spectacular light for all people living in darkness, "the land of the shadow of death" (Matt. 4:16). The prophet Isaiah even foretold of a day when foreigners would be drawn to the God of Israel: "Nations will come to your light, and kings to the brightness of your dawn" (Isa. 60:3).

So what will draw them? The nations will come because of their need and desire to worship. God says, "Be still, and know that I am God; I will be exalted among the nations, I will be exalted in the earth" (Psa. 46:10). Although it never happened during David's lifetime, it didn't stop the shepherd king from singing, "All the nations you have made will come and worship before you, O Lord; they will bring glory to your name" (86:9).

These scriptures are simply spectacular! But they have yet to be fulfilled in their entirety. So when will all the nations arrive at the throne of glory to worship His Majesty on high? Before I answer this question, realize these words speak of God's eternal plan—established before Adam and Eve set one foot in the Garden of Eden, predetermined before the beginning of time itself. God has been moving every second of human history toward the fulfillment of these prophecies.

With the coming of Jesus Christ, we begin to see the brilliance of God's plan more clearly as it unfolds, for "in his name [Jesus] the nations will put their hope" (Matt. 12:21). When Jesus hung bleeding from the Cross, God's love for the nations finally began to make sense: "With your blood you purchased men for God from every tribe and language and people and nation" (Rev. 5:9).Also consider that the full meaning extends even beyond the death of Christ. When all is said and done and we are camping out in the heavenly city, the "New Jerusalem," God's plan for the nations will be fulfilled to perfection. Speaking of heaven, the apostle John proclaimed, "The glory and honor of the nations will be brought into it" (21:26).

So this is God's love, from start to finish, beginning to end. God's eternal plan is to have an everlasting city where His children from every nation gather together before His throne in worship. I can only begin to imagine the anticipation God has for this day to arrive and the excitement that will radiate from His throne. No word or series of words in the English language—or any other tongue—can convey what that day will be like. "No eye has seen, no ear has heard, no mind has conceived what God has prepared for those who love him" (1 Cor. 2:9).

This ultimate reality leaves me with a few questions, which emerge from a deep place within my heart. I hope you're willing to ask them as well. Can we not attempt to do today what we will be spending all eternity doing together? Can we somehow build within our churches a slight taste of the type of community that will exist in heaven? Why are we still so segregated?

The Current Reality

Time Magazine published an article on January 11, 2010, titled "Can Megachurches Bridge the Racial Divide?" The author, David Van Biema, gave a startling report. He said, "Surveys from 2007 show that fewer than 8% of American congregations have a significant racial mix." But the statement that alarmed me most was this: "In an age of mixed-race malls, mixed-race pop-music charts and, yes, a mixed-race President, the church divide seems increasingly peculiar. It's troubling, even scandalous, that our most intimate public gatherings—and those most safely beyond the law's reach—remain color-coded."

Ouch!

Time Magazine is not *Christianity Today*. However, pay attention to the fact that our secular society is interested in this issue, perhaps even more than we are. Whether we like it or not, we are under the world's microscope. The "sinners" are raising questions for the "saints" that strike at the very heart of our credibility and witness. Jesus knew situations like this would arise. That's why He said, "By this all men will know that you are my disciples, if you love one another" (John 13:35).

Have you ever noticed the majority of people tend to gravitate toward those who are most like themselves? Look at the average city in America. Our nation is a melting pot of diversity, but not in the typical neighborhood. Look at the average church. The same principle holds true. Jesus wants us to learn how to love our fellow brothers and sisters in the Lord first, then together spread that love into our eclectic society.

The Future Reality

I'm looking forward to heaven. For years I've studied all the Bible has to say on the subject, preached extensively about our future there, and tried to wrap my mind around what that experience will be like. I can identify with the Sons of Korah, who said, "How lovely is your dwelling place, O LORD Almighty! My soul yearns, even faints, for the courts of the LORD; my heart and my flesh cry out for the living God" (Psa. 84:1-2). One of the many spectacular moments we will experience together in heaven is found in the book of Revelation:

> *Then the angel showed me the river of the*
> *water of life, as clear as crystal, flowing from*
> *the throne of God and of the Lamb down the*
> *middle of the great street of the city. On each*
> *side of the river stood the tree of life, bearing*
> *twelve crops of fruit, yielding its fruit every*
> *month. And the leaves of the tree are for the*
> *healing of the nations. No longer will there be*
> *any curse* (Rev. 22:1-3).

Did you catch that? No more curse! The nations will be healed from the poison of sin and its bitter aftertaste. But even more specifically, they will be cleansed from the toxicity of pride and prejudice—that old stain of segregation and separatism—not just temporarily, but forever. When Jesus returns for His Bride, all of these blessings will be set into motion. As Wilburn Chapman wrote, "One day He's coming—O glorious day!"[8]Until that day arrives, there's something for us to do together now. I love what the angels told the disciples after Jesus ascended into heaven: "'Men of Galilee,' they said, 'why do you stand here looking into the sky?'" (Acts 1:11). God never intended for us to sit on our hands and wait for heaven to come. No. While we're waiting, let's be committed to build the kind of Christian communities that anticipate and reflect what heaven will be like. Perhaps this is what Jesus meant when He told His Disciples, "As you go, preach this message: 'The kingdom of heaven is near'" (Matt. 10:7).

Why Change?

What a witness this would be to our culture! When a black man and a white woman kneel at the same altar, weeping over their sins in the presence of God, something powerful has happened. When an affluent business

---

[8] Public Domain.

executive studies the Bible with a homeless man, something extraordinary takes place. When a PhD holds the hand of a high-school dropout, and together they raise those hands before the Lord of glory, God is pleased.

What would it take for this to happen? Hearts would need to change. Fears would need to be laid aside. Anger, envy, prejudice, and a whole host of things would need to be confessed, nailed to the Cross of Christ, and thrown into the grave. Each of us would need to be intentional, make plans, and then step beyond our comfort zone, perhaps even our own selfishness.

None of this will be easy; it never is. We should pray for courage and an unrestrained heart. We need to reflect on what it means to be magnanimous—spiritual Robin Hoods who take not from others, but from themselves, to give to others what they need most. We should empty some of the non-essential rooms in our lives and make room for someone who is different.

Most of us struggle in this area. We are cliquish, clannish, and cautious. We want to hang out with all the people of common interests and similar notions of what keeps us entertained. Over time, we grow more and more narrow. We limit our exposure to new ideas. If we're not careful, our worldview may become astigmatic.

On the opposite side of this equation, we grow when we force ourselves to stretch our horizons. When we increase our exposure to different cultures and classes of humanity, it's impossible to lose. Even the awkward moments can become teachers. You will learn more by forcing yourself to take risks than by living life like you're packaged in bubble wrap.

All of this has a very specific purpose. The apostle Paul was willing to become whatever was necessary—without moral or biblical compromise, of course—in order to win people for Jesus Christ. He had renaissance attitudes about race and culture that allowed him to break free from convention. Ironically, he was probably one of the most narrow-minded people on the planet before he met Christ on the Damascus Road. But

Jesus changed Paul, and together they changed the world.

I'm afraid all this may sound like "pie in the sky" thinking, but when I build a bridge, I grow. On the occasions I've walked across a room to help someone integrate into a new group, or flown across the oceans to meet people in other countries, I grew both personally and spiritually. Despite the fact that I'm a preacher, I wasn't wired from birth to do this naturally or without a struggle. It was a decision born from a conviction.

When I considered all that Jesus did to reach me, as unworthy and troubled as I was, something happened inside. I came to understand my value to God. He loved me—warts and all. He loves you too—claws and flaws. If we're not shouting it from the rooftops, it's because we know more about our sin than we understand of His grace.

We will never comprehend the gift Christ gives us, nor fully appreciate it, until we share it with someone else. If you want to experience the fullness of the life of Christ, do what He did: give it away. We don't need training seminars, books, and strategies to make this happen. It takes more than pragmatism to build a bridge over difficult terrain. It takes conviction.

Godspeed!

5

BRIDGES

I know You're there, across the great divide.
But how can I reach You on the other side?
Your voice calls gently, I almost hear it now.
I'd come to you, Lord, but I don't know how.

"A Bridge Builder will arise, just wait and see."
The voice was reassuring: "He'll set you free."
With eyes wide open, I searched every day,
Just waiting for the season He'd pass my way.

My hope vanished when the cross first appeared,
Towering on the horizon, the crowds all jeered.
The sky grew dark when the Bridge-Builder died.
I turned the other way, then fell down and cried.

I heard wonderful news after three days had passed.
Someone shouted we'd been saved "at long last."
The Bride-Builder's no longer dead, "He's alive!"
"The chasm spanned, all the way to the other side."

The news was thrilling, nearly too good to believe.
But if it were true, my heart would no longer grieve.
Wanting to see for myself, I turned around and ran.
Yes, I saw a Bridge standing between God and man.
(James Shupp, author)

"How much longer?" I thought to myself.

Mike—a missionary and my new friend—led the way. For a man in his mid-fifties, he moved at a fast pace, posture steady, eyes focused. Behind him was a convoy of approximately fifteen people who had sketchy information about where they were going and why—myself included. We followed Mike through the matrix of bus stops, subways, and pedestrian crossings. Our group moved swiftly at first. But after an hour or so, fatigue grew, and the line began to elongate.

Trailing off in the distance was the expansive skyline of Hong Kong, an economic powerhouse of Asia and one of the most densely populated regions on the planet. As we ambled along, the gradual change in our surroundings amplified my curiosity. The cosmopolitan cityscape—our point of origin—slowly morphed into patchy marshland and outdated apartment dwellings. We were in an older, more provincial section of the island.

Sensing the troops needed motivation, Mike began to share the details of where we were heading. In a matter of moments, we would arrive at the humble apartment of a deceased American missionary named Roy Robertson. During his eighty-seven years of life, Roy spent sixty serving as an international missionary. Strangely enough, we were needed to clean out his apartment and carry everything he left behind to the dumpster.

As this information began to trickle through the line, it caused an immediate reaction. The pace of the entire group quickened. Our interest intensified. We were instantly humbled, yet ready and excited to serve.

When we arrived at Roy's apartment, it wasn't what I expected. The living conditions were meager—two small bedrooms and a tiny kitchen. There were a few bookshelves made of particleboard, a circular table with mirrors surrounding the pedestal, and cloth furniture—all outdated, circa 1970, a "blast from the past." Still, there was something wonderful and magnificent about the place. It was peaceful.

We carried his furniture down four narrow flights of stairs to the dumpster outside. In no time, a small crowd of people gathered to rummage through Roy's things. Although the items had little monetary value, they were quickly scavenged, carried away by people who acted like they'd won an unexpected shopping spree. That's when it hit me. It was poignant when I realized none of those people knew the man—the missionary—whose personal effects they'd clamored to attain. Roy didn't amass wealth or seek notoriety. Until that day, I didn't know anything about his life either. But then I thought, *Roy won't be remembered for the stuff he left behind but for what he did for God's kingdom.*

A growing fascination to know more about this man captured me. So I asked Mike to share with me the story of this noteworthy servant of God. What I heard that day led me to research his life even farther. It's simply fascinating and too important not to pass on.

In 1941, Roy Robertson answered the call to ministry while listening to George W. Truett, the celebrated pastor who spent forty-seven years leading the First Baptist Church in Dallas, Texas. A few months afterward, the Navy sent Roy to Pearl Harbor. He arrived on December 6, 1941. On that day, Roy attended a small Bible study led by the Navigators. It was his first contact with this evangelistic, disciple-making ministry. No one could have foreseen that Roy would later play a significant role in leading the Navigators to spread the gospel around the world.

The very next day, December 7th, 353 Japanese airplanes from six aircraft carriers bombed the U.S. Naval base at Pearl Harbor. Amid the flames and the chaos of that infamous day, Roy submitted to the Lordship of Jesus Christ. He pledged his absolute devotion to follow Him to the ends of the earth. No sacrifice was too great, no price too high.

After WWII, Roy joined the Navigators. For two years he lived in the home of its legendary founder, Dawson Trotman. When Trotman wanted to send the first Navigator missionary to Asia, Roy was his immediate choice. Roy accepted the challenge, left everything behind, and traveled to Shanghai, China. He arrived just five months before the Communist takeover. But through that small window of opportunity, flames were stoked that enabled the underground church in China to endure the hard freeze of religious persecution—this, despite Mao Tse-tung's atheistic reign of terror.

Roy would later serve in Singapore, Hong Kong, Vietnam, India, Indonesia, Japan, and many other places in Asia. While he worked for the Navigators, Roy established another missionary organization called TEL— an acronym for "Training Evangelistic Leadership." Today TEL maintains a full-time staff of more than one-hundred. What a legacy!

The Bridge to Life

Perhaps the greatest gift Roy left behind was a simple but brilliant method of sharing the Good News of Jesus Christ. He developed an evangelistic illustration called "The Bridge to Life." When I was a young ministry student at Hardin-Simmons University, Roy's technique was taught in our evangelism class. In fact, it was the very first training I had on witnessing.

As we cleaned out Roy's apartment, I thought about all the people I'd led to personal faith in Jesus Christ using "The Bridge to Life." Then it hit me: Literally millions of people will be in heaven because of this powerful gospel presentation. "The Bridge to Life" helps people visualize, clearly and simply, how eternal salvation in Jesus Christ is made available to all.

Imagine two landmasses separated by a steep chasm. Man is on one side; God is on the other. The vast expanse that separates us from God is created by our own sin. It is impossible for any man to cross this great divide and be reconciled to God by his own efforts. Even if you devoted all your spare time to performing random acts of kindness, if you fed the poor every day, gave all your money away, and then achieved the "nicest person on the planet" trophy, you still couldn't reverse the consequences of just one sin—any sin, great or small. "All have sinned," the Bible tells us, "and fall short of the glory of God" (Rom. 3:23). Justice demands that somebody must pay the full price for our sin, for "the wages of sin is death" (6:23).

Throughout the centuries, people have tried many ways to escape this penalty of eternal death by bridging the sin gap for themselves. History proves that philosophy has failed to bring men closer to God. It's a broken bridge built by agnostics and atheists. Morality has failed. Why? Because willpower isn't powerful enough to stop people from sinning. Even religion itself falls short of making men good enough to please God. Every solution of man has failed and will fail. The Bible clearly teaches this truth: "There is a way that seems right to a man, but in the end it leads to death" (Prov. 14:12).

So how can a sinful man stand on the same ground with a holy God? Who is worthy to bridge the gap and allow people to have peace with God? Only one Person ever lived a perfect life. One Man never fell short of God's glory. One Man was spotless and untainted by the choice, activity, and consequences of sin. Never once did this Man fail God. His name is Jesus, and He loves us in spite of our sin.

The good news is that Jesus took our place: "For Christ died for sins once for all, the righteous for the unrighteous, to bring you to God" (1 Pet. 3:18). Jesus bridged the sin gap by His work on the Cross. His sacrificial death was enough to satisfy God's justice: "For there is one God and one mediator between God and men, the man Christ Jesus" (1 Tim. 2:5).

God has made the plan for our salvation wonderfully clear and simple. Jesus said, "I tell you the truth, whoever hears my word and believes Him who sent me has eternal life and will not be condemned; he has crossed over from death to life" (John 5:24). With such a great offer on the table, there's really no reason to reject God's free gift of salvation. Many people think they need to wait for a more convenient time or first clean up their lives before accepting this amazing gift. Some people believe the offer is for everybody else but not for themselves. Others are afraid of what their friends or family will think if they become a "Bible-thumping Jesus freak." Still others are afraid it won't work, or they'll fail to live up to their part of the bargain. They don't want to be branded as "another one of those religious hypocrites."

All of these objections are really just excuses. The reality is, God won't accept any excuses on the Day of Judgment. "Everyone must die once, and after that be judged by God" (Heb. 9:27 GNT). The only people who will get into heaven are those who enter by means of Jesus Christ. Jesus is the bridge to God and the key to the abundant life He has designed for us to live: "The thief comes only to kill, steal and destroy; I have come that they may have life, and have it to the full" (John 10:10).

If you haven't already, confess your sins to God. Invite Jesus Christ into your heart as Lord and Savior. If you believe, you will walk across the great divide that separates you from God and be saved … today! The Bible is crystal clear about this truth: "If you confess with your mouth, 'Jesus is Lord,' and believe in your heart that God raised him from the dead, you will be saved" (Rom. 10:9). Don't delay: "I tell you, now is the time of God's favor, now is the day of salvation" (2 Cor. 6:2).

The Bridge to Love

But the good news doesn't stop there. The relationship we enjoy with Jesus Christ has everything to do with our daily lives, right here and now. Some people think of salvation merely as a fire insurance policy to keep them out of hell. Others believe they can live like hell because it doesn't matter what they do, they'll just go to heaven anyway. Both these attitudes are immature and reflect an incomplete understanding of all Jesus Christ did through the Cross.

We're now part of God's forever family, an emerging kingdom of priests and saints. We're free to enjoy the benefits of Christian community. We share a Spirit-filled camaraderie with other believers. It's our choice. We don't have to live in a cesspool of hot-blooded turmoil and relational garbage like the rest of the world. "In this world you will have trouble," said Jesus. "But take heart! I have overcome the world" (John 16:33). One of the many reasons Jesus bridged the gap between God's holiness and our sinfulness is to enable us to live peacefully and joyfully within His family.

The Apostle Paul gives one of the most brilliant commentaries on the power of the gospel to build and unify God's family. He says, "But now in Christ Jesus you who once were far away have been brought near through the blood of Christ. For he himself is our peace, who has made the two one and has destroyed the barrier, the dividing wall of hostility" (Eph. 2:13-14). What thrilled Paul was the fact that Jews and Gentiles, people of different ethnic and religious backgrounds, could be united in Jesus Christ. The barrier between the two had been the Mosaic Law. The Jews had it; the Gentiles didn't. Jesus, however, fulfilled the Law so all nations could come to God *through* Him and be one *in* Him.

Christian fellowship is a beautiful gift. It's free, but it didn't come cheap. Jesus paid the entire amount, first to reconcile us to God, then to each other. This reality is more satisfying than companionship, more fulfilling than friendship, and more enduring than kinship. The deepest truth inside every believer is that he or she is a child of the King. We're one in Christ. We'll reign with Him upon His throne in glory. We're one in Christ whether we speak different languages or live on different sides of the planet. Whether we're slave or free, rich or poor, American or Asian, Republicans or Democrats, we have the most important thing in common. The Holy Spirit sent by Jesus Christ is living His life through us: "And in him you too are being built together to become a dwelling in which God lives by his Spirit" (v. 22).

The New Testament is filled with examples of this fact. The apostle Paul sent a message to the church of Laodicea because He wanted them to be "encouraged in heart and united in love." Why? He continued: "...so that they may have the full riches of complete understanding, in order that they may know the mystery of God, namely, Christ, in whom are hidden all the treasures of wisdom and knowledge" (Col. 2:2-3). Don't miss the point. How we relate to our fellow believers reflects how well we understand the fullness of Christ's life in us.

Jesus was very clear about how believers should behave toward one another. He said, "A new command I give you: Love one another. As I have loved you, so you must love one another. By this all men will know that you are my disciples, if you love one another" (John 13:34-35). Few things strengthen the cause of Christ like genuine love, freely flowing between believers. Everyone's looking for love, but there's only one place to find it—at the foot of the Cross.

Love builds bridges and tears down walls. Love ties hearts together with a cord that can't be broken. The yearning for love is universal. The absence of love makes one miserable. "Love as brothers," Peter said, "... be compassionate and humble" (1 Pet. 3:8). Because love "bears all things, believes all things, hopes all things, endures all things. Love never fails" (1 Cor. 13:7-8 NKJV).

I believe the Holy Spirit is asking each of us to take this issue to heart. Right now your heart should be yearning for what God says "Yes" and "Amen" to. Considering all Jesus did to reconcile us to God, we should willingly and gladly strengthen the bond of unity between one another. Since we've already crossed the bridge to life in Christ, let's build some bridges ourselves. The Carpenter from Galilee has already given us the blueprints and shown us the model. Better still, He's given us a compelling example by which to live.

> *Make every effort to keep the unity of the Spirit through the bond of peace. There is one body and one Spirit—just as you were called to one hope when you were called—one Lord, one faith, one baptism; one God and Father of all, who is over all and through all and in all* (Eph. 4:3-6).

 6

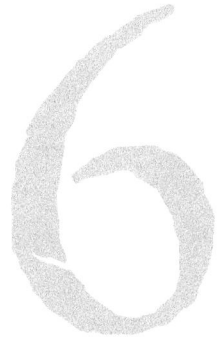

STARING AT THE SON

"But we see Jesus, who was made a little lower than the
angels, now crowned with glory and honor." Hebrews 2:9

A little over a decade ago, the Irish rock band U2 produced a song entitled "Staring at the Sun." Like many of their songs, it was a monster hit. As the DJs spun the song repeatedly on the airways, many people attempted to decipher the puzzling meaning of the lyrics. My first thought when I heard the title brought back my mother's ominous warning as a child: "James," she said, "don't look at the sun. You'll go blind!"

Strange Lyrics

Although my obedience record from childhood is moderately tainted, something instinctive prevented me from looking at the sun for any length of time. Perhaps it was the scorching pain in the back of my eyes when I defied my mother's warning for just a fraction of a second. In fact, Mom was seldom wrong. Consequences always seemed to back up her decrees.

Every living creature with a photosensitive retina naturally avoids fixating on one forbidden spot in the sky. We don't stare at the sun. To do so would fry our retina and destroy our vision. We avoid it like we avoid placing our hand in an open flame. It's intrinsic and reflexive, or as my dad used to say, "Simple common sense."

Therein lies the irony of U2's song "Staring at the Sun." As I listened to the refrain, I noticed the song was actually a metaphor, somewhat abstract but nonetheless fascinating, like most of Bono's lyrics. I can almost hear the Irish tenor's voice now, singing of staring at the sun, and wrestling with the fear of what he might discover if he defiantly gazed upon the forbidden object. Would he be stunned, deaf and dumb, while "Staring at the Sun"? Absolutely. But for Bono, the adventure was worth the risk.

I'm a pastor, not a poet or a lyricist. Though my primary skill is interpreting the Bible, I find some intriguing ideas springing from U2's lyrics. The big idea of the song is to cut your ties with conventional wisdom. Joyfully embrace the consequences. Take a courageous dive into the river of risk. Look at what no one else dares to look at. Pause, gaze, and peer into the great unknown. Stop seeing things through the eyes of others, and gain your own perspective. Challenge the norms. Question the presuppositions. Now take action on what you see, and embrace it with your whole heart.

The people who follow this path lead revolutionary lives. They go blind to all other realities as they focus their efforts on the only thing that matters most to them. Without people like that there would be no Biography Channel. History lectures would put everyone to sleep. The picture of humanity would look like a glass of homogenized milk.

Instead, we applaud the brave ones who had the courage to make a solitary stand and ascend above the darkness. Such men and women have a syndrome I call "spiritual tunnel vision." I would place the Apostle Paul at the top of the list of people diagnosed with this condition.

On April 22, 1991, the cover of *U.S. News & World Report* featured this headline: "History's Hidden Turning Points." This special report—in what must have been a painfully slow news cycle—captured my attention in the impulse aisle of the grocery store checkout line. I wondered what this "secular" magazine concluded the greatest turning point in all of human history to be. Thumbing my way to page 54, I discovered these words in bold font: "Number 1: The Momentous Mission of the Apostle Paul."

Consider these next words carefully. While travelling down the Damascus Road, Paul's *one blinding vision* of the resurrected Jesus Christ created a shockwave that is still reverberating throughout the fabric of human history. One man with a clear and compelling vision of Jesus Christ, combined with the passion to make Him known, launched a missionary movement that changed our world forever.

Could this still happen today? Better to ask yourself this question: "And why not?" God is still on His throne. The needs of our world are great. Sin is just as ubiquitous in our generation as it was in theirs.

Perhaps you are the next in line—the chosen man or woman who will launch *one blinding vision* for our generation. If so, I challenge you to follow the Apostle Paul's example. He said, "But one thing I do …" (see Phil. 3:13a). With a simple and yet clear focus, Paul began the first step in his journey to expand the kingdom of God. Instead of dabbling in many things, he focused on the *one thing*. The Man Paul met on the Damascus Road now commanded center stage in his life. Paul stubbornly refused to be distracted by all the other sideshows of this world. And Paul never turned back—no, not once.

This former martyr-maker and persecutor of Christianity left his past in the dust and kept his eyes glued to the skopós. Paul continued in Philippians 3:13b by saying, "Forgetting what is behind and straining toward what is ahead …" Behind you are memories. Before you are dreams. Paul believed his dreams were greater than his memories. You can too. The future is worth living for. Make history; don't just read about it.

There are things in your life right now that are worthy of risking a deeper look, even if it costs you dearly in the process. Fixate on them. Lock your gaze. Then you will go blind to things of lesser value. Some might call it an obsession, but that's fine. Only one Man in life is worthy enough to capture your focus to take ownership of you.

I remember Bill Hybels, the pastor of Willowcreek Community Church, once saying, "Do you have a vision to die for?" What a question! Martin Luther King, Jr. said, "If you have nothing worth dying for, you have nothing worth living for." The Bible puts it this way: "Where there is no vision, the people perish" (Prov. 29:18 KJV).

Into the Life of Christ

The vision I've written about in this book began as an adventure into the life of Christ. In the process, I've journeyed into my own heart to discover what I was willing to die for … or stare at until it blinded me. For years I sat back and admired people who had already done this in their own ministry, business, or passionate pursuit. In many ways I tried to embrace their fervor and passion for the *one thing* that blinded them to all other things. It didn't take long for me to discover that one man's passion can become another man's pain. At first I was inspired, then merely interested, but ultimately distracted.

What I discovered in the long journey through the murky waters of my own passions was this: If I am willing to go blind over a vision, that vision absolutely has to come from God. I was powerless to borrow it, create it on my own, or have it mysteriously fall out of the sky. I had to do the difficult work of discovering what God put me on the planet to accomplish. I had to know just what attracted me, angered me, and violated my sense of right and wrong. Understanding the meaning of true justice, love, fairness, my personal interests, and primary motivations were all part of this pilgrimage.

Then one day it happened. I saw what I'd been afraid to look at for years. The more I saw, the less of anything else I could see. I was blind, and I was happy to be that way. Now I'm charging up the enemy's hills and stomping through spiritual swamplands. I have a fever to enlist a militia to see it the way God has revealed it to me. No apologies! I would like you to be blinded by this vision too:

- First, deliver people;
- Second, multiply disciples;
- Third, build bridges.

This vision arises out of a quest to understand the mind and the ministry of Jesus Christ. He captivates me. As I read through Scripture, I regain my focus in life simply by staring at Him. I no longer find myself reading words on a page. In fact, I've become a bystander and sometimes a resident character in the gospel story itself. I hear the inflection of Jesus' voice when He calls out to the disciples, the splash of the water as they tie the boats to the shore. I have seen the eyes of the blind opened, and I see Bartimaeus, now blinded by his devotion to follow Jesus on the road to Jerusalem. I see Jesus reading people's thoughts and exposing their motives in parables that sometimes confuse and other times convict.

I have met Jesus in the corner of my mind, and I love Him more today than I ever have in my life. Sometimes like Peter I want to cry out, "Depart from me; for I am a sinful man, O Lord" (Luke 5:8 KJV). Standing in His presence generates some very powerful emotions about my own personal sin these days. It's a good thing!

When the heart opens wide, the imagination soon follows. Scripture comes alive like never before. I can almost hear the sounds and see the expressions on people's faces. Do you remember the New Testament story where those eager men pulled the roof off another man's house? As they lowered their paralyzed friend down before the feet of Jesus, I feel the surprise of the crowd and the shock of the homeowner. But I imagine a smile on the face of Jesus when He said, "Friend, your sins are forgiven" (Luke 5:20). What a powerful moment! Their faith enabled their friend to become a friend of Jesus.

Another thing that has grabbed me about Jesus is the remarkable authority He exudes in everything He does. He teaches with authority. He prays with authority. He has a laser focus on His mission despite the many attempts to sidetrack Him. Where does this type of authority come from? Jesus is consumed by a blinding vision of His Father's will. Every thought, every word, and every action had a singular focus—so the Son may bring glory to the Father (see John 14:13).

One Blinding Vision begins and ends with a focus on Jesus Christ. And it has but one test to pass. The Apostle Paul knew this to be true as well: "For no one can lay any foundation other than the one already laid, which is Jesus Christ. If any man builds on this foundation using gold, silver, costly stones, wood, hay or straw, his work will be shown for what it is, because the Day will bring it to light. It will be revealed with fire, and the fire will test the quality of each man's work" (1 Cor. 3:11-13).

Every vision will be tested by the Refiner's fire on the Day of Judgment. This vision will walk through that fire. It will be examined in the crucible of God's opinion. It survives only if the focus was to bring glory to the Son of God. Anything less, even the slightest focus on building glory for the leaders of the vision, or for the church in which the vision was planted, will disintegrate like pine needles in a forest fire.

A blinding vision of Jesus Christ ascribes glory to God. Such a vision takes our eyes off the things that steal our joy and prevent us from having a real life. Keep your eyes on Jesus, and you'll never sink beneath the waves of self-doubt or self-interest. An unknown author said it best:

> *We mutter and sputter; we fume and we spurt;*
> *We mumble and grumble; our feelings get hurt.*
> *We can't understand things; our vision grows dim,*
> *When all that we need is a moment with Him.*[9]

---

[9] Quoted in Calvin Miller, *A Hunger for the Holy: Nurturing Intimacy with Christ*, (Howard Books, 2003), 117.

The Final Challenge

Let's return for a moment to U2's "Staring at the Sun." Change one word in the lyrics, from "sun" to "Son," and a whole new perspective emerges: I realize I'm not the only one staring at the Son.

No, I'm not the only one who wants to fix my eyes and life on Jesus Christ. I believe you want to as well. You will never have a better focus, see a more beautiful life than His, or live with a greater sense of adventure than when your eyes are fixed on the person of Jesus Christ. I have written this entire book to help you experience this for yourself. If you should burn out your retina gazing upon our glorious Lord and Savior, you will see fantastic things, unrivaled by anything you've ever seen before.

I challenge you to take on this new perspective. Stop living everyone else's life. What about your own God-inspired dreams? Look deep inside. Emerge from your spiritual cocoon. Rise up! Christ in you is the hope of glory (see Col. 1:27). Jesus died so He could live His life through you. That's why He said, "The kingdom of God is within you" (Luke 17:21). It is *near* and *now* (see Mark 1:15), relevant, and all that really matters.

When I look at Jesus, sometimes He takes my breath away. I cannot speak. He is the epitome of masculinity and gentleness. I noticed in Scripture the other day how He looked at people eye to eye. Jesus connected with their humanity at the deepest level possible. I call this the marksmanship of grace.

Jesus looked beyond the obvious targets in the sights of the institutional religionists of His day. He looked past appearances and reputations. He set His crosshairs—skopós—on expressing empathy and compassion. He even felt other people's hurts and shame. It was a prelude to what He ultimately did on the Cross. From the very beginning, it made perfect sense that He'd take this step.

Do you remember the woman who wept at Jesus' feet in the house of Simon the Pharisee? Her story is found in Luke 7:36-50. She was a known prostitute. She wore the original scarlet letter. She was a plaything to most, a woman from whom men become takers and not givers. Her weeping reverberated throughout Simon's house as she agonized over her past. Each painful sob was absorbed by the mercy of Jesus, softly and tenderly.

It must have been quite the contrast watching the host of the dinner party express his obvious disapproval. Fortunately for her and for us, Jesus viewed her differently. He looked into her heart with those sacred eyes. Then He asked Simon if he could see her as well. Not hardly! For that was Simon's biggest problem. His blindness originated from staring too much at himself.

For me, the most wonderful thing about this moment is the way Jesus must have looked at her. As a prostitute, she was surprised to see another man view her, not as a thing or an object but as a person of worth and value, desperately needing forgiveness. When she saw an absence of lust in the eyes and heart of Jesus, she knew He could offer her forgiveness.

Finally, I end our journey together with a reference to the last words to the chorus of U2's "Staring at the Sun," where Bono expresses that he's not the only person happy to go blind.

I agree, for I too am happy! The quest for *One Blinding Vision* has changed my life. My heart's desire is that it will change yours too. This vision is not for sissies, however, and it will never be realized unless we jump in headfirst and do as Warren Buffet says: "Put our skin in the game!"

One thing I've discovered about Jesus is that He never tolerated commitment on a percentage basis. His challenge left no wiggle room. It was either all or nothing, for or against, hot or cold, life or death. Put your hands to the plow. Don't look back (see Luke 9:62). So like Jesus, are you ready to deliver people, multiply disciples, and build bridges? The good news is … you get to answer this question for yourself. The bad news is …

no one can make this choice for you.

Yet, I promise you this. When Jesus is your singular focus—the stellar sight of all you now desire—your life will take on new significance. You will go blind to what no longer matters. Everything in life will be less complicated and confusing. And those things you no longer see? They won't matter much anymore.

Why? You will be happy to go blind.

About the Author

James Shupp is the CEO of www.BriarPatchConsulting.com whose mission is "Helping Churches Thrive." For nearly three decades, he's pastored churches in Texas and Oklahoma. Currently, he serves as the founding pastor of the Movement Church in San Antonio, TX.

When James is not pastoring, writing, or helping another church navigate through a tough challenge, he enjoys mountain-biking and flying. He's been married to Cherry, the bride of his youth, for thirty years. They love their evening walks together, reminiscing about the two sons they raised, and making each other laugh so hard that one finally snorts.

www.ingramcontent.com/pod-product-compliance
Lightning Source LLC
Chambersburg PA
CBHW061426040426
42450CB00007B/913